THE
ENGLISHMAN
THE
MOOR
AND THE
HOLY CITY
*The True Adventures of an
Elizabethan Traveller*

THE
ENGLISHMAN
THE
MOOR
AND THE
HOLY CITY

The True Adventures of an Elizabethan Traveller

JOAN TAYLOR

TEMPUS

For my father, Robert Taylor: traveller, civil engineer and musician

First published 2006

Tempus Publishing Limited
The Mill, Brimscombe Port,
Stroud, Gloucestershire, GL5 2QG
www.tempus-publishing.com

© Joan Taylor 2006

The right of Joan Taylor to be identified as the Author
of this work has been asserted in accordance with the
Copyrights, Designs and Patents Act 1988.

British Library Cataloguing in Publication Data.
A catalogue record for this book is available from the British Library.

ISBN 0 7524 4009 8

Typesetting and origination by Tempus Publishing Limited
Printed in Great Britain

Contents

Acknowledgments

Sincere thanks to the following people, in alphabetical order, who have helped me with this project in small or great ways: Father Athanasius Macora, Luigi Bonomi, Vicky Byford, Rupert Chapman, Felicity Cobbing, Mike Downes, Kenneth Dunton, Shimon Gibson, Greville Freeman-Grenville, Ezz el-Guizawy (who rescued me in Alexandria), Mahmoud Hawari, Ashley Jones, Gerald Maclean, Douglas Pratt, Rachel Timlick, Ian Ward and my wonderful family, especially Emily who helped with the maps. I thank also the librarians and archivists of the British Library, the National Archives Kew, University College London, Essex University, the Palestine Exploration Fund, the London Guildhall Library, All Hallows by the Tower, the Hampshire Records Office, San Salvatore Monastery, Jerusalem, and the University of Birmingham.

For Sailers and Adventurers (as one saith very well) are neither amongst the living, nor amongst the dead: they hang betweene both, ready to offer up their soules to every flaw of wind and billow of water wherewith they are assaulted ... Others would bee ... but feare to expose themselves to dangers by Sea and by Land. It is good (say they) to sleepe in a whole skinne. They cannot abide to bee tossed and tumbled like tennis-bals on the turbulent and tempestuous seas.

Theophilus Lavender

Now, sir, be judge yourself
Whether I in any just term am affin'd
To love the Moor.

William Shakespeare, *Othello*, I. i

Perhaps some will thinke this to be a lie or fable, but to such I answere, I can urge their credence no further then my faith and truth may persuade them: and if thereon they will not beleeve me, let them take paines to make their owne eies a witnesse, and when they have paid as dearely as I have doone, their judgement will be better confirmed.

Henry Timberlake

Prologue: An Old Book

I had absolutely no idea when I performed a key-word search on the University College London library catalogue one afternoon after teaching a class that I would be pulled into adventure. After entering the word 'Alexandria' for a current project, I trawled down the results and all of a sudden an item sprung from the screen like an invitation to a party:

> A strange and true account of the travels of two English pilgrims some years since, and what admirable accidents befel them in their journey to Jerusalem, Gr. Cairo, Alexandria, &c, published by Nath. Crouch, London, in 1699...

Admirable accidents?

Pilgrim accounts, I knew, could be quirky things. You had to be a strong-minded, mildly obsessional and dare-devilish individual to traipse off from Western Europe to the Middle East in the seventeenth century. Northern European society of this time was full of religious tension, blood-baths and bigotry, and the practice of pilgrimage to holy places was identified by Protestant leaders as a Catholic activity they spurned in favour of reading the word of God in freshly translated vernacular. Even Catholics had got cold feet about it because of the dangers. The Ottomans had held Palestine since routing the rival Muslim empire of the Mamluks in 1517, and, under the rule of Suleiman the Magnificent (1520–66), Jerusalem had been improved, but the land was rife with highway crime, and – still stung with memories of the Crusades – Muslims were deeply suspicious of Christians. It was no wonder that these pilgrims had 'admirable accidents'.

The entry gave me the publisher's name: Nathaniel Crouch, and I soon established that Crouch (1632?–1725?) was a bookseller and printer who, under the name of Richard or Robert Burton (R.B.), churned out cheap (plagiarised) histories and compendia for the general edification of the growing literate public. He would not have published anything that was not eminently readable, and with pictures.[1] Crouch's volume appeared in Britain's online catalogues with publication dates from 1683 through to 1796.

Before long I was walking up Hampstead Road to find the UCL Special Collections building. Arriving there, I was issued with Crouch's pocket-sized, leather-bound publication on a factory-shaped, grey foam support. To open the cover of a very old book can sometimes be a delicate thing. The pages – as befits a cheap edition were very thin. There was Nathaniel Crouch's information: the book was printed at the Bell, in the Poultry, near Cheapside. I imagined the environment: coffee shops, booksellers, printers, haberdashers, milliners, barbers, apothecaries.

Turning further the brittle pages, nervous I was going to rip them, I noted a frontispiece showing a bearded man in a turban sitting slightly precariously on top of an equine camel, with a whip held upright (Figure 1). The accompanying caption read: 'The manner of Travelling upon Dromedarys' and immediately established the contents of the work as dealing with the oriental and exotic. I found the account, originally a letter written by the mysterious 'H.T.', and read it quickly. Yes, this was truly adventure: a story of an English sea captain who – somewhat accidentally – found himself surviving one of the worst journeys in history. He travelled from his ship in Alexandria, to Cairo, across the deserts to Jerusalem and back, fired by curiosity, a desire to take measurements and a certain zing of espionage. This letter was not intended to be a ripping yarn for general entertainment, yet clearly it had become exactly that.

It was also something else. Twice H.T.'s life was saved by a Moroccan Moor, who became his fellow-traveller. This Muslim saved a Christian's life, protected him, outdid him in compassion, and the Christian in turn was not shy to chronicle the circumstances. Their story was situated in a much bigger story of Muslims and Christians and the way they related in the era just before our own, and it was a positive story in terms of the dynamics between the two men. Given some of the rhetoric of today, you might be forgiven for believing that the relationship between Muslims and Christians throughout history has been a tale of unending mistrust and dire misunderstanding. Not so.

'H.T.', I realised also, was the product of a much earlier time than I had thought. He mentioned 'the Queen'. He was *Elizabethan*, a man from the age of William Shakespeare, Edmund Spenser, Francis Drake, Walter Raleigh. This was the time of merchant adventuring, discovery, daring exploits, cultural energy. I suddenly had an image of someone dressed like Hamlet standing, utterly amazed, in front of the Dome of the Rock.

I had to go to the British Library.

Outside, in a big empty forecourt, there is Edouardo Paolozzi's magnificent sculpture of Newton measuring the universe, symbolic of scholarly quests. Inside the British Library, I sat at a numbered table on my own search for knowledge. Here I found that 'H.T.' was one Henry Timberlake. A self-standing edition of his account had first been published by the London publisher Thomas Archer in 1603. *A True and Strange Discourse on the travailes of two English Pilgrims* had run through numerous editions, long before Crouch picked it up.[2] 'Travailes' was right, I thought; in those days 'travel' and 'travail' were the same word, not without reason.

Before long I had a miniature tower of books: all the British Library holdings of Timberlake's work. This old book had been buried away for centuries, mentioned by few. It seemed a miracle that I had found it, or found him: refreshingly, Henry Timberlake was not some pious pilgrim in awe of every holy grotto he was led into. He was a businessman and mariner, robust and hearty. The sacred sites were clearly meaningful to him, but he had a practical approach and, apart from saying the Lord's Prayer whenever necessary, he clearly liked to measure things and take notes. Timberlake's travels, undertaken in 1601, were more like a whistle-stop camping tour in which he must have wondered what he had got himself into: the experience of the journey was perhaps more important to him than the sacred shrines, as was the experience of keeping his own identity when the world turned upside-down, in a place in which he feared some of the other Christians more than Muslims.

Timberlake, while fiercely proud of being an Englishman, possessed an enterprising New World soul. In the course of time, he would voyage to America, and be one of the first English landholders in Virginia and Bermuda.[3] His descendants would be among the oldest families of Rhode Island. In 1601, in his journey towards Jerusalem, he would encounter – in all its vast complexity – the old world of the Middle East. In that enterprise, Henry Timberlake also seemed like a hero of a Monty Python film, going off boldly and optimistically into the unknown without the foggiest idea of what he would be getting himself into. There was something fresh and naive about him, in his simple notion that being an Englishman was an identity he could happily rest proudly on as he travelled in Ottoman lands.

And what about the Moor? Who was he?

'Moor' was a term used rather loosely by the English, but strictly speaking it referred to a Muslim from the Berber civilisation of North Africa, a 'Maghrebi' in Arabic, and more widely to any Muslim of the Mediterranean and Middle East. The old sophisticated Moorish civilisation of North Africa – which had ruled southern Spain until the fall of Granada in 1492 – had retained autonomy from the super-power empire of the Ottomans, at least in Morocco, under the fabulously wealthy Sultan Ahmad al-Mansour. The Moor was of this resplendent society.

Today when we think of a 'Moor' it is usually Shakespeare's Othello who springs to mind. He is described as 'black', 'lascivious', 'rude' in speech, 'changeable' in will, 'warlike', 'base', 'jealous', 'eaten up with passion', 'angry', 'rash as fire', 'ignorant as dirt', 'cruel', 'unfortunate'. Yet the bard also defines Othello as 'fair', 'noble', 'brave', 'valiant', 'worthy', 'good', 'free', 'constant', 'loving' and 'great of heart'. Othello is the antithesis of English reserve, as dark is to light, and is therefore dangerous, a mixture of negative and positive traits. Shakespeare could have depicted the alien Othello as totally without redeeming qualities – as he did with the Moor, Aaron, in *Titus Andronicus* – or as a clown, like the Prince of Morocco in *The Merchant of Venice*, but instead he injected Othello with noble virtues. The English representation of Muslims had, by the time Shakespeare wrote, become slightly nuanced by appreciative descriptions of Moors and 'Turks'.[4]

The Moor of Timberlake's *True and Strange Discourse* is – through and through – a good man. This was the estimation of a Muslim by a Christian at a time when Christians and Muslims could more easily view each other as misguided infidels doomed to eternal punishment. Some of those who saw the play *Othello* performed at the Globe Theatre, or Blackfriars, would have already read Timberlake's account. Perhaps Shakespeare himself read it as he formed his characterisations. As I sat in the British Library I thought of Shakespeare holding the same book as I held, ruminating. Who was this Muslim whose path crossed with Henry Timberlake? What motivated him?

The British Library proved a resource where other treasures could be uncovered. There in the Manuscript Reading Room I traced the loopy scrawl of a handwritten version of Timberlake's account.[5] Historians always want to work with the most reliable, authentic sources, ideally an 'autograph': something written down in the author's own hand. Armed with the facsimile copy of the 1603 edition, I compared the manuscript's words to the printed version, but there were some omissions and mistakes: for example 'Arabians' for 'Armenians' at one place, misreadings of the place names, a wrong date, an underline where the copyist could not read a word, or did not want to, and so on. The paragraph that should have been at the beginning was tacked on to the end. There was a huge lacuna, beginning half way through a sentence about Bethlehem, where the copy was missing a folio. The pages were unfolded (when a letter would have been folded and sealed), and it concluded with 'A well willer [sic] to you all, Henry Tymberly', not, accurately, his name. Someone copied the letter, but it still seemed better than any printed version, given the penchant for creative editing among publishers in the sixteenth and seventeenth centuries. Printed versions could be wide of the author's work. To take but one glaring example, the endings are quite different between the 1603 and 1609 editions of Timberlake's account, clearly because Archer continued to 'improve' the text, to make it more exciting, or to answer criticisms. A hand copier was not interested in impressing readers/buyers: the copy was made for private study or for a circle of friends, and this meant that a copyist would leave out chunks if need be rather than improve the language or story.

I discovered also that in Samuel Purchas' great compendium of travel stories and documents, published in 1625, an epitome (abbreviated version) of Timberlake's letter appeared. Purchas introduces it slightly incoherently as:

After so often mention of Master Timberley, I have here given you some Extracts of his Journall (the whole the Reader may see printed) before the impression I writ out of a Manuscript many yeers agoe.[6]

So Timberlake was known as 'Timberley', and people did copy his letter (though Purchas was wrong that it was his journal). The manuscript had to be one of the copies made of Timberlake's original letter, probably before it came to be available in print, or the copy of a copy. Or the copy of a copy of a copy.

This manuscript became the basis for the journey that followed: my journey to reconstruct and visualise the context and events of Timberlake's adventure, the result being this book. I use the manuscript, rather than the printed editions, aside from where there is a lacuna, and form my extrapolations from this basis. It is my aim here not to provide a scholarly enquiry, but to bring Timberlake's story to life in an interesting narrative for those unfamiliar with the period of early modern travel and adventure. In order to do this it has been necessary to synthesise a wealth of mainly English but also other European travel accounts, and the insights of specialists, in order to supply information and images. I am unashamedly fond of the Perfect conjugation with the modal auxiliary 'would', to allow a deeper and more exciting view than is possible via positivist history. There is much that Henry Timberlake would have felt, done and seen. This is a journey to recreate an English experience.

1

Henry Timberlake

Captain Henry Timberlake was not a man who spent his days quietly and contentedly at home. He had been seafaring for years. In 1597 he co-owned a ship called the *Edward Bonaventure*, and sailed it as Master to Russia carrying freight belonging to the Russia Company. The normal sailing time was late May or June, 1597, when ships could navigate a course west of Norway northwards to the Arctic Sea, down the temporarily thawed and appropriately named White Sea, and arrive in the Russian port of St Nicholas. This journey took about a month and was deeply hazardous, with a chance of being blown off course and being frozen to death in the early winter, as had happened to the entire crews of English ships in previous decades, leaving eerie refrigerated wrecks replete with well-preserved dead men for later voyagers to find.[1]

Fortunately for Timberlake, in September 1597 he was successfully back in London with 145 tons of goods: cordage, wax, tallow, flax, hides and fur.[2] After this the ship continued south, calling in at the Florentine port of Leghorn (Livorno), and then the island of Zante (Zákinthos), which was a Venetian dependency. Such a voyage, up to the icy seas of Russia and down to the warm Mediterranean, was repeated in 1599. To take Russian products to the Mediterranean, and Mediterranean goods to Russia, was a remarkable feat in the late sixteenth century. Timberlake was clearly a fit, feisty, brave man who thrived on danger, and a challenge.

Henry Timberlake was both a sea captain and a businessman. This was a time of a rising merchant class in England, when merchants were making fortunes through new trading contacts, in frenetic competition with other Europeans, especially the French, Venetians and Spanish. In her last address to Parliament in the year 1600 Queen Elizabeth stressed the need for new trade routes and further markets for local products. Such trade was undertaken by companies of merchants who, with a charter from the Crown, were given a licence to trade and a monopoly over given areas. For example, if you were trading with Russia you had to do so under the auspices of the joint-stock Russia Company, or else the Company had the right to tax you on your individual adventuring. A portion of

the company profits would then go directly to the treasury.[3] Even within a company merchants often traded with their own capital, making profits and losses.[4]
Shipowners would be paid for freighting goods, and they might also have their
own stock.

In the Mediterranean Timberlake was associated with (though not a member
of) the Levant Company, a regulated company, which meant that all the members
traded with their own stock, making individual profits and losses. The Levant
Company had the right to fly the English flag – red cross on white – on foreign
seas and set up consuls in major towns that acted not only for the Company but
also for the Queen. Small 'factories', consisting of a group of agents ('factors'),
were established in various places and English ships were used by the company
to sell goods such as wool and tin, and buy in Levantine exotica: raw silk, mohair,
cotton, carpets, drugs, spices, currants and indigo. Profits of up to 300% could be
made on a successful voyage.[5]

The English abroad were intent on striking good trading deals, avoiding
pirates and privateers, and making their mark on the economy at home. Trading
abroad and increasing markets was not simply for revenue, but the success of
these ventures, conducted by men held to be heroes of astonishing resilience and
courage, contributed to national pride. The sea adventurer was the quintessential
Englishman: a character that had been affirmed with the publication in 1589 of
a compendium of amazing voyages made by Englishmen over time, edited by
Richard Hakluyt. This was so popular that it was expanded and published in three
volumes in 1598, 1599 and 1600.[6]

If nothing but, Timberlake was indeed proud of being an Englishman, and
he had a passion for Protestantism. There was absolutely nothing problematic
with feeling that way at this time, of course, as long as you stayed in England. In
business, a certain urbane carefulness about national pride would, one imagines,
have been wise when visiting countries who viewed England, and in fact all of
Europe, as a place of inferior beings. Much of the Mediterranean and Middle
East was under the rule of the Ottoman empire, the 'Turks' to the English, their
spread eastwards halted only by the Persians, who resisted their expansion fiercely,
and their spread westwards floundering around Hungary. The 'Turks', with their
base at Constantinople (Istanbul) were at war with half a dozen countries as they
struggled to expand the empire.[7] They were the world super-power, ruled by a
Sultan the English would call 'the Great Turk' or 'Grand Signior' (in the lingua
franca) to whom they would look with a mixture of fear, wonder and inferiority.
Likewise, in the Ottoman empire a non-Muslim foreign ambassador could be
introduced as 'the naked and hungry barbarian' who had dared to 'rub his brow
upon the Sublime Porte', and one French ambassador of 1666 was reportedly
greeted by the Grand Vizier in Constantinople by the words: 'you are a *Giaour* (=
infidel), a hogge, a dogge, and a turde eater'.[8]

The ship Henry Timberlake commanded in his journey of 1601 was called the 'Troyan', i.e. the *Trojan*. This name suggests Aeneas of Vergil's *Aeneid*, who flees from burning Troy to sail, with many adventures, through the Mediterranean Sea in search of a new Trojan home. On a merchant vessel on the Mediterranean, travelling from strange port to strange port, he perhaps recalled Aeneas' many stops around the same sea, but unlike Aeneas he had a homeland he would return to and anticipate its further glories. Despite the dangers of sea voyages, trade was booming.

Timberlake owned the *Trojan*. He had organised and funded its construction. There is a record dated January 22, 1597, in which Queen Elizabeth issued a warrant to pay 1,240 crowns (£310)[9] – the Queen's usual reward – to seven men, one of whom was Henry Timberlake (here Henry Timberley), who had recently built ships.[10] Such remuneration did not mean that the Queen owned the *Trojan*: it was simply a reward, an incentive, and it assumed an obligation on Timberlake's part. If England had to face another armada from Spain, Timberlake and his ship would be called upon to make up the forces of the navy.

So Henry Timberlake was a captain and a reasonably wealthy shipbuilder. He was an entrepreneur, a businessman, a man of sea and trade, educated well enough, yet no scholar. He was a man of action, bold and vigorous, hearty and open, sensible and reliable. He made friends. He got things done. Perhaps he entertained a table in the famous local pub, the Crooked Billet, where sea captains and adventurers would drink ale. It was said that all men spoke well of Henry Timberlake, and that he was very honest and judicious man.[11]

His personal circumstances are scantily recorded. In 1600 he had a wife named Margaret, and four children: three daughters – Ester, aged six, Marie, aged five, Sara, aged three – and a baby son, Thomas, aged a couple of months. His second daughter Frauncis had died aged only a few days and was buried on 8 September 1596. His first-born son, who had – as was customary – taken his father's name, had died at less than eight months old, in November 1598. This information is preserved in the register[12] of All Hallows Barking, near the Tower of London, Timberlake's parish church, where he is called 'Harry Tymberly'. This was clearly the name everyone called him colloquially, though it was not how he would sign his name formally. Londoners then, like now, cut corners of pronunciation.

Maybe there was some solace for Timberlake in travelling far away. After the death of two children, he could drown himself in a sea of unknowing, fill himself with adventure, grand goals and new experiences, detach himself from the pain. Leaving baby Thomas in his mother's arms – leaving his wife for God knows how long – could have been, in some ways, also a relief.

Where did he live? He had a house somewhere just west of the Tower of London, within the parish boundaries of All Hallows Barking, with all the densely packed timber-framed buildings with thatched roofs, all the buzz of a city brimming with merchants and hawkers, street performers and vagabonds, drunk sailors and street children, wealthy aristocrats and cobblers, horses and carts, piles of animal excrement, chickens, cows.

Today we call this area of central London 'the City', a name that is a legacy of what went before, a shorthand for 'the City of London', which was in fact part of a twin metropolis, with the City of Westminster – the true capital – lying to its west. It was a kind of semi-autonomous state within a state, ruled by the Lord Mayor and a council of aldermen (generally wealthy merchants) with tremendous power. There were ancient walls and gates to the City of London, and Londoners were conscious of their occupation of a town with a venerable history. In 1598 John Stow published the fruit of eight years' labour, the great *Survey of London*, which must have given everyone a sense of living in a place that was a pinnacle of world civilisation. There was the great Norman cathedral of St Paul's, 593ft long and one of the largest in England. There were the wondrous Inns of Court and their gardens, Bridewell Palace, the Guildhall, the commercial hub of the Royal Exchange. London had 109 churches and fifty-two company halls: Ironmongers, Fishmongers, Clothworkers, Mercers, Vintners, Tallow Chandlers, Grocers, you name it.[13] Everywhere you went the City burst with confidence, theatre, poetry, music, dance, buying, selling, chattering of news, eating, drinking, watching, commuting.

The City had sprawled out, as cities do, and was not only tied to Westminster but to Southwark, across the river at the southern end of London Bridge. 'The Bridge', as it was called (as 'the City', or 'the River'), was a twelfth-century feat of engineering, and actually 'more of a continuous street than a bridge', says Stow. It was a jam-packed, built-up thoroughfare over the Thames which boasted of the English island's love of the waves. The Bridge, with its 60ft-high arches, was so strong it could accommodate a load of fine buildings that seemed a tribute to creative architecture, with their centrepiece, Nonesuch House, like something from a Russian tale: four storeys high, onion-domes on towers, and all the walls painted in bright colours. At the northern end, huge water wheels generated power from the Thames' current. At the southern end, at the Great Stone Gate, the heads of decapitated traitors were positioned like olives stuck on toothpicks, marking the border between the City and the ribald world beyond.

Southwark, the ribald world, was home to the Globe Theatre, built in 1599, and other playhouses: the Swan, the Rose, and also the Bear Garden for bear-baiting. It boasted taverns, brothels, gambling dens and Borough Market. It was in Southwark that visiting sailors could find an ale, a meal, a game and a whore.

As an affluent merchant, captain and shipowner, Timberlake would have had a reasonably large residence, with servants and horses, perhaps a house overlooking the Thames as shown in wide-angle views carefully sketched by visiting Dutchmen (Figure 2). High dwellings rose up from the great Thames, and hugged the ships moored at the 'legal quays' beside them like mothers clasping children prone to stray. The 'legal quays' were where foreign ships would unload and pay the duties at the nearby Custom House.

The river was a watery highway alive with vessels calling into port from the Continent, Scandinavia, North Africa, the Italian states. The section of the Thames partly abutting the parish of All Hallows Barking was known as the 'Pool of London'. It was the main harbour. Boats went off to look for the succulent eels that were the delight of customers in taverns and markets. Fishing boats sailed out to bring in some of the 118 species of fish in the river. Wherries hustled for customers who would sail from the wharves of the City to Bermondsey or Southwark. Flat-bottomed row-boats called 'lighters' unloaded cargo from elegant ships and transferred it to warehouses and markets in Eastcheap or Cheapside, thereby making the ships lighter (hence their name). New galleons from far-away places arrived with strange flags and stranger-looking sailors. The Tower sat stolidly square overlooking the scene, an ancient antithesis to the dazzling Nonesuch House, and a symbol of the Queen's sensitivity to anything smacking of treason.

In the winter of 1600, however, Timberlake's home was also his prison.

In June 1600, Queen Elizabeth – briefed on what incredible profits certain members of the Levant Company had made through their monopoly – wanted more of a share paid to the Crown. The Company refused. In June the Queen's charter to the Levant Company was abruptly withdrawn, leaving the Company literally high and dry: a withdrawal of the charter meant a withdrawal of their right to trade, and their monopoly. In July, they promised to pay the Queen £4,000 per annum.[14] It was a tax indicative of the lucrative Mediterranean trade, selling English wool, lead and tin for spices, drugs, currants and wine. The Queen got what she wanted. A renewal of the charter was promised in August, but the Queen dragged her heels, toying with the fortunes of the entrepreneurial merchants by not issuing a new charter. By December the Levant Company merchants must have been desperate. Usually ships for Syria sailed before 1 June, but Timberlake's *Trojan* was stuck.

The Levant Company in its general court accepted tenders from the owners and masters of vessels, and would decide on which to take on. Terms were made for freightage by the court and Timberlake would have signed an agreement, which also included a bond of £500 for his due performance, an enormous sum indicative of the money he could in fact command. He had agreed to take the stock belonging to Levant Company merchants, including that of Richard Staper, the co-founder (in 1581) of the Company, a former governor, and one of the leading merchants of London.[15] The date of departure was fixed by the general court.[16]

Timberlake must have been in an awkward position. He himself was a private trader, and a shipowner. Clearly, he was anticipating good remuneration for his services as Master, and for transport of cargo. A job with the Levant Company was an excellent deal, as a rule. Ship captains were allowed to trade a stipulated quantity of goods in their own name, without membership of the Company. But Staper had to wait for the new charter. Timberlake did not sail at the time he should have sailed, in the summer. He ended up sailing very late, on wintry seas.

He was held back, when timing was everything. Soon the cooler weather would end on the Barbary Coast and Egypt, and sales of English woollens would dwindle drastically. Without the sales of woollens Timberlake would be able to buy no drugs or spices. The leading men of the Levant Company could look at the grey Thames and the forest of ships waiting there like those incarcerated in the Tower could look through thin slit windows out at the same scene, with the same yearning for royal remission and sense of utter powerlessness. Timberlake could walk the streets, down Tower Street towards Eastcheap market, as a supposedly free man, but he could not sail. And if he could not sail he could not earn money, after parting with such a colossal bond for his ship and his services, which he had probably had to borrow. He was trapped, and being trapped was something that Henry Timberlake could not endure. As we shall see, it was his Achilles' heel.

Timberlake was not the only one who was trapped. Oddly, there was another group of people likewise stranded in London whose situation was even more uncomfortable: the Moors.

There were sixteen Moors in the delegation, sent by the Sultan of Morocco to Queen Elizabeth, apparently on a trade mission, who wanted to go home. Instead, they too were walking the streets, unable to leave. They wandered around the markets in their strange apparel, weighing different products out of interest, and making careful notes on everything. London marketeers did not understand why there was this embassy, which never seemed to leave, and people considered the men of the deputation to be spies. The Moors seemed too interested in gaining a precise knowledge of English economics. The purpose of this, so people said, was to work out how high they could raise their prices for sugar. They gained a reputation for fierce bargaining and uncharitable behaviour. It was one thing to have visiting merchants stay in London for a few weeks, buying up produce for their homeward journey and to sell back at home; it was another thing to have a kind of permanent embassy installed, nosing about and asking endless questions for reasons no one understood, with a manner that many Londoners thought superior, stingy and cold.[17]

Queen Elizabeth herself had not intended on holding them captive for months in her grey country, but in a striking display of lack of omnipotence, she was unable to coerce any mariner to take them where they wanted to go. True, they were being housed in the elegant residence of Alderman Radclyffe, in a swanky street near the Royal Exchange, but they were effectively as stuck as Timberlake, because they had asked the Queen to convey them to Aleppo in Syria, and the

Queen had asked the shipowners if they would equip a ship for the purpose, to no avail. With her particular stand-off with the Levant Company presumably causing bitterness, procrastination and confusion, the ship captains all refused, understandably being in no mood to do the Queen any favours under the circumstances. What was the point of a voyage if you did not have a charter to trade? So then the Queen decided to equip one of her warships instead. However, the Moors objected that sailing an armed English warship – as opposed to a merchantman – into Ottoman waters might look a little provocative, and the plan was abandoned. So the Moroccan deputation was marooned in London, for months. They wanted to be taken to Aleppo, and Elizabeth could not arrange it.

The Queen's advisers put it about that no one would take the Moors home because merchants and mariners thought it odious and scandalous to be seen as friendly towards infidels. This was complete rubbish. All the operations of the Levant Company depended on merchants and mariners being, in some way, friendly to infidels. The problem they had was not with the Moors, it was with the Queen, who seemed to be holding all the merchants of the Levant Company hostage by her delay with the charter, while apparently very much wishing to sustain the trade with the Grand Signior.

Mutterings about the Queen aside, there were even more about the Moors. Most Londoners were both repelled and fascinated at the same time by their deputation. The Moors had caused a sensation at the Queen's coronation anniversary festivities, on 17 November 1600, when they shared a platform with the Russian embassy. Imagine: the exotic Russians and Moors, side by side. They were as exciting as a visiting group of pop stars. But there were rumours of murder, passion and vice. It seemed that Londoners could believe anything about them. Villainous intrigues and lustful shenanigans: that was what was going on there in Alderman Radclyffe's house, and everyone proper and respectable *knew* it.

No one knew why they were *really* there. The mission from Morocco was a complete mystery. The public, and even the Levant Company, was kept in the dark. Passing the Moors in the street, Timberlake would have had no idea why they had come in the first place – a strange matter we shall return to in due course.

Of course, time tends to resolve all things one way or another. The Moors eventually decided to abandon the plan to continue towards Aleppo, and found passage back to Morocco. As for Timberlake, after months of deadlock, the dispute between the Crown and the Levant Company resolved itself. A new charter was issued on 31 December 1600 in the form of letters patent that granted 'priviledges, liberties and immunities' for fifteen years, backdated to Michaelmas, 29 September, which presumably allowed the Company to deal with goods that had arrived in the port, and supposedly ships that had sailed willy-nilly.[18] Richard Staper could breathe a sigh of relief and allow his stock to go out on the high seas.

Timberlake was free.

He would leave London some weeks before Essex's disastrous rebellion, full of confidence and loyalty to his Queen. His wife, Margaret, and the children would be left alone again. Now the Captain's thoughts would focus on his other woman: his ship, the *Trojan*.

2

The Ship and the Sea

The *Trojan* was not a large ship by today's standards, but larger than the *Mayflower*, the old merchant ship that took Puritans to New England in 1620, having worked around Norway and the Mediterranean. This was 180 tons, 113ft long, 25ft wide and took 102 passengers on board, all tightly squeezed in. Timberlake's *Trojan*, on the other hand, could take 300 passengers. In the 1609 edition of Timberlake's account, it is stated that he had a crew of sixty. Records of the Levant Company indicate that initially its chartered ships were 100–300 tons, and carried crews of twenty-five to sixty men.[1] That makes the *Mayflower* a medium, rather than small, ship, but the *Trojan*, with sixty men, was large, like the ship that appears at the frontispiece of the account of the primary voyage of the East India Company (Figure 3): it was a four-rigged, low-charged galleon, perhaps with two gun decks.

The *Trojan* was one of many. By 1599 the Levant Company had twenty ships in Italian waters alone, and in the following year it had freighted sixteen additional vessels, even with the hiccough in its activities.[2] So Timberlake would have been busy with meetings with the Levant Company merchants, especially Richard Staper and his sons, making agreements, organising supplies, negotiating freight charges, ensuring he had a fit crew of mainly grown men (apart from the cabin boys), hiring a pilot, boatswains, a clerk for the accounts, carpenters, a cook and assistant, a barber-cum-surgeon, a cooper, gunner, the sailors, apprentices.

He could reclaim the Thames. He would be again on the water, which linked all the continents of the globe in its embrace. The Thames, to a mariner, was a single meandering avenue in a huge labyrinth of shipping lanes. There the *Trojan* was prepared for sail: a magnificent tall ship polished, proud, like a fine horse ready for a race.

Finally, there was the day of departure. Timberlake would now have been firmly the man in charge, commanding and energetic, ready to be gone after all the months of waiting. You can see the scene. A huge winch hoists the last cargo on board from the shore. Ropes are untied pinning the ship to the shore, and the ship manoeuvres out, as sails are quickly unfurled to catch the slight breeze that will take them through to the English Channel. The crowd shouts and cheers. People wave their arm. And among those arms there are those of Timberlake's wife, Margaret, and his young family. Timberlake leaves them all, to voyage towards Barbary, and Egypt, looking for good trade and fair winds, to bring back a fortune and tales of wonder.

Many aspects of a sea-going voyage in 1601 seem primitive or slightly strange. You might imagine a captain at the wheel peering into the distance through a telescope. Timberlake did not have a telescope. It was decades before these became small enough to be used on board ship. He would have had to rely upon a lookout sitting in a crow's nest high on the mainmast or foremast to search for enemy ships, rocks, land, or other hazards. Steering in 1601 was done by whipstaff, connected to the tiller, and a man would have to steer it according to the instructions from the Captain, the Master, or Ship's Mate.

The Captain and the Master need not be the same person. The Master, actually, could often be more the man in charge of the ship than the Captain. The Master was a career sailor, responsible for navigating the ship, and controlling the crew. The Captain might be a gentleman, a patron, a merchant and adventurer, and some were more adept at seamanship than others. However, Henry Timberlake was Master and Captain and shipowner all rolled into one, a man whose knowledge of the oceans was sound, a man who took command, and knew the business of navigation. The top career sailor here would be his Mate.

Navigation was a complex and secret science, and there would have been a table spread out with charts and equipment. Latitude was determined by means of a quadrant, which meant lining up the top of the instrument with the pole star, the end star of Ursa Minor. You needed a clear sky and keen sight for the instruments essential to Elizabethan navigation: the mariner's astrolabe, sundial, quadrant. Perhaps the ship also had two pocket globes: one terrestrial, showing the known continents and principal ports, and the other celestial, where colourful constellations danced across a world turned inside-out.

What guided Timberlake initially would have been experience, a compass, the position of the sun glimpsed through clouds, and a rutter. A rutter was a nautical guide book, with descriptions of navigations, and it was a top secret document. It was considered essential that the crew did not actually know how to navigate, in case of mutiny. Best they never knew quite where they were. All the instruments, equipment, charts and the rutter would have been kept away from prying eyes, in a room under lock and key, for Timberlake's own use. He alone could look at the shape of France and Spain drawn on the chart in front of him. The shores were inked with bold black lines, and all the ports were listed, with their names jutting out like an edge of frayed cloth. Then he could pull out another chart: the coast of North Africa, sweeping along to Egypt, where the continent of Asia and the continent of Africa met, with the Nile River as their border. This was where he could make his fortune.

Such maritime charts were used by Abraham Ortelius in 1570 to make the most accurate maps of the world. It was possible then to see how nations fitted together, how seas were connected, and the relative proportions of everything (more or less). But away from the coastal cities Ortelius knew little of what there might be in Africa or Asia. Ortelius' map of Europe is quite detailed for the western lands, but south and east were large expanses with names only around the seas, apart from a few exceptions: Cairo, Jerusalem, Damascus (see cover illustration).

Timberlake also had to know about war. Perhaps he had been old enough to have taken part in the repulsion of the Spanish Armada in 1588. Certainly, there was a gunner on board to be ready to fire cannon. A ship loaded with cargo from England was vulnerable to attack, and if needs be the crew had to fight. The rows of cannon on both sides would have enabled the *Trojan* to fend off pirates. Ships of this time were resilient and armed for both defence and aggression, and they could be fast and fleet. The only problem with a wind-powered sailing vessel like the *Trojan* was if no wind blew: then a galley – a ship that could be drawn by oars – had the upper hand, and a galleon was a sitting duck.

This was the era of the swashbuckling adventurers. 'Swash' was the sound made by the sword swishing down and striking the shield, the buckler. There was practice of the techniques on deck, when time permitted, so that all would be ready with their skills to fend off pirates. Swordsmanship, gun practice, wrestling: that was part of the routine training. Rifles and pistols had to be made ready in advance with shot, and could not be reloaded quickly. Once your shot was fired, you had to rely on traditional fighting methods.

As for Timberlake's crew, seafaring had its thrills, but the mortality rate was very high. Men went to sea because their life options were so miserably limited they had nothing much to lose. Victuallers, who supplied the food for long voyages, were not always reliable, and the standard salt beef, pork and fish, the cheese and biscuits, beer and wine were sometimes bad at the outset. Food poisoning and disease were more likely to kill a crewman than attack by enemies. Their quarters were congested, dark, smelly and unhygienic. Discipline was usually strict. Then there was the unfortunate possibility of death or enslavement at the hands of pirates and privateers.

Edward Webbe, master gunner of the ship *Henrie*, left Alexandria in 1576 and:

> sodeinly in the way, wee met with fiftie saile of the Turkes gallies, with which Gallies we fought two daies and two nightes, and made great slaughter amongst their men, we being in all threescore men, verie weake for such a multitude, and having lost fiftie of our 60 men, faintnes constrained us to yield to them, by reason wee wanted winde to helpe our selves, and the calme was so great unto them, as there was no way for us to escape.[3]

Webbe was taken prisoner, beaten, shaved, put in cotton clothes, manacled by wrists and ankles, and set to row an Ottoman galley for five years, before being forced into the Ottoman army. He did not manage to return to England for thirteen years, after experiencing grisly horrors wherever he went. His was not a tale to inspire confidence in seafaring. There were other similar stories, told by ancient mariners in crowded port taverns, and some were written down, with plenty of poetic licence to spice up the narrative, and a heavy emphasis on sex: if you were lucky you might get to be the slave of a Sultan, and find yourself servicing the erotic whims of his concubines; if you were unlucky, and young, you were buggered by a gang of pirates and castrated.[4]

Seafarers and passengers of old went through abject misery to get from one place to another: sheer travail. John Rawdon, a traveller en route to Syria in 1607, managed to get a ship from Venice to the island of Zante but then waited four months for another ship to take him on to Alexandria since the winds had turned unfavourable. On his way home the following year he had wanted to make an overland trip to England from Naples, but the ship was so blown by winds that it did not manage to stop there, and did not put to port until it reached Alicante. He then managed to get a small Scottish vessel of the Leith, bound for Dover, which was then becalmed and set upon by Ottoman privateers in two oared galleys. Rawdon writes:

> we thought it to small purposse for us to withstande them, yet knowing that if they toke us that the shippe & goods wer not sufficient for them, but ourselves [would be] made slaves, therfor [we] resolved to fight it out so longe as we coulde, & then to blowe up ourselves & shipp together.[5]

Fortunately, they decided to talk before opting for this radical course of self-annihilation, and when the 'Turks' demanded it the Scottish captain put down the ship's sails. Then there passed a conversation. The privateer commander 'demaunded what she was laden with, which indeed was salt, & so we toulde them, at which they did spitt & semed to be angrye therat'. The commander then wanted to know what else was on board: 'besides salt also what passingers we had aborde, whether ther wer any Spaniardes or Florentes' and so on. Rawdon might have thought his goose was cooked, but amazingly the assailants:

> wer loth to trobbe themselves with so mean a prisse, consideringe they must of necessity put some of ther owne men into her which woulde disable ther gallees somethinge, or otherwisse go directly home with her into Barbarea, wherby they should then loose the benefitt of som better purchasse.

After three or four hours of indecision, the privateers decided to let them go and wished them, '*Bon Viagio*'.

Despite being wished, incredibly, 'bon voyage' from a group of ruthless privateers, Rawdon gives a completely woebegone summary of conditions on board
the ship as it travelled from Alicante to England, a journey 'most unhappye' that
took seventeen weeks, in which '[we] wer often times driven backe further in
on[e] night then we coulde fetche up againe in a weeke, but always contrary
windes [blew so] that indeede the iourney proves very tedious & evill to me
for many respectes'. Rawdon was so deprived of food that he thought fondly of
ship's biscuit rather than stale bread.

Storms on the English Channel could blow so fiercely that they would send
galleons to their doom. There are numerous accounts of ships being thrown off
course the moment they hit open sea, such are the vicissitudes of this stretch of
water. The ship *Hector*, in which was Thomas Dallam, an organ-maker who had
the difficult job of accompanying the clockwork organ he made, as a gift from
Queen Elizabeth to the Ottoman Sultan Mehmet III in 1599, was so buffeted
by winds and sea that it was thrown off course towards Ireland, and the Captain
managed to turn south only with a huge amount of labour, and sheer luck.[6]

Nevertheless, the English could not complain about the weather all the time.
It was the weather that had foiled two recent – massive – attempts by Spain
to conquer England: in October 1596 the Governor of Castile had sailed from
Ferrol with over 100 ships and 16,000 men but the fleet was scattered by a storm
off Cape Finisterre; the following year an attempt with 136 ships and 9,000 troops
was likewise dispersed by foul weather, this time close to their target, off Brittany.

In other words, travel by sea in a northern autumn or winter on a heavily
laden galleon was extremely dangerous, and great courage and skill was needed to
adjust the sails with strong winds and huge waves. Sodden through with sea and
rain, Timberlake himself had to control and navigate the ship, barking orders to
his men, as the swell turned them this way, that way, sinking low, pulling high. A
winter's storm, the freezing wind and sea, put an end to many ventures.

When the wind blew fairly, ships kept a course wide of land, beyond sight of
France, at an average speed of about 7 knots, all going well, until they reached the
southern coast of Spain, and the town of Territh or Tenerith (= Tarifa), close to
the sea. Then there was Gibraltar, with 'Ape Hill', on the side of Africa, and the
Trojan sailed through the swift current of the Strait of Gibraltar into the calmer
waters of the Mediterranean.[7] Now the sun would shine. It was here, for the
English, that the exotic world began.

3

The Moor

The first port of call was Algiers, a Barbary port that was officially ruled by the Ottoman authorities but in reality was loyal to no one but pirates.

Algiers was a walled city in the shape of a topsail, broad below and narrow above, which stretched up the side of a hill. The walls were double, with a ditch as well. Near the edge of the sea was a great castle. Such defences were needed against Spain, which had in the past invaded. England being also an enemy of Spain, Algiers was considered a friendly port, a place where the luxuries of North Africa could be bought, and there was a chance for rest and relaxation. This was despite the fact that the English would sometimes end up there as slaves. In the late fifteenth century the slave Treasurer to Hassan Bassa, the King of Algiers, was from Bristol, a man named Samson Rowley. The story goes that he was a boy on the *Swallow*, sailing from England in 1577, travelling with his merchant father Francis, when pirates attacked the crew and passengers were seized and taken to Algiers as slaves. Samson Rowley was taken off, castrated, and sold as a eunuch to high officials. He was encountered in 1586 as Assan (Hassan) Aga.[1] A slave could go places in the Ottoman administration, but at a price.

Taking slaves being a prime business of pirates, Algiers had a booming slave market trading in white- and black-skinned victims as well as the main markets for everything else, where the provenance of booty was not an issue. The Barbary pirates were extremely successful. Sometimes, the booty they seized was colossal; a single ship might in total have a cargo worth up to £180,000.[2] In this time, maritime trade was the big business of the world, and the costs and profits were beyond imagining for ordinary people who earned a shilling a day and who bought a loaf for a penny, people who lived in an era where wages were low and food was expensive. No wonder there were pirates. Between 1609 and 1616, seven years, 466 English vessels were captured and all aboard enslaved.[3] The figures would have been the much same in previous decades.

Pirates were, as in popular imagination, flamboyant, knowing no loyalty to anything but their own ships, and they knew no outside law. Among pirates, you could have Dutch, Turkish (from Ottoman lands), English, French, Spanish,

Moorish (Maghrebi), Arab all in the one boat, united by the wish to plunder. The English had more of a reputation for piracy than just about anyone else: when an English ambassador to Constantinople in 1583 was told by an Ottoman official that the English ships were nothing but common pirate vessels, he rather proved the point by punching the accuser rather than engaging in polite diplomacy.[4]

As for the *Trojan* and Captain Timberlake, Algiers was deemed safe enough. There was an English Levant Company consul, John Audellay,[5] waiting for news from London, and it is with him that Timberlake would have stayed. Here, on the Barbary coast, the crew could go ashore, provisions could be bought, and sales made. A warm ambience after the cold of the north tended to loosen the English into lasciviousness. Algiers had its lures, not only foreign whores, but also opium dens. There at the markets twice a week Timberlake could begin selling his stock of woollens, lead and tin, and perhaps some Russian ware as well, and buy in more victuals.

Timberlake as Captain had to think of ways to make money to finance the voyage. One of the ways to do this was to accept paying passengers, who were usually crammed into any spare space below. It was here, at Algiers, that Timberlake took on board up to 300 people – Christians, Jews and Muslims.[6] Timberlake seems to have crammed in everyone he could, for the sake of extra cash in hand, estimating that he could deal with a heavy ship.

The unnamed Moor who would play an important part in Henry Timberlake's adventure was one of these passengers. Who was he?

There are a couple of clues. He was, like Timberlake, a merchant, because he spoke the lingua franca, 'Frank',[7] a fusion tongue that facilitated trade in the Mediterranean. You learnt it fluently in order to talk with foreigners, to do business in the lucrative markets of maritime trade. It was a little-recorded language based on Italian, with Provençal French, Spanish, Portuguese, Greek, and a smattering of Turkish and Arabic, that enabled international deals to be conducted smoothly and diplomacy to function. In North Africa the Arabic-speakers despaired that the Europeans – the *Frangi* (= Franks) – had at least twenty-five languages and none could understand another. Unless European traders had interpreters, then there had to be some effort on the part of Europeans to pool their languages into a single form. English did not feature as a significant tongue at all, since England was marginal in terms of the main trading harbours. You might as well have spoken Icelandic in terms of its value. Once there had been Latin to use, but Medieval Latin had become the property of scholars and ecclesiastics: no one spoke it for trade. English merchants might additionally know other languages, depending on their main trading contacts, but the lingua franca went everywhere, including English ports, where it ultimately gave England such words as 'savvy', 'palaver', 'bimbo' and 'lingo', from sailor-speak that went into the theatre and travelled with players. '*Sabir parlar?*' you might ask, 'Do you know how to talk [the language]?'[8]

The other clue about this man is that he was on the *hajj*. This Moor, while still fit enough, undertook the holy pilgrimage to where the Prophet Mohammed lived and died. He had already travelled over 435 miles from his home city of Fes, a great university town, renowned for being a centre of culture, theological study and the arts, where donkeys loaded with fresh hides for tanning swayed along ancient alleys lined with great containers of fluorescent spices, metalwork, jewellery, ceramics, carpentry, textiles, leatherwork and carpets. In its labyrinthine streets men talked of high things, as well as business, and valued beauty: the curves of the intricate arabesques, the geometrical patterns of doors, ornate calligraphy, the orchestrations of colour.

It was and is the duty of every Muslim male to undertake a pilgrimage, the *hajj*, to Mecca once in life, though travel at this time being what it was, only the most devout and determined dared make the journey from *al-Maghreb al-Aqsa*, 'the farthest west'. Pilgrims needed a certain amount of money to finance the *hajj*, an amount beyond the reach of most. It was not a usual mid-career move. With good fortune it might take as long as twelve months to complete: a gap year that few men could afford, given the responsibilities of feeding your family while you were away. You were not expected to trade en route, but rather to come back with nothing but the vision of sanctity and sacred mementoes.

Once you made the *hajj*, and if you returned, then you became a special, respected person in the community, a *hajji*, someone with a holy aura, who was expected to live a better life than anyone else. But very many did not return to a place as far away from Mecca as Morocco. To travel to Mecca meant to surrender everything you knew of normal life, to give up on your business, to relinquish your ties to those you loved, and to trust yourself wholly to God. Everything was in God's hands – life and death, travel and rest – and there was a meaning to it. The *hajj* was the ultimate surrender to God's will, the ultimate surrender of the self to the forces of the universe.

After leaving Algiers, the next stop for the *Trojan* was Tunis, some 560 miles eastwards, and there was the continual rhythm of shipboard life to surrender to also: the cleaning, the shifting of sails, the routines of cooking and training, the observations. Passengers could not be accommodated on deck all in one go, and were permitted only in small groups, in shifts. This Maghrebi would then at times have been stretching his legs on deck, perhaps watching the Captain instruct a couple of young mariners in self-defence. This is how you stab your dagger. This is how you wrestle a pirate to the floor. But whatever active part he had once played in the martial arts was now relinquished. He too could shoot a pistol, and wield a sword. He too knew how to speak to foreign traders, and talk of money, exchanges and quantities. But all this was gone, far away, into a past left behind in the streets of Fes, where his family lived out their lives without him, amid the white-washed walls and blue doors, the wrought-iron gates, splattering fountains and gleaming glass.

Clearly, from what follows, the man from Fes liked Captain Timberlake. In the way he dealt with his crew and passengers there was perhaps nothing of the arrogant swagger of some other Europeans. The Moor would have listened to the melodious and yet clipped language of English, noted Timberlake's careful checking of the seas for pirates, and observed as a friend of his talked with the Captain. But he, apparently more reserved by nature, stayed a little reclusively apart on board the merchant ship, and managed not to make a strong impression on Timberlake. He would wrap himself up in robes against the chill sea winds, and watch.

The journey eastwards 1,864 miles from Algiers to Alexandria was often slower than the trip south from England, since the winds could be slighter, and at times ships were becalmed. It might take a week to reach Tunis, where they stopped for a time, and then another fourteen days to reach Egypt, if they were lucky. While the Mediterranean in winter is generally less hostile than the Atlantic, strange things happen at sea, in the form of erratic winds, and waterspouts. John Locke of London, travelling eastwards in 1553, describes such a phenomenon:

> The same day in the afternoone we sawe in the element a cloud with a long tayle like unto the tayle of a serpent... and we did see the water under the sayde cloud as if were like a smoke or myste.[9]

Locke also in his account shows how passengers did not take navigation for granted. In 1601 you very much hoped the Captain and Mate knew where they were going, and felt very grateful to them if they did. Locke set off to Palestine on a pilgrim ship departing from Venice on 16 July 1553 (by 1601 these ships did not sail, as there were too few pilgrims), and they successfully managed to get to Cyprus, departing there on 14 August.

However, as they neared Jaffa (Joppa) on the Palestinian coast, they ran into trouble. That is, they got lost. On 17 August the mariners reported that they were six miles from Jaffa, but this proved wrong. Uncertain, they dropped anchor seven miles from shore and sent a boat with the pilot and master gunner 'to learne the coast, but they were returned, not having seen tree nor house nor spoken with any man'. However, they had scrambled up a hill and thought they had seen Jerusalem in the distance, which meant they had overshot Jaffa by fifty miles. On 18 August they remained at anchor waiting for wind, and on the 19th they set sail, but the current was more forceful than the wind and they drifted in the wrong direction, until about 4 o'clock in the afternoon, though then there was panic when the ship's cat, owned by their patron, fell overboard and had to be rescued.

By 20 August, things looked grim. 'It was still calme, and the current so strong still one way that we were not able to stemme the streame. Moreover, we knew not where we were.' The Captain (Master), pilot and others held a meeting and decided to send another party to shore, and still found no one to talk to. They set sail again, came to anchor again, went on shore again, and finally they spotted some human beings. Unfortunately, these men, seeing the Venetians, took to their heels in terror. Only with 'much a doe' did the Venetians manage to convince the 'Moors' (= local Muslims) that they should stay and speak with them 'which men when they came together were not able to understand ech other' seeing as the Moors spoke Arabic, and the Venetians did not, though they tried Turkish. They had to use sign language, and drawing on the sand. Finally, the Moors understood that the Venetians wanted to get to Jerusalem, and told them that they were eighty miles north of their target. Eighty miles! They must have been somewhere between Acre and Tyre, and if they had not found someone to 'talk' to, they would have kept going the wrong way.

Many of the Muslim passengers would have congregated together, five times every day, to pray, up on deck and below. It would have kept them focused on the purpose of the journey. Here, there was no call from the *muezzin* to tell the faithful the right time for prayer. There was no *mihrab* to indicate the *qibla*, the direction of Mecca, the direction in which to pray. They had to rely on one of their number with expertise in the art of the determining the *qibla* and the times. For this there was an instrument: an astrolabe. A compass was built into a round brass plate, and the expert had to make a small adjustment each day to the pointer. This was the world made into mathematics, an applied instance of spherical trigonometry. Prayer is timed with the sun: daybreak, noon, mid-afternoon, sunset, evening. Like the ship's Captain, or the pilot, the expert in prayer times knew the heavens, and navigated by the sun and the stars. Needless to say, they shared the common assumption that the sun moved around the earth. Copernicus was known and respected by few. Galileo's discoveries were still to come.

The time returned again and again to kneel and bow, to submit to God, to focus on surrendering oneself. The Muslims purified themselves with water, and prayed together in a well-rehearsed ritual: standing, kneeling, bowing down, throwing their bodies into the rhythm of the universe, of the stars, sun and moon, of the times. The English seamen were also called to prayer, morning and evening, by their Captain; it was his duty, as it was for Francis Drake in his voyage around the world, thirty years earlier. It was the English way. The other Christians, from North Africa, would have had their own prayers, and then there were the Jewish prayers, and their Sabbath rituals.

How strange, to see this ship, the *Trojan*, not only as a vehicle of transport but as a kind of universal temple, a floating locus of prayer and praise: different languages, different rituals, all directed towards one shared God that everyone understood in different ways.

At night, below deck, passengers were packed in tight – men, women, children, babies, goats, chickens, donkeys, luggage – and sleep can only have been fitful. During the day there was not much to do but rest, or watch the crew and the sea, when passengers came up on deck. William Biddulph writes of his own experience:

> About these parts we saw flying fishes, as big as an Hearing, with two great finnes like unto wings before, and two lesse behind; who being chased by Dolphines and Bonitaes (= striped tunnies), fly as long as their wings are wet, which is not farre, but oft a gables length. Porpices and many other strange and deformed fishes we saw in our voiage, the names whereof we knew not. We saw also sword fishes and threshers: which two kind of fishes are deadly enemies unto the Whale. The swordfish swimmeth under him and pricketh him up, and then the Thresher, when hee hath him up, belaboureth him with his flayle or extraordinary long taile, and maketh him roare.[10]

Perhaps such aquatic warfare resulting in roaring whales is not a case of completely accurate scientific reporting, but marine life was clearly a subject of conversation. A sea voyage does that. The tiny changes in the waves and the wind, a plop of a fish in the water, the shape of clouds, seagulls, all become very interesting after a time. To be accompanied by dolphins is a sensation, and any self-appointed marine biologist would have gained rapt attention at once.

With the same eye for natural phenomena, Thomas Dallam wrote – with archaic spelling – of whales with great spouts, before coming into the Mediterranean and, east of Algiers, an extraordinary display of lightning, 'for we myghte se the eayre open and a fier lyke a verrie hote iron taken out of a smythe's forge, somtimes in liknes of a roninge worme, another time lyke a horshow, and agine lyke a lege and a foute'.[11] Along with this there were great claps of thunder.

So there was the Moor, watching the Captain as he ordered the furling and unfurling of sails, shouting directions, talking to one or other of the passengers. The Moor watched as his companion spoke to Timberlake, also in Frank.

'The Moor'. I use the term here as an epithet that represents the English experience that I am here concerned to present, but otherwise he is unnamed in Timberlake's account. In Arabic, his formal name would actually have been associated with the name of his eldest son: 'the father of Abdullah', for example. Then he would have been identified by his father, his tribe, his city, or perhaps the Muslim legal rite he followed: Abu Abdullah Athil bin Omar, al Lawati, al-Fessi, al-Maliki, for example. However, al-Fessi is the best I can do for his name: 'the man from Fes'.

What did he know about the Moroccan delegation to London? They cannot have returned before he left. Perhaps that is what the Frank talk was about between al-Fessi's friend and Timberlake: how they fared, what the Londoners had thought of them, what the Queen had done. To the Moroccans the English were considered friends.

The English fought the Spanish, the enemy of Morocco. Spain was, to the Sultan, a kingdom of infidels that had, just over a century earlier, brutally seized the beautiful Muslim lands of the north, in al-Andalus, and the magnificent city of Granada. As a boy perhaps al-Fessi had seen the arrival of the English ambassador, Henry Roberts, and his grand train.

There had been favourable relations between the Moroccans and the English for years, with English merchants selling tin, lead and cloth and buying Moroccan sugar and salt-petre. There is correspondence preserved in the Hakluyt compendium about the dealings between Elizabeth I and Sultan Ahmad al-Mansour, whose name is given there as Rey Mulei Hamet, in 1585. Henry Roberts, the ambassador, remained in Morocco for three years, before his return with 'Marshok Reiz', the Moroccan ambassador. It was a case of very good diplomacy. Moroccans had been overjoyed at the defeat of the Spanish Armada by England in 1588: Spain was rightly chastised. The Sultan issued an order that, regarding the English in his domains, 'our princely counsaile wil defend them by the favor of God, from any thing that may impeach or hurt them in what sort soever they shal travaile'.[12]

Sultan Ahmad al-Mansour was the epitome of Arab elegance and culture: he traced his ancestry to the Prophet Mohammed (the Saadians, of whom he was one, were purportedly invited to Morocco years back in order to create a positive influence over the date crop of the south) and had a library of over 3,000 writings. He was also victorious in military matters. Under his rule Morocco was secure, confident and rich.[13]

So here is where we come to the real reason for the Moroccan delegation to London in 1600, a reason few people outside a privileged circle actually knew. The secret diplomacy was truly extraordinary. The embassy from Morocco that was sent by Sultan Ahmad al-Mansour was not, in fact, checking out on English commodities and measures. Those sixteen men of the highest standing in Moroccan society came to England with a very important proposal: that Morocco and England would join together 20,000 strong armies each to attack and defeat Spain, not only in Europe but in the Spanish colonies of the West Indies.[14] Given the recent attempts at Spanish invasion of England, foiled by the weather, the obliteration of the source of such terror would have seemed tempting.

The ambassador leading this mission was the Sultan's secretary, 'Abd al-Wahid bin Ma'ood bin Mohammad 'Annouri, from Fes. He was a sharp-witted, intelligent and literate man whose attitude to the English is very well caught by the unknown Elizabethan artist who painted his picture during his London sojourn (Figure 4). In this portrait, Abd al-Wahid (named as Abdul Guahid) both frowns and smiles at the same time, and his gaze is penetrating, critical and astute. His right hand is on his heart, and his left hand is poised on his sword. What must a clever, educated man like him have thought of Tudor London, or English xenophobia? It is all summed up in his expression.

No one understood why the delegation was in England, because the Queen was certainly not telling, and both the Moroccan Sultanate and the English Crown were determined to mask their real purposes by pretending the visit was a trade mission. The Queen was, in fact, quite tempted for a time by the war proposal, and one of her advisers noted: 'her Majesty in using the King of Fes, doth not arm a barbarian against a Christian, but a barbarian against a heretic.'[15]

Morocco was angry at Spain not only because the Spanish had seized Moorish lands in al-Andalus and dealt appallingly with Muslims there but because the Spanish were continually capturing Muslims to serve as slaves in the Spanish colonies in the Americas.[16] Sultan Ahmad al-Mansour was serious about his plan. With English ships and Barbary horses they could stand a good chance, and Spain could be overthrown, forever.

No one knew of this proposal but a small elite around the Sultan of Morocco and Queen Elizabeth of England, who would eventually reject the suggestion, but relations between Morocco and England were extremely good. There was a peculiar alliance in spirit. Together they might have waged war on Spain: Protestants and Muslims united against the Catholics. It is by this peculiar alliance that we can see how definitively the Crusades had ended in the English mentality. Had these two nations gone forward and been successful, their project would have made the history of the Americas a very different story.

Eventually, perhaps forty-five days after leaving England,[17] the *Trojan* arrived at Alexandria, sailing past the great fort which guarded the eastern harbour. It was not an easy port to enter. Alexandria had two concave ports on either side of a narrow peninsula of land, but the western port was reserved for Ottoman galleys 'as too full of shelves and rocks for deepe bottomes', as Henry Blount observed.[18] There would have been huge relief as they reached their destination. They had avoided piracy, foul seas and navigational errors.

Their sails were spied from far off, and the procedure that followed was always the same. As they came near to the port ships were met by a small boat carrying a pilot who knew the local conditions. He would guide the ship to an anchorage.

A party of officials arrived with documents. All the cargo was recorded by scribes, and every passenger listed, before anything was offloaded.

Such was the form, repeated time and time again.

The hours passed.

Eventually, money was paid, and the officials departed. Barges drew up along the sides of the boat. Everyone would now be transported to the Customs House.

The *Trojan* was one of the largest ships to enter this harbour, and there would have been excitement on land. The scene can easily be imagined. On the wharves, a mass of people assemble. Sounds travel. Street hawkers shout to the passengers about accommodation, places to eat, things to buy, holding up fruit, coffee, water, necklaces. Merchants call out that they have the best price for spices. Whores flash a glimpse of leg and arm from top-floor windows. Officials ensure they are not jostled, by keeping janissaries in a tight phalanx around them.

Janissaries. This was 'Turkie', land of the Ottoman empire, whose inhabitants were the 'Turks' of European eyes. The areas of the Barbary Coast still had some limited autonomy, but this was the heartland: Egypt was the jewel in the Ottoman crown.

Being on board such a ship is like being in a capsule. Your mind has adjusted to accepting that your personal territory is the small rectangle where you spread your mat to sleep each night, and every part of the boat has become familiar, safe even. As a passenger there has been nothing to do but watch faces, listen in to other people's conversations, contemplate the journey ahead, note the activities of the crew as they follow orders, joke and squabble, remember home, watch the sea, the sky, the stunningly bright stars. There are other stars too on a sea voyage – the people you cannot help but notice – and there are the people you see for the first time when you are preparing to leave, even though they have slept only a few metres away. You have become used to the rock of the boat, and its creaking, the waves swishing, breezes fingering your face and the wind bumping in the sails. There is an integrity about it.

Suddenly the alien world of land appears there before you, and it seems loud, and difficult, and not part of reality at all. A part of you is aching to be gone from the ship, to walk out to the newness. People laugh, chat excitedly, knowing that an adventure begins. A part of you recoils, and you look around sentimentally at the mesmerising sea, the familiar vessel you will never see again, and the people who have become, not necessarily friends, but characters in a drama you have been watching with the utmost attention, a drama that now ends, without an ending.

So al-Fessi would have prepared to leave, smoothed down his beard, adjusted his turban, and stood with the other pilgrims bound for Mecca. Now they would move off together, first towards the Customs House, where they would be searched and charged for possessions and goods brought into the country – collected on behalf of the Ottoman authorities by Jewish officials – and then towards a mosque, to thank God for a safe arrival.

He would have said farewell cordially to the Captain. His was not a face that would be immediately remembered by the Englishman. Al-Fessi had made no effort to impress the man in charge of the *Trojan*. There was no reason to think he would ever see Henry Timberlake again.

4

Alexandria

From Herodotus (fifth century BC) onwards it was quite customary for travellers to begin the accounts of their journeys by assuring their readers that everything was absolutely true. They then went on to recount some not very reliable information, intermixed with the truth, leaving their readers to try and pick out the pieces. Edward Webbe, for example, as an eye witness in the 1580s and '90s, wrote that in the court of Prester John (the Abyssinian emperor), there was a beast called Arians having four heads shaped like wild cats. Travellers could also recount information in a way that was both true and untrue at the same time. Webbe's unicorns in the garden of Constantinople are quite clearly rhinoceroses (though the accompanying picture indicates the classic horse variety) and two examples of 'wilde man' (and cannibal) with 'all over their bodies… wonderfull long haire' were possibly crazed chimpanzees.[1]

From Timberlake's own use of flashback, his journey prior to arrival in Alexandria, and the journey of al-Fessi, are known, but the account as printed in the 1603 edition begins with the following greeting:

> Although it passe as a generall proverbe, that travailers may tel leasings (= untruths) by authoritie: yet I being no way daunted by that bugbeare-thunderbolt, but confidently standing on the justice of my cause, my kinde commendations to all you my deare friendes.[2]

The addressees are plural, leaving us to wonder at who the recipients actually were. Timberlake is characterised here as a traveller, not as a Captain and merchant, signalling that his letter had to do with journeying rather than business. This may not in fact have been how Timberlake's letter actually began, but rather it is a fitting introduction to the printed version of it, designed by Thomas Archer. The manuscript has the beginning tacked on to the end, and it runs as follows:

> Since my deptinge from Grannd Cayro to warde the holy land I wrote a letter from Ramoth Gilliad of all my proceedings to that place and sent it with 7 other with it

to Damaskco in a Carravan to be sent from thence to Constantinople and doubtinge
that it is not yeat come to your lands I thought good to write againe.[3]

In other words, the surviving account of his travels is a second letter to his
friends in England, following one which told of the preliminary part of his
travels. It is not some well-crafted literary piece: it is just the second letter in
a sequence, in which it is apparently the only survivor and the only one to be
printed. With letters from foreign parts you never knew whether a letter was
going to arrive at its destination, so it was a wise move to create back-up letters
just in case, sketching some of the same material with some new additions to
make it sufficiently important in itself. By the time Timberlake wrote his second
letter, his first impressions of Egypt had been overwritten in his mind by new
experiences.

At any rate, 'the wonders of Egypt' were reasonably well known to people at
home in London already. The educated writers of Elizabethan England echoed
the Greeks and Romans in seeing Egypt as a fantastical place full of the strangest
things on earth, and had written about it already at some length. The mysterious
rise and fall – and the source – of the Nile; the pyramids; crocodiles; mummies;
hieroglyphics; animal-headed gods; cone-shaped dovecotes where pigeons were
bred for carrying messages, also for dung and food; reliefs of scantily-clad girls; the
ancient ruins: these things were frightening, awesome, voluptuous, secret, entic-
ing. The figure of Cleopatra, in Shakespeare's play, encapsulates the Elizabethan
image of Egypt as a whole.

It is possible, however, to reconstruct what Timberlake would have done in
Alexandria from what his English near-contemporaries did. George Sandys, in
January 1611, arrived at the port of Alexandria, where customs officials levied a
10% charge on all goods and 0.5% of all money before they were allowed ashore.
An earlier account notes how the busy Alexandrian officials, after writing down
all information about goods and persons, despatched documents by homing
pigeons to the authorities in Cairo, so that they too were kept up-to-date on
any new arrivals.[4] Sandys proceeded to the house of the French sub-consul,[5] and
perhaps Timberlake and his assistant Waldred did the same.

There was much to relate over a meal of Egyptian fare: hummous and auber-
gine dips, dates, pomegranates, yoghurts and white cheeses, bread, onions, bananas,
spicy rice with pistachios, lemons, bean salad, avocados, olives. The Alexandrian
courtyards of today are not much different from those of yesteryear, where men
would sit and discuss trade: airy places where great clouds of crimson bougain-
villea provide shade. During conversation, discussion would have turned to the
current trade situation in Egypt, which was not good, for fair weather made foul
trade in English woollens. The Egyptian winter had ended.

Then there was the Levant Company consul in Cairo, Benjamin Bishop himself. Rumour had it that the misnamed Bishop was a whore-mongering gambler,

an extortioner, and a trafficker in high-alcohol *aquavitae*. For Timberlake this cannot have been the best news to receive when he was relying on the consul not only for accommodation but for help in selling stock. Bishop had not long been in his post, but the consul had – by all reports – sunk into a state of embarrassing depravity, and could not be trusted. In this dissolution Bishop went the way of many a representative of England when placed in a warm country far away from the social mores of the homeland, being in a fairly isolated position, with no one to bother him about what he could and could not do.

For some days Timberlake would have stayed in Alexandria, arranging his onward journey and the shipment. Had he visited this town before? The way Timberlake describes his journey, it is with the tone of a new experience. For all his trading, whether with Russia, Barbary or the Levant, this seems to be the first time he had gone to Egypt. As a newcomer, he would have wanted to see what this place was like. What might he have looked at?

The greatness that once was Alexandria was sure to be on the minds of any visitor with a classical education, but Timberlake never quotes a single ancient author, and his only scholarly allusion is found in the name of his ship. When Timberlake had sailed past the great fortress, Borg al-Zafr (Kait Bey), built in 1480, he may well rather have thought of Anthony Munday's account of Englishmen, including a certain John Fox, captured by Ottomans in 1563, used as galley-slaves, and housed in an Alexandrian jail when not at sea. After fourteen years, all the 266 occupants of this jail, apparently entirely composed of captured Christians, staged a mass break-out, commandeered a galley, and sailed off to freedom.[6] It was a kind of 'escape from Alcatraz' of the sixteenth century.

William Lithgow, a Scot who visited in 1612, wrote that Alexandria 'hath two havens (= harbours), the one whereof is strongly fortified with two Castles, which defend both it selfe, and also Porto vecchio.'[7] The harbour was busy with, as John Rawdon notes, 'the shippinge which doth make theer provisione therof, which ar many, though fewe or none English, yet greatt store of French, Venetians & Mitinezes (read: Milanese?) likewisse greatt store of ther owne & of the Gran Seniors shipping & principallest that he hath.'[8]

Alexandria as a town was an old, faded queen. Once it had been the New York of antiquity and the Christian Byzantine Empire, but now it was a crumbling, unpopulous sea-port with little vitality, and had a strange position of being neither here nor there. The Romans called it *Alexandria ad Aegyptum*: Alexandria *by* Egypt. With the Mediterranean Sea to the north and Lake Mareot in the south, it was a strip of limestone white in between blue, and by 1601 that liminality was even more extreme, as the town had crept even further seaward, occupying land that had once been water, and now was built with houses, mosques and markets.

The long sandy beaches were viewed with anxiety by William Lithgow: 'The fields about the Towne are sandy, which ingender an infectious aire, especially in the moneth of August, and is the reason why strangers fall into bloody fluxes, and other heavy sicknesses.' The advice is: 'to keep my stomacke hote, to abstaine from eating of fruit, and to live soberly, with a temperate diet'.[9] More likely, what made Alexandria unhealthy was the huge number of underground cisterns (rather than wells). It enabled a ready supply of water, but the water was not necessarily very good, and in summer they were, it was said, 'fenny' (= swampy): they festered, breeding mosquitoes, bacteria and other unwholesome life-forms.

Loaded with grand visions of its classical spendour, visitors tended to note to the ruinous state of Alexandria. The gentleman scholar Henry Blount, visiting in 1634, described the town as 'almost nothing but a white heape of ruines'.[10] Goats grazed among them. Encircling these ruins and the town itself were walls punctuated by small turrets, which stood up high over the steep rocks against the sea. Actually, Europeans liked presenting great cities of the past as being 'ruinated' in the hands of Muslims, but in this sweep of nostalgic rhetoric they do at times manage to present a different reality as well. John Rawdon mentioned that on the side:

'neer the sea, right against the baye or harbore the which is a place of greatt bewtye, is a fayre Campo in which they usually meet, discoursse & take the aire, about yt ar many faire auntient buildinges in which the Turkes of the best sorte do live which buildinges ar somewhat repayred by reasone that they ar such as doth comande & governe which be manye, for that it is so greatt a place of merchandisse & traufficke.'[11]

But past splendours now gone were what interested Europeans. There were pillars everywhere, some fallen, some still standing, mostly made of porphyry and marble, the most remarkable being a huge pillar, 27 feet high, made of reddish-grey marble which stood close to the then shore on a square foundation outside the walls on the south-west side of the town. Reputedly, and wrongly, this was where the ashes of the first-century BC Roman general Pompey were laid, and the pillar was raised in honour of him by Julius Caesar. Another story was that one of the Ptolemaic rulers (fourth to first centuries BC) erected the column at the furthest extreme of the harbour, as it was, to defend the city from naval invasion. At the very top was a kind of laser-gun: Ptolemy placed a magical steel mirror which, when uncovered, would set enemy ships on fire. Subverted by the foe – the Romans – the mirror lost its power, and that was the end of the technology. Imagination has always worked wonders with ancient Egyptian monuments. In fact the pillar was erected by the Emperor Diocletian at the end of the third century AD.

On the north side, within the city towards the sea, were two great obelisks covered in hieroglyphics, one standing, called 'Pharaoh's Needle', and one fallen, 'halfe buried in rubbidge'.[12] Later, in the nineteenth century, these twin

'Cleopatra's Needles' (actually made by Thutmosis III, *c.*1500 BC and originally erected in Heliopolis) would be given by the Egyptian government to London and New York respectively.

A self-appointed local guide and interpreter (*tarjaman*, often rendered 'dragoman' in English), given some *bakshish* (= remuneration, money), would give the travellers a tour and duly they wrote down what they were told. 'Here, Sir, are the ruins of Cleopatra's palace! See – the gate where she received Mark Antony after their overthrow at Actium! And look, over there, the ruins of Alexander the Great's palace, the greatest general of all time, who founded this magnificent city! And do you want to buy drugs? Do you want antiquities? Coffee? My uncle has a shop...' All a guide needed was a pile of pillars and a few walls to weave the myths around, while leading his captive audience to a helpful trader.

Visiting Christians could not go everywhere, however. Owing to attacks over time by the Cypriots, French and Venetians, the Ottoman administration ordered that they were not permitted to ascend any mounds of ruins that gave them a good view over the city, but local antiquities dealers sold them artefacts that local fossickers dug up from these mounds, and impressed the visitors especially with collections of finely made seals and rings in which tiny figures were cut into precious stones. On top of one of the mounds was a high watch-tower where men constantly scanned the seas to give notice of approaching sails.[13]

Christians could, nevertheless, visit a very important site in Christian history: the place where, reputedly, St Mark (identified as the author of the Gospel of Mark) was once buried. St Mark had established the Church in Egypt, and was the first leader and martyr there. Legend has it that in his old age he suffered a gruesome death by being burnt alive (*c.* AD 98). The Venetians sacked Alexandria early in the ninth century and took the bones of St Mark, their patron saint, to Venice. Protestants regularly visited the Greek Patriarch of Alexandria, who lived in a house adjacent to the Church of St Mark. The Patriarch, named Cyril, was very well disposed towards them. Patriarch Cyril insisted that the differences between Greek Orthodox religion and Protestantism were 'but shells' while the difference between the Greeks and the Roman Catholics were 'kernels'.[14]

This was a statement more diplomatic than true. Alexandria was a town in which Muslims, Jews and Orthodox Christians lived together, and they looked out collectively at the Roman Catholics of Europe with suspicion, and some hostility.

The vicious split between the western (Catholic) and the eastern (Orthodox) Church was the eventual result of the later Roman Empire being split into western and eastern parts, with two main languages: Latin (western) and Greek (eastern). Both sides considered themselves thoroughly 'Roman' in tradition, an identification reflected in the Arabic term for Christians of the Greek Orthodox church – the '*Rumi*'. The Catholics (and now Protestants) of Europe were collectively referred to in Arabic as the '*Frangi*', the Franks. The Catholics, on the other hand, could talk about the 'Latins' (themselves) and the 'Greeks', as if language was the key to everything.

The two sides of the Church had evolved different rituals and norms, but ultimately it had been the refusal of the Patriarch of Constantinople to submit to the Bishop of Rome (the Pope) in 1054 that led to the schism: the Pope promptly excommunicated the Patriarch and vice versa. The nadir of relations came when in 1203 the Doge of Venice led the Fourth Crusade of knights on Constantinople, and sacked the great Christian city in 1204, stripping it of its treasures, including those of the ancient Hagia Sophia church. Patriarch Cyril's assurance to visiting Protestants in Alexandria that their differences were minor was a clear case of someone wishing to make friends of those with a common enemy.

The Greek Orthodox Church in Egypt had another rival at home that Protestant visitors were warned to steer clear of: the Copts (from Arabic *qibt*, from Greek *Aiguptios*, Egyptian), who outnumbered the Egyptian Greek Orthodox Christians, and had their Patriarch based in Cairo. While the Greeks had formal links with the other Orthodox churches throughout Christendom, and had accepted the dogmas of the Council of Chalcedon (451) that Christ has two natures (divine and human) in one person, the Coptic church was fiercely independent, and Monophysite, in that Copts believe that Christ was of one nature (for his humanity has been absorbed into his divinity like a drop of wine in the sea). The two-natures-in-one versus one-nature Christologies had split the Church into raging parts by the sixth century, and the Copts were accordingly considered by English visitors to be plain weird. After all, apart from being heretical, they continued the ancient Egyptian custom of circumcision, and in their church services, they 'conjoyne in savage noises, to our judgements not articulate', wrote George Sandys, and 'professe some knowledge in Magicke'.[15]

Timberlake therefore may have visited the fraternal Patriarch Cyril and the Church of St Mark, but avoided the peculiar Copts. But he was surely extremely distracted as he toured the town and heard the stories. He was not a tourist on a learned journey. His mind was clearly not on antiquities, whether Ptolemaic, Roman or Christian; his mind was on his goods, finances, and the sheer logistics of the operation ahead.

At last, Timberlake would have obtained a *tescaria* (= permit) from the Qadi (= judge) to leave Alexandria. He paid a fee at the gate and departed with Waldred, and his stock, on 20 February 1601, guarded by a party of janissaries.

The party went into desert, where round, black pillars showed the way through the trackless sands, interrupted by clusters of palm trees and plants used for the crystal glass Venetians would make into fine objects.

The usual route was to head eastwards towards the Nile River rather than to go overland through all the arid landscape. People went forty miles eastwards to Rosetta, where later Napoleon's army would find the trilingual inscription of the Rosetta Stone (which in due course would unlock Egyptian hieroglyphics). Travellers passed on the left further ruins, unsurprisingly identified as the royal mansions of Cleopatra, and the ruins of ancient Bucharis 'onely shewing her foundations,' wrote Sandys, 'where grow many Palmes which sustaine the wretched people that live thereabout in beggerly cottages'.[16] They then encountered a guard station, where the caravan was charged a fee per head. Seven or eight miles on, they ferried over a channel of the sea, by raft, including all animals. Then there was a *khan*, a very simple, quadrangular, arched courtyard, where the members of the caravan could unload cargo, cook and eat what they have brought with them, drink and nap. By midnight, as with Sandys' party, they would have departed again, journeying on until dawn, with the 'Moors' keeping themselves awake by telling the same tale, over and over.

Rosetta was reached: a 'pretty little Citie', writes Henry Blount, upon the Nile, four miles from the sea, wanting nothing but 'art, and a soft government'.[17] The houses were made of brick with flat roofs that jutted over the street for shade. The uncomfortable experience of the trip from Alexandria made visitors experience Rosetta as a huge restaurant: 'I thinke no place under heaven is better furnished with graine, flesh, fish, sugar, fruites, roots &c' enthused Sandys.[18] There was another *khan*, this time for Europeans, with a basement room, dark and dusty, with no windows, and just the floor to lie on.

At Rosetta, Timberlake hired 'jerbies' (*yermi* = river boat) with a crew of seven per vessel for twelve dollars each, to transport his stock, himself, Waldred, and his guards. This was actually a lot of money: a dollar was equivalent to 2 ducats. The expense indicates the stock's value. A jerbie was flat-bottomed to negotiate an ever-changing sand-bar, and held a maximum of twenty passengers. The journey against the Nile current took five long days, and involved various hazards, generally to do with one or more boats being grounded in the shallows. The jerbies were pulled against the current by boatmen using ropes from the shore, a laborious, slow process, which was not always successful. Sometimes boats were overturned by the current. The passengers looked out at the simple mud dwellings of the Egyptians, often built high on mounds for protection against the annual flood in August. They observed the water wheels turned by oxen, and irrigation methods, the towns of Abdan, Foua, Pharsone and Salomona, and were told of a stone named Aquiline which keeps a woman from experiencing pain in childbirth. They ate fish and sampled sugar cane.

The views from the Nile over the Delta were lush. It was a place of villages, cultivations in the black earth, gardens, laden donkeys. In the water, children played, men fished, and women washed clothing. The fertility of the region was dazzling; there was an abundance of beans, grains, Paradise fruit, and, says Rawdon, 'greatt store of dattes of the best that be in the wholle worlde, pharoh figges, oringes & lemondes, likewisse almondes, poumgarnetts & many others, great store of cashoe,

& sugar caines likewisse: to conclude it is wholye a garden so as the greatest wante they have is wine which to them is none, for that the water of Nilus is so good & doth to all the lande of Aegypt searve for their drincke.' The descriptions are exotic. How very far away and sterile wintry England must have seemed as the travellers journeyed through this sunny world.

It must have been odd for Timberlake to have had to accept such passivity. For other travellers of this time who wrote of the journey, they were used to being the passive load that got taken from place to place, from start to finish; but Timberlake was the Captain of the *Trojan*, and a merchant adventurer. He was a man of authority, action: a man giving orders, taking responsibility. From steering his ship and navigating its way from England to the coast of Africa, now he was a passenger himself, watching colourful birds dip around the trees, with no orders to give. These boatmen knew how to operate their ropes better than he did.

What did the local people think of the sight of these English merchants and their boxes being pulled along the Nile? The river itself was the old equivalent of a motorway, and they had seen all kinds of odd things upon it. This area was called Errifia, and the inhabitants were, according to Sandys, 'civill... as more conversing with forreiners'. [19]

In 1601, not all the locals were friendly. Blount's party in 1634 were attacked by a group of 'wild Arabs' with lances, on horseback. Fearful that the ropes would be seized, the accompanying janissary on the jerbie fired a pistol, twice, while the armed passengers indicated they would do the same. With that the highwaymen backed off. John Sanderson records that (on 11 June 1586) a jerbie was taken by thirty 'Arabs'. Five Turkish janissaries were killed and four Jews robbed, but spared. [20]

There were other hazards too, in the form of crocodiles, 'very bad animals... like to the dragon,' as one traveller would say. [21] The possibility that floating logs might be such dragons had many passengers far from relaxed. Rumour had it that people would be snatched and eaten in a split second by such creatures. There were eye-witness accounts.

At last, five days after their departure from Rosetta, Timberlake and Waldred arrived in Boulaq, a large town by the river from which the road led directly to Grand Cairo. Boulaq was Cairo's port, a thriving, busy madhouse of arrivals and departures where the world met and mingled, the men of each religious group and ethnicity identified by distinctive clothing. This port contained every hue of skin, every strange attire. There were Moors from Barbary with white turbans, and 'green-heads', men with green turbans, who by this means advertised that they were descended from the Prophet. There were Jews in yellow turbans, and some Jewish doctors with high, brimless maroon hats. Local Egyptians wore side-coats of linen tied at their waists and scarves around their necks. The poor men who scrambled to be porters wore goat-hair garments striped black and white. The Copts wore caps, scarves around their necks, striped garments and wide sleeves. Then there were Persians with baggy trousers, and women with different wrappings and shoes, all well-covered in the hurly-burly, trying to be unseen. Clothing defined you.

The two Franks were easily recognisable here, with their wide-brimmed black hats, paying a gold coin, a *sultani*, each. Then there were further duties levied on the goods.

The janissaries from Alexandria would have organised transport to take them to Benjamin Bishop, hiring horses and asses. This was the customary system. Other visiting merchants could stay in Boulaq, where there were huge caravanserais for the selling of linen, grain, and other goods. These caravanserais were shopping malls: the largest in the world, with up to forty shops in each one. There were hundreds of small boats riding at anchor alongside vast houses built along the Nile.

But the Levant Company base was in Cairo itself, and they departed on the road which led past immense palaces and magnificent palm trees to the greatest city on the planet, a leviathan of urban creations, a city larger than Constantinople. Cairo was where Asia and Africa met, a huge cosmopolitan hub and commercial entrepôt. In this cultural crossroads and massive trading centre Timberlake hoped he would sell his English stock. Trade worked on the simple basis of trying to sell your goods for as high a price as possible and buy in choice local and Asiatic goods for as low a price as possible. If he could do it in Russia, Florence, Venice and North Africa, he could do it here.

5

Grand Cairo

Europeans, arriving in Cairo, tended to explode with superlatives at the extraordinary sights they saw in a place that was, to them, completely 'other': exotic, fascinating, frightening, alluring and Africo-Oriental in character. However, despite the proposals of Edward Said's influential study on European attitudes to the 'East',[1] it is very hard to see that the experience of visiting Elizabethan and Jacobite Englishmen was founded on imperialism, exploitation and a wish to subjugate. If a desire to trade is defined as essentially exploitative then English visitors were guilty of that, but this would be to see their projects in a very negative light; and the foreign (Ottoman, North African, *et al.*) merchants coming into London would have to be also so designated, an analysis that surely presupposes a certain rarefied Marxism. England did not look to the Ottoman empire from a position of power and superiority, but from a position of marginality and inferiority. The 'oohs' and 'aahs' we can detect in the sources may be seen as Orientalist preludes to cultural and economic domination only if we retroject later imperialisms. The very opposite seems to be the case. It was the Ottoman empire that was dominating and powerful. As Robert Irwin notes:

> Until the late seventeenth century the West's interest in the Turks was mostly driven by fear. The Ottomans in the seventeenth century ruled over almost the Balkans. Only the tiny mountain principality of Montenegro preserved a nominal independence. The Turks had twice besieged Vienna, in 1529 and 1683. The Ottoman navy dominated the eastern Mediterranean. Richard Knolles in his *General History of the Turks* (1603)... described the Turks as 'the present terror of the world'.[2]

Arriving in Cairo, European travellers put fear to one side and allowed themselves to be humbly overwhelmed, awed. They tried to provide a sense of the enormity and wonder of the place by giving numeric values: there are 35,000 churches and chapels (= mosques and shrines), wrote Blount, 24,000 streets, some which are two miles long, each one guarded and locked at nightfall; the city is guarded by 28,000 men; the whole circuit of the city is between thirty-five and forty miles.[3] Lithgow decided to walk around the city, and estimated the circuit to be twenty-two miles, not counting the suburbs, with its length twenty-eight miles and breadth fourteen.[4] It was so populous that even with a plague that killed 1,800,000 people there were more than ever five years later.[5] Juan Perrara in 1553 enthused that there were 30,000 horses and mules, 60,000 riding asses, 3,000 windmills, 14,000 mosques and shrines, forty Christian churches and 14,000 shopping streets.[6]

Edward Webbe wrote that Cairo 'is the greatest Citie in the worlde'. The 'king' of Cairo is second only to the 'Great Turke', the Sultan Mehmet III, residing in Constantinople.[7] The houses were very old, built of lime (plaster) and stone. Blount noted that when the old buildings crumbled, which were built high, of large stones, they were rebuilt lower, with mud and timber, and were poorer. The quality of life, for most ordinary Egyptians, had apparently fallen under Ottoman rule; though fabulous wealth was concentrated in the hands of the few.[8] People lived in apartment blocks, usually three to four storeys high.

It was said that you could not ride a horse from one end of Cairo to the other in a single day, such was its immensity. John Rawdon, however, had another explanation:

> many make report that a man cannot ride through it in on[e] daye... although he woulde ride post (= fast), to that I answer the reason is not for that the grounde is so much or the waye so longe, but the crokednes & narrowenes of the streetts, some of them, being but entrees & to a horseman evill, likewisse the infinitte number of people, by reasone of the abundance of merchantes & traufficke which ar continuallye in such troopes and multitudes, as a man can hardlye ride at all much less poste.[9]

The concentration of people and houses created urban nightmares beyond any known European scale also. The water was bad. Blount complained that during a southerly wind the air 'is odiferous as any Spanish Glove, and so hot, as when it held long, it corrupted my stomacke'.[10] Plague killed thousands.

As for the people, Webbe noted that they are 'for the most part of a reasonable stature, yet of a brounish and swart complexion: their women goe muffled'.[11] This did not suggest to the visitors that Egyptian women were submissive or downtrodden; quite the opposite. Sandys writes that 'the women [are] too fine fingered to meddle with houswifry, who ride abroad upon pleasure on easie-going Asses, and tie their husbands to the benevolence that is due; which if neglected, they will complaine to the magistrate, and procure a divorcement.'[12]

Cairo was a melting-pot of different ethnicities, and you could see all kinds of different types of dress and skin colour, just as at Boulaq. There were Christians: from Italians, French, Greeks, Copts and Georgians to Armenians, Abyssinians, and Nubians, together numbering more than 100,000 people. There was an entire Frankish quarter. Of the Muslims, there were, in addition to the local 'Moors', also 'Turks' (from other parts of the Ottoman empire, and/or the Ottoman elite), other 'Moors' (Muslims), identified as black and white in skin colour, Persians, and people whom Lithgow terms 'Arabians, Barbarians and Sarazens' for want of more accurate descriptive nouns.[13] Here also were large numbers of Indians and Jews. In the Jewish Quarter there were Karaites (who rejected the Rabbinic Judaism of the Mishnah and Talmuds) as well as Rabbinites, and Samaritans as well. The different peoples would all congregate and interact in the bazaar, where also there were horses visitors could hire, with a guide, to see the sights. The Copts were respected as goldsmiths, silversmiths and woodworkers. Jews likewise worked in precious metals, and were bankers and money-changers. Greeks and Armenians were tailors, jewellers and clock-makers.

To enter Cairo was to arrive in a consumer frenzy. There were huge markets and shops and street hawkers. Markets spilled out into streets dedicated to one thing or another: the coppersmith street, the rice road, the sugar lanes. Cairo was also a processing centre: there were areas for milling, vinegar-making, spinning, weaving and dyeing, leatherworking, woodworking, metalworking, especially in the southern suburbs. A three-storey covered market, the Khan al-Khalili, with fine pillars in its centre, was dedicated to precious goods: exquisite jewels and luxury spices.[14] Palestinians dealt with soap in the caravanserai of the Jamaliyya quarter. Indians and Persians had their own caravanserai. In the different areas for each group, you could find different clothing, food, religious rituals, languages, customs.

In the area of merchant houses adjoining the main markets lay the residence of the Levant Company consul, Benjamin Bishop. He was, by this time, known to be 'as badd a fellowe as bad maye be', selling the alcoholic *aquavitae* to wayward Muslims for money, and abusing his creditors in England.[15] There was some reason for him to branch out into other commodities given his situation, especially if the expected number of ships from England did not arrive as a result of the crisis with the Queen. While the consuls in some cities of the Ottoman empire were paid (Constantinople, Aleppo, for example), in Cairo, Cyprus and Tripoli the consuls did not receive a salary, but retained a 2% 'consulage' from goods belonging to members of the Company that passed through their spheres of influence.[16]

When far away from home, you become particularly reliant on your hosts. To enter a house that was, under Bishop's care, a den of iniquity cannot have been very heartening. Bishop would have asked, 'What news?' and presented himself in clothing atypical for England. It was common for Frankish consuls and factors at this time to wear local fine attire, so as not to stand out too much, and to be accompanied outside their residences by a retinue of guards, to avoid any jostling and elbowing from the type of Muslims who did not welcome any infidel traders in the Dar es-Islam.[17] To blend in was considered the wisest course. A year on, after Bishop was dismissed from his post, he would in fact 'turn Turk' entirely.

It was at Bishop's house in Cairo that Timberlake met a traveller named John Burrell, though this was not the John Burrell who met an unfortunate end recorded in the pages of Hakluyt.[18] In the 1609 edition of Timberlake's letter, he is called a 'gentleman of Middleborough'.[19] This could be Middlesborough, then a small village in the north of England, or it might be Middelburgh, Zeeland, the foreign headquarters of the Merchant Adventurers of England. The former is more likely, since gentleman would be identified by their provenance (e.g. Shakespeare's *Two Gentlemen of Verona*), not by their place of work. Additionally, he does not appear to have been a merchant, but someone of a more scholarly disposition. He spoke Greek, perhaps not 'as naturally as pig's squeak', as Samuel Butler describes his scholar doing in *Hudibras* (I, i, 51), but at any rate well enough. For this he may have spent time in Athens, which was still a place that attracted scholars rather than merchants. It seems to have been his purpose to go to Jerusalem – and beyond – for pure edification: there was no other good reason for a Protestant to go. It was not on the merchant trail other than as a waystop between Cairo and Damascus.

If John Burrell was a scholar, then perhaps he had followed an overland route to Athens like that of John Rawdon, which allowed for more knowledge-gathering than a sea voyage. This prototypical backpacker went from Dover to Calais, then to Montreuil, Abbeville, Amiens, Reims, Chalons, and then out of France – with whom England had a treaty of friendship – to the Duke of Lorraine's territory – to Nancy, Strasbourg, on the Rhine River, and then to High Germany: Ulm, Augsburg, Innsbruck, where they reached the Alpes. Rawdon crossed the Brenner pass to Bolzano and Trent, and on into 'the territories of the Venetians', where Rawdon's party was halted 'for that ther feare of the plauge is much'. They went through Verona, Vicenza, Padua, and then finally arrived at Venice, a journey of some 1,000 km that took nine weeks. Rawdon stayed a month in Venice and then managed to get a ship to Zante, a journey lasting twenty days. At this island, as noted above, he was stuck for four months before getting a ship to Alexandria.[20] Athens was four days' journey from Zante. 'Greece', incidentally, did not exist as a country at this time. From Zante you crossed into Morea (the Peloponnese). The eastern side of Greece was Albania and the west was Macedonia.

Whatever the case, Burrell, now in Cairo, had a new ambition: to go to the Holy Land. His enthusiasm was probably not shared by Bishop, or the factors in Cairo. While for Catholics, the spiritual significance of pilgrimage to holy places had been cherished for centuries, Protestant leaders had defined themselves against the Church they had rejected by stressing the utter uselessness of the endeavour. Since Protestants should not engage in veneration of Christian holy places, there was not much point in going to Terra Sancta, the Holy Land, unless you were of a scholarly disposition and wished to see the sites out of historical interest, or to improve your Biblical exegesis. Those who did go to Jerusalem risked life and limb on a hazardous journey, and there were precious few pilgrims after the loss of Rhodes and Cyprus to the Turks. In 1596 Gianfrancesco Alcarotti noted that holy pilgrimage (from Europe) had been 'reduced to oblivion'.[21]

The Ottoman military activities on the borderlands of their vast empire, east and west, meant that a certain amount of manpower was drained from areas like Palestine. There were not enough janissaries to keep the roads safe. Brigandage was rife. Travellers, both Christian and Muslim, were mugged in transit. They would also die of diseases like dysentery or from food poisoning.

Pilgrims from Europe had to make their way as paying passengers on merchant ships, and were terrified not only of pirates, but also of Ottoman sailors which, seeing a ship of a foreign nation not under their dominion, were not averse to taking Christians as slaves, or 'imposing great exactions, and doing foule injuries to them.'[22] If a Protestant was on board a ship belonging to 'Papists' (= Catholics), there was also the unfortunate possibility of being thrown into the sea during a storm to assuage the wrath of God against heretics, a sort of Jonah scenario.[23] Most Protestants who went to the Holy Land did so out of sheer curiosity, but you had to be seriously curious to risk death or injury to sate your interests. Today the foreign office would issue a warning against travelling there. You risked your life.

An eager pilgrim scholar may have seemed a little incongruous in the mercantile context of Cairo and anything smacking of pious holiness was not exactly in vogue among the European 'factories' of the Ottoman world. Merchants entertained themselves by putting on sumptuous dinners to which other merchants were invited. At these they could show off their splendid residences, furniture, ornaments, horses, wines and foods, and indicate how many servants they had. The 'jolly cup' was offered even to the local wealthy Muslim merchants who also came to enjoy the entertainment. The arrival of newcomers was usually the excuse for such banquets. At these a certain amount of gambling was in vogue, and of course a certain amount of sexual entertainment as well. Neither the French, English nor the Venetians in Cairo were renowned for their exemplary commitment to Christian morality when it came to sex, and the Levant Company at times had to send out admonitions against vice and sensuality.[24] It was among these merchants that the myth of the erotic Egypt (and other realms) first took hold. In fact, Egypt was not more licentious than Europe; it was the Europeans who were licentious once they were ensconced there.

Timberlake would have handed over the stock he had transported belonging to the merchants of the Levant Company to the team of factors in Cairo, and breathed a sigh of relief. But he had his own stock to sell as well. At the beginning, Timberlake, as a merchant, was surely interested in selling his stock well and spending time in the market. This market of Cairo was described with wonder by every European traveller who ventured there. It was dense, with shopkeepers calling out, people milling around, bedraggled donkeys, performers: talking ravens, performing dogs and goats, dancing camels, charmed lizards (entranced by music) and trick-making asses. The tropical fruit was – to the English – heavenly: oranges, pomegranates, lemons, figs, Paradise Apples (= bananas), dates, almonds. Huge bunches of roses were offered for sale. The pungent smell of coffee wafted over the street from great sacks of coffee beans, and mixed with the smells of fast-food stalls and restaurants. Chameleon lizards changed their hues cunningly. The people were decorative, colourful, clinking. Women wore jewels in their noses, through their cheeks, and under lips,[25] and shone with bracelets and anklets of gold, silver, copper or iron, with coins on their foreheads and necks. Their chins were tattooed with knots and flowers of blue. There were also beggars, singing and playing on drums to attract attention, many afflicted with diseases of the eye, from the sun, the dust and the pox.

Men sold a salve made from snake's venom. Sad leopards sat in cages, for sale with other caged beasts: monkeys, musk cats, gazelles, ostriches and Nilotic monitor lizards. There were antiquities: gold, glass, alabaster figures, hieroglyphic pieces, inscriptions, mummies. The mummies, or parts of them, were sold to Frankish merchants, who would sell them in turn to apothecaries, who would grind them up for medicine.

The air was dusty. The streets were unpaved, and the dust was continually stirred up by the traffic of people, horses, camels, donkeys, mules and other stranger creatures.

Timberlake, with his great stock of woollen cloth, could not have failed to be bedazzled by the textiles here: silk woven in miraculously fine ways with stunning colours, linens of different grades, bright cottons. There was so much gold and silver, so many jewellers and precious stones, copper vases, glass from Damascus, honey, magical balsam oil, peppers, spices, sugar, herbs, beans.

Then, as in Algiers, there was the slave market.

Muslims were not allowed to be enslaved, and so the slaves for sale were Christians, Indians and – most predominantly – the pagan tribes of Africa untouched by the Religions of the Book.

It was said that the slave market was so huge in Cairo and slaves so cheap that even the poorest artisan or merchant in the city would have three slaves to help him.[26] A Spanish–Belgian visitor of 1665–6, Father Antonius Gonzales, saw 800–1,000 slaves for sale in the market on one single day.[27] Cairo was one of many great slave-trading centres in the Ottoman empire, like Constantinople. Of that emporium, William Lithgow wrote: 'I have seene men and women as usually sold heere in markets, as Horses and other beasts are with us: the most part of which are Hungarians; Transilvanians, and Bohemians, captives, and of other place besides, which they overcome.'[28] They were stripped naked and even their private parts were examined in public, with trade continuing every day except Friday, the Muslim holy day.[29]

Leonhard Rauwolf writes of the slaves for sale that there were: 'amongst them young and old, men and women, some wherof are white, and others black; thither come the chapmen (= pedlars) and cheapen (= haggle for) them; they have liberty to look upon their naked bodies, as if they were beasts, and to feel them, whether they are sound in their limbs, or whether they have defect, which they always fear.'[30] Old men were sold at 20–30 ducats (gold coins), old women at the same rate or less; strong young men fetched 60 ducats, young women and beautiful girls 50 to 70, and little children 4 to 10 ducats.[31] A Spanish ducat was worth between 6.8 and 9 shillings in this period.[32]

It is ironic to think that the Europeans who write with such revulsion of the slave markets of the Ottoman empire would soon learn from these slave-traders themselves, and go to West Africa for their own purposes. In 1601, however, the English traders of the Levant Company were faced with a traffic in human beings that was, to most of them, shocking. The way they write indicates that they had yet to lose their moral sensibilities.

Elsewhere in Cairo, unbeknownst to Timberlake, al-Fessi was also walking, discovering this astonishing, traffic-congested megalopolis. There were encampments of foreign Muslim pilgrims in Cairo at khans and madrasas, waiting for the departure of the great *hajj* caravan. It would set off at the prescribed time, with each people in convoy, across the great desert and down, southwards, to the holy city deep in the Arabian peninsula. Cairo was the key point of departure, though of course caravans left from other places also, like Damascus, or Baghdad. Slowly, the pilgrims would assemble to make the journey all together. Till then they remained in Cairo, visiting the great mosques of the city, in prayerful anticipation.

They could also take advantage of the university. Cairo was not just a city for commerce, it was a city for the intellect. The university attached to the al-Azhar mosque had attracted the elite of the Muslim's world's teachers. Here both the theological and the physical universe would be explored.

Classes could be visited. Perhaps then the Moor was there, sitting at the feet of one of the university's great Maghrebi teachers.

As time went on, Timberlake was stymied. He could not sell his stock. The weather was against him. He had arrived too late in the season, and interest in warm clothing had waned. The only thing to do was wait, wait for visiting merchants from Persia, or India, to take an interest in building up their supplies for the next winter. Stuck in the house of the degenerate Bishop, in the bustling chaos of Cairo, he was back in the same position he was in months earlier, in London. He had to wait, be patient; and he was so not a man to wait and be patient.

As the days wore on, John Burrell's prospective journey to Jerusalem clearly intrigued him more and more. Burrell was a lone traveller, and had investigated his route thoroughly, learning that he would have to travel north-east to Bilbeis to connect with a large caravan that crossed the dangerous desert towards Gaza. Perhaps he was waiting though until he could have at least one companion on this enterprise. The whiff of adventure caught Timberlake as he talked to this man from Middlesborough. It started to become irresistible. In the 1609 edition of his account Timberlake affirms that he had no intention at all of going to Jerusalem when he went to Cairo.[33] It was an idea that seized him when he was there.

The stress of staying in Cairo was acute. Sandys wrote when he visited in 1610 that English merchants were getting thoroughly fed up trying to sell woollen broadcloth in Egypt: 'But the English have so ill utterance for their warme clothes in these hote countries, that I belieeve they will rather suffer their ships to rot in the River, then continue that trade any longer.'[34]

Timberlake had stock worth £1,200. In selling it and buying in the resources of Cairo he would hope to triple its value at least. He had to wait to sell it. But he was a man of action, not of patience.

With time on his hands, Timberlake would not have neglected a visit to the pyramids. They were dubbed 'the World's Wonders', and seeing them made all onlookers gasp at their 'admirable greatnes... excessive hugenesse and height',[35] except for moralistic George Sandys, who stiffly calls them 'the barbarous monuments of prodigality and vain-glory'.[36] Journeying into the desert about twelve miles south-west of the city, across the Nile, in a small party, they would have been informed that the pyramids were the storehouses built by the famous Joseph, son of Israel, in anticipation of the famine he predicted in a dream. This false notion had been held by Christians for over a millennium, but most visitors were convinced they were tombs.

A picture of (armed) Franks with their janissaries riding past the pyramids of Giza and 'colossus' (= sphinx) appears in *Sandys Travels* (Figure 5). While at first all one sees in this picture are five pyramids, sand dunes, the head of the sphinx, and a party of five Europeans on mules with four guards – two janissaries on asses and two walking – the picture also shows silhouetted figures in the background, and small clusters of buildings. These small background figures are very telling, for the place was occupied by the 'wild Arabs'. In the picture the janissaries at the front are much more concerned with two figures at the base of the sphinx, both of whom hold long spears, than with the wonders of the world. On closer inspection, none of the figures seems to be gasping at the pyramids at all. The first European is turning back as if to say over his shoulder something like, 'We've got trouble.'

As the seas were full of pirates, the land was full of highwaymen. They were everywhere in the world of the sixteenth and seventeenth centuries, and your best protection – bar never actually travelling anywhere – was to ensure you were heavily guarded, carried a weapon, and went in a group. The 'wild Arabs' were considered to be 'uncivilised' and distinguished by not caring too much about such fundamental laws of Christianity, Judaism and Islam as 'do not steal' and 'do not murder': hence, they were wild, even though they were, to varying degrees, Muslim. Law, order and religion could proceed within cities, towns and villages, but outside these centres were vast tracts of wilderness, uncultivated and untamed, and full of nomads who supplemented a peripatetic, sheep-goat herding existence with the bounty provided by visitors who happened to trespass on their domains.

Having avoided attack, the pyramids themselves became a challenge: they could be entered through long, dark and airless tunnels or they could be climbed. Ascending to the top of the pyramid of Cheops was a very popular tourist activity, despite the fact that a few people plummeted to their deaths every year.

So we see Timberlake pulling himself up, stone after stone, measuring them occasionally, determining the average was five foot broad, nine foot long. William Lithgow later did the same, hauling himself up, 'by degrees, with great paine', to the top, where he was 'mervailously ravished, to see such a square plat-forme, all of one peece of stone, which covereth the head: each side whereof extendeth to 17 foot of my measure. It is yet a great marvell to me, that by what engine they could bring it up so safe, to such a height. Truely, the more I beheld this strange worke, the more I was stricken in admiration'.[37] What seemed a sharp point like a diamond from the bottom was a (sloping) platform that could contain a hundred men.

So let us see Timberlake standing there, surveying the vast, flat landscape before him: the string of pyramids stretching into the hazy distance, the glittering Nile which was considered to be the division between Africa and Asia, and the other division between fertile land and the buttery desert. Does he, at this point, get some sense of his own smallness, or his finiteness? Does England seem far off and very young in comparison with the ancient culture that had produced this marvel of architecture, a marvel that no one in his own day could possibly match?

Perhaps, but if he looked into the distance there, the horizon called.

6

The Caravan and the Chickens

Trading English goods for the great treats of the Cairo market – silks, dyes, spices, coffee, drugs – was not easy. The cost of living in Cairo was high in comparison to England. On arrival of a plethora of European ships the prices of spices always went up. To get a good deal, the rise had to be outlived, by keeping a ship at the port of Alexandria long enough to see the prices fall. It could take over a month.[1] The English wanted so much more from Egypt than Egypt wanted from England. New caravans and traders from the Red Sea could arrive at any time, and provide such a glut of eastern goods in the marketplace that the prices had to drop.

Instead of waiting, Timberlake decided to accompany John Burrell to Jerusalem, and leave Waldred to do the work, with Bishop, in Cairo. It was a surprising and reckless thing to do. Waldred was suddenly loaded with a breathtaking responsibility, given the huge amount of money involved. He would have to let Captain Timberlake go his own way, to Jerusalem. This was said to be a ten day journey at least, rife with dangers. Timberlake must have been full of positive reassurances: he would be back within a month, he would have insisted. After all, any longer and the men could mutiny. He was well aware of that.

As for Bishop, he had no authority over Timberlake. He could not forbid him from making such a hazardous trip, even though he was the Captain of a ship bound to the Levant Company and had parted with a significant bond. Timberlake could be captured by 'wild Arabs' and sold on the slave market, and the consul would not be able to intervene outside Cairo. Then it would be down to Waldred and Bishop to rescue the operation. Did Timberlake really understand what he was doing?

It is hard to guess what motivated Henry Timberlake to accompany John Burrell to Jerusalem. Did Timberlake want to go out of a kind of residual piety he was not supposed to have had, despite being fiercely Protestant, for all intents and purposes? At this time, in English society, there was no such thing as being irreligious. All English subjects of the Queen were expected to be members of the Church of England, and to deviate from that required deceit, or a firm stand.

On the other hand, English religion was Protestantism of a peculiar kind. Since England had become Protestant not so much from popular sentiment but from the initiatives of the Crown, English Protestantism was conceptualised as the decent, nationalistic, right way of thinking. It did not overall have the zealous theological fervour of Protestantism on the Continent, though there was a sector of society that certainly held up those values. In 1601, Protestantism was not as austere as the Puritans would later have it. At the crunch, it was also obedience to the monarch. Catholicism smacked of treason. But personal piety could manifest itself in myriad ways.

Protestant leaders did not think it right to think of there being a Holy Land on earth. To be a pilgrim meant having faith, travailing dutifully in life's hardships, working diligently, being good, in anticipation of God's providence and a spiritual home in the hereafter won by the merits of Jesus Christ's sacrificial death on the cross and subsequent resurrection, but personal piety was not necessarily straight-jacketed into correct thought and practice. Timberlake, for all his anti-Catholic prejudice, seems in his account to have had an idea of the 'Holy Land', and was drawn to that idea, when Protestants were supposed to be circumspect and critical.

Did the experience of seeing the shipboard piety of the Muslim pilgrims on the *hajj* make some impression upon him? Did he see a different kind of pilgrimage to that which he configured as the corrupt Catholic veneration of relics and sacred sites? Had he thought of seeing Jerusalem, when talking to them? Was their piety contagious? You get that kind of Muslim challenge felt by Protestants in the writings of the Augsburg physician and botanist Leonhard Rauwolf, whose work was first published in his Swabian German dialect in 1582 and then translated into English in 1693. Rauwolf was no fan of Islam, but he was impressed by the way Muslims prayed, throwing their entire bodies into it, and notes: 'If we Christians did but mind the fervency and zeal of the heathens and superstitious in their prayers, we should see what reason we have to awake from our laziness and coldness in our prayers, and to pray with earnestness.'[2]

Or was there something Timberlake wished to conquer, on some personal level? Pilgrimage was sometimes done to wash away sin. Catholic pilgrims earnt indulgences, which would exempt them from their due time in Purgatory. Protestants did not believe in Purgatory, or indulgences, and trusted that their sins were washed away through the sacrificial blood of Christ, God's Only-begotten Son. Yet perhaps the echo of what pilgrimage had been for so many centuries still sounded.

There was also the sheer adventure of it. The Holy Land was so little understood by the English. Pilgrim voyages seemed rather archaic, the stuff of yesteryear, and the descriptions of the places visited by English pilgrims were likewise old now.

The sixteenth century was not full of contemporary pilgrim accounts in English. In 1506 Sir Richard Guylford made a difficult journey there and died (it had been left to his chaplain to tell the tale), and the story was printed in 1511.[3] The Rector of Mulberton in Norfolk, Sir Richard Torkyngton, wrote a diary of his visit in 1517, but this was not on release to the Elizabethan public, existing only in manuscripts.[4] John Locke visited in 1553, but his account published in Hakluyt's compendium of voyages is about travel to and from but not in Palestine.[5] Likewise printed in Hakluyt was the visit of Laurence Aldersley in 1581. This was in fact the most detailed recent description, though it was exceedingly brief.[6] Publishers churned out the same old fourteenth-century account by John Mandeville to satisfy the public curiosity.[7] Timberlake and Burrell may have read the short and astonishing tale of the gunner named Edward Webbe, published in 1590, which recounted how he had been captured and enslaved by the 'Turks' and forced through Egypt and the Holy Land in the service of the Ottoman army, but his story reads like someone's report today of being kidnapped by extraterrestrial aliens.[8]

The short impressions of Aldersley and Webbe were, nevertheless, all the Elizabethan public had in terms of contemporary English travel accounts, which must have acted as aperitifs for those of an adventurous spirit. Englishmen were visiting Palestine now and then in the latter part of the sixteenth century, but not necessarily writing descriptions of what they saw, or not writing these for the public, or not making it home to tell their tales.[9] The (originally Latin) account written in 1596 by Fynes Moryson, whose brother died on the trip, did not get published until 1617.[10] However, in terms of an academic summary of the Christian holy places of Jerusalem, the Elizabethan public did have the stolid work of Christianus Adrichomius, who published his tome in 1584 in Latin. The work was soon translated into other languages, including, in 1595, English.[11]

Elsewhere in Europe a revival of pilgrimage literature at the end of the sixteenth century appears to parallel a dearth of actual travellers to the Holy Land; it was as if the rarer it was the more the public wanted to read about it.[12] Among these there were, for example, important works in Italian by Bernadino Amico, a Franciscan Custos of Bethlehem (resident 1593–7) who published detailed plans of sacred places, Jean Zuallart (visiting 1586), or Gianfrancesco Alcarotti, Canon of Cathedral of Novara (visiting 1587); in Spanish, by Francesco Guerrero, Master of the Chapel of La Sancta Inglesia de Sevilla; in Portuguese, by Pantaleao d'Aveyro, a Franciscan monk (visited 1563–5); in French, by Pierre Belon, who looked at the natural science of the region (visited 1547), or the traveller Jacques de Villamont (1588); and in German, by Leonhard Rauwolf (visited 1575), mentioned above, whose research was largely botanical, and Melchior Lussy (visited 1583).

In 1601 Terra Sancta was also Terra Incognita to the English: an ancient land, heavy with mystique and importance, and visited by Europeans only really if they were Catholics, who wrote piously about the holy places in languages most English people could not understand.

The maps that existed of the Holy Land were not hugely informative either, with information on the layout of Palestine deriving more from what was in the Bible and classical authors such as Strabo and Josephus than on current observation. Abraham Ortelius' map in *Theatrum Orbis Terrarum* (1570) (see cover illustration) was much better for the coasts than anywhere else, because he could draw on a tradition of maritime maps. In Africa and the Middle East he archaised the nomenclature of the land, and for Palestine he used the word 'Iudea' for the south, below Jerusalem, and 'Soria' ('Syria', extending to Aleppo) for the north. 'Judaea' was a term not used past AD 135 (at which time it referred to a large part of inland Palestine, including some of the coast, not just the small, landlocked tribal lands of Judaeans/Jews in the central south), but Europeans could sometimes subdivide the region into Philistina (the coast), Judaea (inland central south), Samaria (inland middle) and Galilee (inland north), to fit things into the template of familiar scripture. Good maps of contemporaneous Palestine were actually not available until the nineteenth century. Even Napoleon's map, drawn by M. Jacotin in 1799, would be drawn largely from supposition and second-hand reporting.[13]

Timberlake, the Captain, would have had no map. All his nautical charts would have been left behind on the *Trojan*. He could remember the sweep of land upwards to Syria, the strands of the Nile, fanning out over the Egyptian Delta, and the main ports: Gaza, Jaffa, Acre, Tripoli, Alexandretta (Scanderoon). But inland: what was there, really? There was only one way to find out.

Timberlake took only the barest essentials with him on his journey, and dressed in a set of pilgrim clothes, what he calls his 'pilgrimes weeds'.[14] The 1603 edition values these at 10 groats, which was next to nothing, and the 1609 edition mentions a 'haire cloth Coate'.[15] Haircloth was sacking material, usually made out of goat hair in the Middle East and North Africa, and was abrasive and unpleasant to wear, unlike wool. Cotton or linen shirts would have protected his skin, but it would still have been slightly uncomfortable. It was also thin. He would not have had much warmth from it at night. He had also 'hose',[16] by which he means stockings, and also breeches, which were the common attire of an Englishman of the period. He would have had sturdy leather shoes, and a black wide-brimmed hat. Pilgrim clothing was simple: a bag, a hat, very basic attire, Christian badges.

Strictly speaking, you were not supposed to be armed, but many pilgrims were. He would have had a knife in his belt. The crucial thing was not to look military or mercantile, which probably explains why Timberlake and Burrell dressed in such clothing, even as Protestants. They wanted to be recognisably *not* wealthy merchants.

Most Europeans nevertheless could not help but look wealthy, since they often travelled in large parties with considerable baggage and guards. Timberlake and Burrell had no guards. They would travel alone.

For now, Timberlake and Burrell lay aside their association with ship, with wealth, and merchandise, with everything familiar, and became equalised and anonymous.

Initially, however, they went off in a group. On 9 March 1601, Timberlake and Burrell set off from Cairo, northwards, probably on horseback, in company and with a guide. Timberlake writes that they travelled first with a merchant named Anthony Thorpe and some others, probably part of Bishop's team of factors in Cairo. These companions allowed themselves a day's excursion to the place 'where it is said the Virgine Marye did stay with ower Savior Christ',[17] to see Timberlake and Burrell on their way. In this prologue to their real journey everything was peaceful and quiet. Unlike in a thriller adventure, they did not immediately encounter a dire threat the moment they set off.

The reference to the Virgin Mary's abode is to the Gospel of Matthew 2:13–15: an angel comes to Joseph and tells him to take Mary and Jesus to Egypt because King Herod will search for the child and kill him; and the holy family depart from Judaea that very night, and stay in Egypt until Herod is dead. When pilgrimage to holy places became a Christian imperative, from the fourth century onwards, with the rediscovery of Christ's tomb in Jerusalem and (ostensibly) the wood of the cross on which he died, there had been a concerted effort to identify all kinds of sites mentioned in the Bible. This effort would reach to Egypt, with Mt Sinai (Horeb) identified in the desert, and the pyramids confidently deemed to be the granaries used during the famine of Genesis 41:53–7. Eventually, the Christian imagination worked on the few verses in the Gospel of Matthew. Some time after Cairo superseded Alexandria as the major metropolis of Egypt, i.e. after the ninth century, a series of sites were plotted out.

In Matariya, a fertile area five miles north of Cairo where wealthy Cairo residents had villas, a chapel was established to honour the holy family. At the chapel, a guide would point out the exact house where Mary and Joseph lived, the sycomore fig tree (*Ficus sycomorus*) under which Mary rested with Christ in her lap, and the well opened by an angel where she washed him.[18] Some said the well was opened miraculously when Mary left her child lying on the ground while she went into a nearby village to ask for water, only to return to find pure water welling up near Jesus' feet, for his holy heels drumming on the ground had brought the pure water to the surface.[19] The story goes that Mary washed Jesus' clothes, and where they were hung the bushes turned into fabulous, and lucrative, balsam plants: a little like something changing to gold.

Matariya's significance was that it was a place where this bush was cultivated. *Commiphora Opobalsam* was one of the rarest and most highly prized plants in antiquity, and its sap continued to be greatly esteemed both as a perfume and a medicine: brilliant for curing headaches, lung problems and skin disease. Some said the plants themselves came from Palestine, from distant En Gedi, next to the Dead Sea.[20] Once it was grown only in an adjoining plantation, watered by the wonderful supply of water that bubbled up from the Christian shrine. Elsewhere in the village, the wealthy residents also once had access to a bath-house so huge that it could accommodate 300 bathers at one time.[21]

By the time Timberlake visited, the balsam garden had been partly destroyed by the Ottomans, who had overthrown the former Mamluk rulers of Egypt in 1517. They had their balsam crop planted closer to Cairo, enclosed in a guarded garden.[22]

English travellers were not entirely convinced of Matariya's authenticity in terms of the life of Jesus. Henry Blount, in 1634, upon having the very fig tree the holy family rested under pointed out to him, asked his attendant janissary how long fig trees actually lived for. He was told 'halfe a hundred yeares, or thereabout'. Blount 'noted that if this tree should faile, nevertheless that place hath many others of the same kinde, ready to take the reputation upon them'.[23]

The tree in 1601 was healthy, shady, and the garden full of other trees, and planted with flowers and bushes, with water running by. Coptic priests closely attended, telling their stories, offering water to travellers to drink. It was said that the Sultan of Grand Cairo himself would only drink this water. It was the best in all Egypt. The Pasha (= Governor) of Cairo would come here, as would other wealthy Cairenes, for rest and relaxation.[24]

After this little hiatus, Timberlake and Burrell farewelled their companions and went onwards, alone: two Franks on the road in rural Egypt. But the sweetness of Matariya faded as they found their first khan. By nightfall, they reached a village 'where we lodged in ayarde upon the bare grounde wantinge neither fleas nor lices'.[25] This village, which Timberlake calls Canko (the manuscript has 'Canto'), is now the modern town of al-Khanika, twelve miles north of Cairo near the Ismailiya Canal.

It is about nineteen miles from al-Khanika to Bilbeis, which Timberlake calls 'Philbites': for him an itchy journey after fleas, lice and the rubbing of the hair-cloth coat. There, at Bilbeis, they met up with a 'companie of Turkes [= Muslims], Jewes, and Christians', and some 750 camels, bound for Damascus over the deserts.

They stayed in Bilbeis 'ii dayes and one night' before the caravan was ready to depart. During this time Timberlake had a wonderful experience. He encountered a radical new technology involving chicken-hatching.

This does not sound quite as exciting to us as it did to Henry Timberlake. It was not of interest to the British Library manuscript copyist either, who left out the entire section, indicating the omission with a gap on the page. But it provides some insight into what most interested Timberlake, who is more excited by this than he is by anything else on his journey. Two of the twenty-six pages of the 1603 edition are dedicated to the description of the process.[26]

Timberlake writes that when he was in the town of Bilbeis, while he was looking around finding provisions to buy for the journey, he 'went into a house, where I sawe (in my judgement) a very strange secret of hatching Chickins, by artificiall heat or warmthe: the like I had seene before at the Grand Cayro, but not in such extraordinary numbers or multitudes as heere.'

So Timberlake in Cairo had also visited a chicken hatching centre as part of his mercantile explorations. In Bilbeis Timberlake was so excited that he asked for a tour of the facility, and, with payment, got a complete overview of the entire process. He was not the only Englishman to be fascinated by this. Artificial incubation of chicken eggs ranked with homing pigeons as one of those things that Europeans found amazing in Egypt.[27] As a merchant, however, Timberlake could see the cash-flow potential.

The incubation was done by heating camel's dung. Ash was mixed with this dung (and some pigeon's dung) and placed on earth, under which was a concave hollow place, three foot wide, under which was another layer of green camel's dung laid on branches of dead trees, and under that was a fireplace where embers yielded a temperate heat. The heat from the embers passing through the initial layer of dung and branches 'delivereth forth an extraordinary vapour' which then enters the hollow concave part under the layer of earth and ash the eggs rest upon. 'This artificiall heate gliding through the embers whereon the Egges lie, doth by degrees warme thorowe the shelles, and so infuseth life by the same proportions of heate: thus in seven, eight, nine, ten, or sometimes twelve daies, life continueth by this artificiall means'.

But was it foolproof? The furner dampened Timberlake's enthusiasm. Out of 100,000 eggs, he may get only 30,000 chickens, and in bad weather maybe only 20,000. Not only that, but weird things could happen: the feet may have five claws, or two before and two behind.

Timberlake was both excited and dismayed by the risks. He thought long and hard about it, and concluded that the incubation of chicken eggs was 'in vaine to be practised in England, because the ayre there is hardly ten daies together clarified: neither is there any Camels dunge, though they have dunge of other beasts every way as hote'.

Pondering upon thoughts of the lucrative financial potential of artificial chicken incubation and the heat of dung, rather than on sacred shrines, Timberlake scribbled in his notebook. The next day, the tents were taken down, and, by the afternoon, they were ready. They would ride all night.

7

The 'Wild Arabians'

Travelling parties through the Sinai Desert went by night for several reasons: it was cool, it was considered safer and it was not necessary to stop for prayers. As long as you were heavily armed and kept to well-worn paths, by way of guard stations where you had to pay protection charges and duties, you were doing all you could to ensure a safe trip. However, despite there being 1,000 people and 750 camels in the caravan, this was one instance where protection in numbers only went so far. They were like a herd of wildebeest moving into the territory of hungry lions.

Timberlake writes that the caravan went from Bilbeis at night to a place called Boharro, perhaps al-Buha, south of Kafr Sakr, where they pitched their tents at 9 o'clock in the morning of the 14th. The fact that he tells us the time indicates that he kept with him some chronometrical instrument, perhaps a miniature sundial. He may have had a small clock, though clocks, driven by a coiled steel mainspring, were not amazingly accurate. It was not until 1657, when Christiaan Huygens invented the pendulum as a regulator, that seriously accurate time-keeping began.

The travellers set off again that night, going as far as Salhia, today's Es-Salihiya. Timberlake writes that Salhia is 'Eastwarde of the Land of Gozan', the Biblical name for the Delta area, on the edge of the 'desartes of Arabia'. From here the way was extremely dangerous, and 'here we stayed ii dayes for feare of the wild Arabians'.[1]

John Rawdon described the desert they travelled through as being made up of 'all or mostly deepe sandes amongst which sandes [there are] some little smoothe or levell places being harde & [they] ar as if they wer frozen, though not with coulde but rather with heatte'. When rain falls 'yt washeth from amongst the mountaines of sandes a kind of coursse salt & falinge downe to thosse leveller places... doth by the heatte of the sunne congealle into an Isle of Salte, as yf by frost the water wer cleane frozen up into a little crust or haess of Ice.'[2] Such eerie shapes in the flickering haze of heat would prey on your mind. And somewhere in this place lurked people who were ready to pounce and take you and your possessions captive.

Bedouin (*Bedou* = desert dweller) were often called 'wild Arabs' or 'wild Arabians' by European visitors, to differentiate them from the settled or semi-nomadic 'civil Arabs' of the region. The word 'Arab' was not used as it is today to refer to everyone speaking Arabic and participating in Arab cultures throughout the Middle East and North Africa. Nationalistic pan-Arabism was a phenomenon still to come. Arabisation in the spread of early Islam had meant that diverse people were adopted into an Arab tribe upon conversion (with all the linguistic and cultural ramifications that involved), but Renaissance Europeans distinguished between the dwellers of the Arabian peninsula and Sinai, the 'Arabs', 'Arabians' or 'Saracens', from the Muslim population of the Arabic-speaking Dar es-Islam as a whole, whom they could call 'Moors' or, usually in Ottoman lands 'Turks'.[3]

The Bedouin were distinctive. They lived in deserts and wilderness regions as nomadic tent-dwellers and herders. The Bedouin considered these places their territories, and the roads their roads, despite the successive empires that claimed the areas. They did not acknowledge the imperial authority of Constantinople, unless there had been some specific agreement between the Sublime Porte and an individual sheikh.

Nomads had been wandering through to the Levant from the Arabian Peninsula ever since Biblical times, and from the Middle Ages they had defined tribal territories, not without some internecine warfare. Bedouin traditionally could be brave warriors, both fighting other Bedouin tribes – led by rival sheikhs – and also battling against various rulers who had encroached on their areas. Some sheikhs saw travellers as easy prey, though they may also have resented caravans for ruining grazing regions and consuming and polluting water sources.

Bedouin society is close-knit, hierarchical and ordered, with a finely developed sense of justice, and Bedouin have traditionally practised strict hospitality to strangers. It is hard to reconcile this hospitality tradition with the pillaging 'wild Arabs' presented in the sources.

Also, there may have been different degrees of robbery, and different types of 'wild Arabs'. The Augsburg botanist Leonard Rauwolf, visiting in 1575, distinguished between thieving 'Arabians' and 'some Arabians called Balduini [who] keep in the desarts... have no certain abode, but live continually in the fields, and go from country to country in great numbers, wheresoever they find good pasture for their beasts and camels. I have met with many of them in my travels, and have time staid with them all night in their tents.'[4]

John Rawdon makes this distinction too. He writes that there were 'troupes of Arabes dispearced in that parte of the countrey' which the Turks (here Ottoman authorities) could not control. The Turks could not pass in security without a mighty convoy. There was also 'in thosse places, a wilde people caled Pedewines [= Bedouin] which people doth never come in howsse, but liveth in mountaines & on the sandes amongst the datte trees, being abundance standinge on heapes and mountaines of sandes on which they live mostlye'. The Bedouin could well attack a party of travellers, but the large prey of a caravan was attacked not by them but by these other thieving 'Arabes which ar a gallant or braver people in compare of the Pedewines, [who] doth come downe in such multitudes, that they have somtimes caried awaye prisoners to the mountaines, hundreths at once, as well Turkes as Jewes & Christians, & theer [they] make them herdesmen to keepe sheepe goattes & camels 2 or 3 hundreth milles off from the place that they take them, if they be not able to ransome themselves.' In other words, the Arabs, according to Rawdon, came from far away especially to attack the large caravans. He writes of them:

> thesse be of themselves a very greatt people, of them be also greatt men, & mightelye rich, yet few of them seldome or never com in howses, or that I am suer the most part doth live in tents in great multitudes as if they weer in tribes disperced, some into on place & some into another accordinge as they make choisse of ther places, ther heardes of cattle which ar mostlye, camels, gootes & sheepe, every night brought home, & layed aboute ther tents being in compasse as a greatt cyttye, ther cattle being in number infinitte; ther horses that they breed be many, & of the best in the worlde, likewisse every night brought home & layed aboute ther tents, but ther older & best horses at within closse by themselves.

He seems to be referring here (in stream-of-consciousness colloquial English) to the Arabs of the Arabian peninsula, who took pride in their Arabian horses, with individual sheikhs holding great wealth. These were not quite the poor Bedouin of the Sinai.

He writes of their religion being 'little differinge from the Turke & likewisse in ther habitts', but notes that they make their attacks on horseback, and use bows and arrows, pikes, shields and a kind of Turkish sword called a 'Cangeire' which was 'stickinge right before them betwixt ther bellye & girdell servinge for a dagger'. They could cast their pikes as they rode at great speed. The bow was short, but very strong, and the arrow was heavy. The arrowheads were long and broad and once in the flesh, writes Rawdon, could be 'hardlye pulled out, without cuttinge a greatt holle in the fleshe'.

While the Ottoman Sultan was the master of the Sinai in theory, these Arabs:

> care not for him, for as they at ther pleasure came downe out of the mountaines, into the places of pleasure, being plaines or vallees, fertill & pleasant, so upon any occatione betwixt the Turke & themselves they do presantlye remove ther tents, families, goods & heardes of cattle, unto the mountaines, where no bodye will followe them, or if they shoulde ther wer nothinge to be gotten but blowes.[5]

A caravan loaded with food, goods, animals and money would have been impossible to resist. The attackers were indeed ruthless, but no more ruthless than an English privateer.

Perhaps Timberlake understood that. Had he ever robbed a Spanish galleon, loaded with oil, currants and wine? Privateering – boarding another vessel and absconding with its cargo (with a bit of collateral damage to be expected) – was not considered murder and theft, or even piracy, by those who did it. For an English privateer – like Walter Raleigh – it was raiding for honour, resources and pride, raiding for national self-protection. You had to have a licence from the Crown to engage in it, but from then on you were not a pirate so much as a speculator undertaking a fine enterprise, gaining extra profit for your venture, useful resources and improving security for friendly ships. One man's theft was another man's successful business operation. Take, for example, this account from the anonymous 'Letter Written to the Right Worshipfull the Governors and Assistants of the East Indian Marchants in London' concerning a voyage of the East India Company fleet:

> The 21. of June [1601]... wee tooke a ship of Vianna bound for Brasill, of the burthen of 130. tunne, her lading was Wine, Oyle and Meale, which hath stood us in great steede in this our voyage: five or six dayes after we turned her off after we had pillaged her as we thought good.

Or, alternatively, from the same voyage:

> The 3. of October beeing Sunday about five of the clocke in the afternoone we saw a saile and gave her chase, about nine of the clocke wee fetched her up and hayled her, and found her to be a ship from Goa and bound for Mallaca laden with Portingals goodes, as Pintados, Calicottes and other stuffes great store, a great part of her loading was Rice and Victualls, and in her about seaven or eight hundred persons men women and children, we had out of her 958 Fardils: and diverse chests with other things as Canistees: wee were forced from her by force of weather beeing put from our anchors.[6]

The accounts of English voyages and explorations are rife with proud descriptions of the looting of foreign ships.

On the edge of Egypt, with the sea to the north and the great Sinai desert to the east, the caravan halted. The thought of venturing out into a darkness in which you might be attacked by robbers would not encourage you to make haste. It cannot have been a relaxed wait. Few of the travellers knew what their destination would be like, or where they would stay, even if they managed to get through unscathed. It was a voyage to the unknown, in the dark. Even if they succeeded in withstanding an initial attack, there might well be other attackers further up the road. Perhaps they looked around at each other thinking of the chances of survival: how many would live, how many would die, how much would they lose?

Men with pistols would have spent some time preparing them. In Jacob de Geijn's *Book of Weapons* from 1608, there is an illustration which shows the forty-two loading motions necessary to fire a match-lock pistol. Under attack, by the time you got to position number thirty-five you might have found yourself run through with a blade. Basically, in 1601, you pointed your pistol and had one good shot, and then you drew your sword. Some of the pistols had nifty combinations of daggers and guns, so if you missed with your shot you could always charge your enemy with the same device. These pistols were heavy and would also have been very useful for clobbering someone on the head. Both the janissaries and the 'wild Arabs' favoured lances that could be thrown very effectively, and the Arabs also were experts with bows and arrows.

Everyone has had the experience sometime of seeing someone you know in a situation you do not expect to see them. You recognise the face, but since it is not in its usual context, you do a double-take, and cannot think where you have seen the person before. It causes a weird mental dissonance. You search through your memory, straining to put the face in the right box, but the mind resists. Perhaps this is how al-Fessi felt when he first saw Henry Timberlake dressed as a poor pilgrim in a party of Greek Orthodox Christians on their way to Jerusalem. Perhaps he doubted his eyes. Timberlake was with a stranger, John Burrell, not with Waldred or anyone else from the boat. There was nothing about him to associate him with the *Trojan*. Al-Fessi would have been justified in assuming that he was seeing another Englishman altogether who bore a remarkable resemblance to the Captain. Whatever the case, al-Fessi made nothing of seeing Timberlake at this stage of their journey, if he saw him this early at all.

For indeed, al-Fessi and his friend, the one who had spoken more animatedly with Timberlake on the *Trojan*, had decided to go to Jerusalem, Damascus and Baghdad before journeying to Mecca.[7] They clearly wanted to see as much as they could now that they were so close to such famous places. The Dome of the Rock in al-Quds, Jerusalem, was the third holiest shrine in the Dar es-Islam. Jerusalem had once, for a short time, been the capital of all Islam. The ancient mosque built on the Haram esh-Sharif, on the very rock where the Prophet was taken up to heaven, was supposed by some to be the most beautiful in the world. At Baghdad, another great *hajj* of pilgrims would begin the journey to Mecca.

By a remarkable coincidence, the two Moroccans and the English Captain that had taken them from Algiers to Alexandria were travelling companions in the same caravan.

Eventually, the caravan loaded up and prepared to depart. It is quite cold at night in the desert at this time of year, and people would have wrapped in the warm woollens of northern lands. Women and children were kept in the middle of the group. Around the outside, though mainly at the front, there were janissary guards, with harquebus rifles and lances. This long worm of people and camels slowly moved off on the night of Tuesday, 17 March, 1601.

The demarcation line between what was considered to be safe land and the wild world of the deserts was Lake al-Sibeita. Timberlake was told that this lake was the result of some botched canal-building by one of the Ptolemaic kings. Instead of a neat canal the sea had flooded 150 miles into the mainland, and over this there was a bridge.[8]

They crossed over the bridge.

But, as Timberlake writes, 'we had noe sooner past this bridge, but we were sett upon by the wild Arabians'.[9]

It must have been utterly terrifying. Suddenly there were showers of arrows, huge pikes landing, spearing animals. The commotion: people falling, donkeys baying, shouting and crying, camels panicking and bolting. Chaos, fear and nowhere to run to but the embrace of pitch darkness and shadowy sands.

Then Burrell was attacked. Timberlake does not describe the details, perhaps because he is covering over modestly his own part in rescuing his companion. It was considered good gentlemanly form to be humble about one's valour in battle. But there was some kind of skirmish and Burrell was the target. It was no wonder. Europeans were the best prey for the highwaymen. A Frankish hat simply spelt money, for it more likely signified a rich merchant than a poor pilgrim. The saddle-bag of a European was worth having, and even better the European himself, who might have money-pouches, drugs, gold and other wonderful things hidden on his person, and, additionally, he could be sold.

The Arabs' ambush strategies worked on the basis of quick, surprise attacks, snatch-and-grabs, and equally quick disappearances. Their best weapons were bows and arrows, sling-shots and pikes thrown from a distance. They did not want to engage in fights, and had nothing of the required expertise, despite their fine looted weapons and brilliant horsemanship.

Timberlake later would write of the encounter: 'In the uprore in the nyght past my fellowe Mr. John Burrell escaped very hardly,' and 'not with standinge our greate companie, for we were then one thousand persones, yeat had we a camell laden with callicowes taken away, and 4 men sore hurte, and one of the 4 mortally wounded. Soe the Arabill. rann away with theire praye, and wee could not remedye it, for that it was nyght.'[10]

The 'uproar' he calls it, as if the most striking thing was the noise. 'We could not remedy it' is a line that implies some kind of personal involvement in the fighting: 'we', not 'they'. The fighters in the caravan could not get the booty back, though Burrell was saved. Unlike other travellers, Henry Timberlake was no passive passenger, looking to janissaries for protection. He was a merchant adventurer, a ship's captain and a gentleman, skilled in fighting. He knew what to do, and there was reason to make sure the attackers knew they had skilled men to fight against.

Like the pirates of the seas, these highwaymen showed no mercy for their victims. For example, Laurence Aldersley's party encountered a great number of 'Arabians' between Ramle and Jerusalem. They stopped the travellers and would not let them pass until they had paid '20 shillings a man'. Aldersley's Palestinian interpreter, who had paid the money, was 'stricken down and had his head broken because he would not give them as much as they asked'.[11] Nearly every European traveller's account has some story along these lines. William Lithgow, travelling south from Palestine to Egypt in a caravan of 800 people, found the area south of Gaza 'sorely distressed by the Arabs'. After they went 'forward to that fearefull Wildernesse' by night (with Lithgow on foot), 200 of the attackers broke out from holes and bushes, and shot arrows until they were given money to depart.[12] Lithgow tells another story of an ambush in which nine women and five men were killed, and thirty 'deadly wounded'. They buried the dead in deep graves with piles of stones on top to prevent jackals from excavating the bodies and consuming them.[13]

George Sandys' caravan was also attacked, at the rear (most of the guards/soldiers being at the front):

> The clamour was great; and the passengers, together with their leaders, fled from their camels. I and my companion imagining the noise to be onely an encouragement unto one another, were left alone; yet preserved from violence. They carried away with them divers mules and asses laden with drugs, and abandoned by their owners; not daring to stay too long, nor [en]cumber themselves with too much luggage, for fear of the souldiers.[14]

Sandys tells another story of a caravan of 300 camels that was entirely taken.[15]

Ottoman sources likewise testify to Bedouin attacking caravans, including pilgrimage caravans bound for Mecca.[16] The Egyptian pilgrimage caravan took a route to Gaza, before going east. In 1545 Bedouin burnt pilgrims' tents, including babies who were in them sleeping in their cradles. The historian al-Jaziri (died around 1568) said that the assailants attacked returning pilgrims because of the goods they had brought from Mecca. The Ottoman authorities paid them allowances to ensure they did not molest the pilgrims, but these were sometimes not considered enough.[17]

After the affray, the caravan regrouped and went on quickly. There was no point in flaffing about in the night wailing about the terror. They had to get to some kind of safety as soon as possible, given that the attackers could return at any time. They pitched their tents in the morning at a well of brackish water, probably the Wells of Duedar, where the dead man would have been buried, and left at '3 of the clocke in the after noone',[18] according to Timberlake's clock. They just had to press forward to get away as soon as possible and hope for the best, aiming for properly defended castles.

The first of these was the 'Castle of Catia' (Katya, wrongly copied as 'Cattap' in the manuscript) where there were a few solitary palm trees and a garrison of soldiers. For the safety it provided, high charges were made on all people and animals. At each stop each traveller had to pay between ten and sixty small pieces of silver. The water at Katya was so bad that the Captain in charge of the soldiers brought his water from Tina, a town bordering the sea twelve miles away.[19] It was a rough place and the garrison lived by demanding high payments and hunting wild boar.[20]

On 19 March, ten days after they had left Cairo, they pitched at another brack-ish well, probably the Wells of Slaves (*Bir al-Abed*), but did not stay long. From there, they covered almost fifty miles during the following night's journey and arrived on 20 March at the second castle, named Arissa, modern al-Arish. This castle was two miles from the sea, with a few houses around about, and had a garrison of 100 soldiers and good water. Further payments were given (twenty pieces of silver a head and thirty for a camel). Next night they went off again, accompanied by many soldiers, and travelled twenty-four hours together to the third castle, resting perhaps briefly by the Wells of Fear. They came to Rapha, which Timberlake calls 'Raphael' ('Rapell' in the manuscript), also 'the Castle of Haniones', by which he means Khan Younis, a thirteenth-century fort not actu-ally to be identified with Rapha. The next morning, 22 March, they pitched close to the city of 'Gaza in Palistina'.

Gaza in the sixteenth and seventeenth centuries was a booming town. Set in lush orange groves and plantations, the Ottomans, in 1516, had made this city a capital of one of the sub-districts of Damascus (al-Shams = 'the left' meaning Suriyya): al-Quds (Jerusalem) was another such sub-district, but Gaza was the greater town. The governor was the fabulously wealthy and influential Ahmad Pasha, who would be renowned for his endowments for the North-West and North-East prayer cells on the Haram esh-Sharif. Mustafa Pasha, Ahmad's grandfather, had been a Christian slave of Suleiman the Magnificent, from Circassia or Georgia, but had ascended to greatness. Ahmad Pasha was famous not only because of his riches and the high-standing of his family, but because he was in charge of the Syrian pilgrimage to Mecca.[21]

Gaza was a very important trading post, where the caravans from Egypt bound for Damascus, Aleppo, and other cities of Syria would stop, sell and buy. It was also the site of the great twelfth-century al-Umari Mosque, in the centre of the city, and many of the well-made streets by the market were full of busy merchandising.

The people of Gaza had had a long and colourful history. Once a Canaanite town, it had been the pre-eminent city of the Philistines, a people who colonised a large swathe of the coastal region in the thirteenth century BC, at around about the same time the Israelites established themselves in the central part of the area, and as time went by the inhabitants became Hellenised (Greek in culture). They traded so successfully with the Mediterranean world that the Greeks came to know the entire area as 'Palaistina', from Philistina, the country of the Philistines, and this became the standard western geographical term for the land. When the Romans included this region in its Empire (from the first century BC onwards) Gaza was a very important Graeco-Roman cultural, mercantile and intellectual centre. The inhabitants then had the religious swings of most of the peoples of the Levant, converting first to Christianity in the fourth–fifth century (which they did in Gaza kicking and screaming) and then to Islam (with Arabisation) from the seventh–eighth century, thereafter facing the various waves of Islamic (and, briefly, Christian) conquerors who sought power from holding the land corridor of Palestine and exacting duties on caravans. But the Gazans had endured, retained their love of trade and culture, and kept themselves flourishing, rebounding time and again from adversity. Gaza was, in 1601, still confident, lively and bold, with a grand old mosque and the burial place of the Prophet Mohammed's grandfather, Hashem bin Abdulmanaf, as well as ancient churches and synagogues.

George Sandys, visiting in 1610, describes Gaza as being upon a hill surrounded by valleys and hills planted with all kinds of delicious fruits. The buildings of the town he found not so impressive, after Cairo, noting that the average house was usually made of undressed stones, with an arched interior. It was flat-roofed, with a courtyard and walls around the roofs topped with potsherds resembling mounted cannon. He noted that people used the roofs as extra rooms, for there they had mats and wooden frames. As for ancient Gaza, he could see marble columns reused in the architecture, and other relics, and there was an area of ruins in the north-east. A castle had been erected here by the Crusader king Baldwin III, and this was where the greatest Ottoman governor of the region resided; the Sanjakbey of Jerusalem was his inferior.

As a trading centre, the Gazans relied on land transport. Goods from Arabia and further east would arrive here, en route to Cairo, or Damascus. Gaza had a cosmopolitan air, with all the visiting traders. In 1601 it was part of a great network of trade routes. And it was a religiously diverse place. Jews, Samaritans, Greek Orthodox Christians and Muslims lived here together.[22]

Rawdon, ungrammatically, effused over the lushness of the place: all around the town there were 'orchardes & gardens of greatt lardgnes & likewisse in the towne being places of greatt pleasure, & to conclude a worlde of fruitte of all sortes, or best in the world.'[23] Timberlake calls the Gazan area 'a goodley fruiteful cuntry beinge nowe cleare of all the desartes'.[24] Here, he writes, 'in the towne I did see the place (as they say) that Sampson did pull downe' as in the Biblical story told in

Judges 13–16, 'which in my judgment must neede be the towne by the situation of the cuntry'. It is interesting here to note that he is assessing what he is told: 'in my judgment', he writes.[25] The place of Samson was actually the al-Umari mosque built – reputedly – with the stones from the house that Samson pulled down with his bare hands, though in fact this mosque is witness to the changing religions of the inhabitants. Once, 2,000 years ago, there was a gorgeous temple of the local god Marnas, which was destroyed and replaced by the Eudoxiana church (fifth century), which was turned into a mosque (seventh century), which was destroyed and rebuilt as a church by the Crusaders (twelfth century), which was turned into a mosque (thirteenth century), which is what Timberlake saw (seventeenth century): old stones in the walls could be easily given a very ancient history by eager guides.

Timberlake here shows an investigative attitude quite different from pilgrims of old. He is not going to believe everything he is told. At Rapha, for example, he had already doubted. Someone had said it was here that the kings of Egypt and Judaea had fought 'many great battels'. Timberlake scoffs: 'but it is very unlikely for theire is nothinge to feede an army with but sand and salt water.'[26] Timberlake could chuckle at the credulity of listeners. He knew how to feed an army, as he knew how to feed his crew, and trusted his own judgement before so-called tradition. He was a hard man to convince, or to attack.

8

The Dwelling
of Abraham

So where was al-Fessi in all this? He too endured the terror of the ambush. He too drank the brackish waters from the wells, and journeyed on the back of a camel together with his friend from Morocco towards Palestine. Timberlake was completely unaware of his existence in the crowd, but perhaps the Maghrebi was looking for a glimpse of the Europeans, wondering again and again if this man in the company could be the Captain, Henry Timberlake, who had taken him as a passenger from Algiers. He would surely have talked with his friend about it. But even if they had overheard Timberlake and Burrell speaking English together, they were not convinced. Why would the Captain be here anyway? It was completely off his course, and not his concern. He was a man of the seas and trade, surely. What business could he have in Jerusalem, dressed as a pilgrim?

The way from Gaza was easier than through the deserts. Timberlake writes that he departed from there on 22 March, the same day he arrived, and made camp at a place called 'Canuie' in Arabic, 'Bersheba' by Christians. 'Canuie' sounds like the name of a khan; the name of the town in Arabic is Bir es-Seba. Here Timberlake states that it is 'upon the borders of Judea',[1] using the template of the Books of Samuel, Kings and Chronicles (reflecting the Iron Age II, 1020–586 BC), whereby the border of Philistina and Judaea ran about here. The caravan followed the road eastwards, across the Negev to Beersheba.

Departing at night from Bir es-Seba, on 23 March, the caravan headed northeast, skirting the Wadi al-Khalil to Hebron, al-Khalil in Arabic. The area around Hebron is fertile and green, especially in March. It was covered in vineyards. Sandys describes this as 'the most pregnant and pleasant valley that ever eye beheld' after his journey from Gaza through 'continued hills, beset with variety of fruits'. Here the landscape was 'full of flowrie hils ascending leasurely' and valleys 'with groves of olives, and other fruites dispersedly adorned',[2] and yet he also noted that, given this bounty, there could have been much more intensive farming and a greater number of villages.

The Ottoman system of governing 'Turkie' at this time did not encourage villagers to invest time in agricultural operations. They were under the thumb of the sipahis, the Ottoman cavalry, who had the rights to a portion of the income of villages, and would dictate what would be farmed and what would not be farmed. Sandys writes that the sipahis used the fields to graze their horses: the sipahis 'are billeted in these rich pastures for the benefit of their horses, [the sipahis] lying in tents beside them, committing many outrages on the adjoyning townes and distressed passengers'. Both the Palestinian peasants and European travellers likewise greatly feared the sipahis, who would ride around as lords, ensuring everyone gave them due obeisance and revenue. It was not a case of travellers relaxing once they quitted the areas of the Bedouin; Ottoman sipahis could be bad news. Fynes Moryson tells a typical story:

> For it happened that a spachi (or Horse-man under the great Turke's pay) riding swiftly, and crossing our way, suddenly turned towards us and, with his spear in his rest,… he rushed upon us with all his might, and by the grace of God his speare lighting in the panell of the Asse, never hurt the French-man his Rider, but he did much astonish both him and us, till our Muccaro [= donkey-driver] enquiring the cause of this violence. He said, 'Why doe not these dogges light on foot to honour mee as I passe?' which, when we heard, and knew that we must here learne the vertue of the beasts on which we rode, we presently tumbled from our Asses (for we had no other stirrops then knotted ropes) and bended our bodies to him.[3]

The Palestinian villagers worked on the principle of keeping their heads down, not appearing rich, keeping their houses modest. The worst thing that could happen was if the sipahis thought them rich enough to pay more taxes. Any individual initiatives on the part of the farmers and villagers (the 'fellahin') to gain extra revenue by land cultivation would be relatively worthless, given the charges levied by the sipahis. The fellahin would frustrate the sipahis' intentions at times by leaving fields fallow, but in doing this they would risk being brought to an Ottoman court and punished.[4] There were covert industries, however. Sandys writes of Christians in Gaza, that their houses had low doorways to deter the swift entry of sipahis, but they had vineyards, and secretly fermented wine underground in 'long vessels of clay' to prevent it being eaten by worms.[5]

The caravan would have gone through Hebron, but the encampment was further north. 'The 23rd in the morninge we pitched one a greene under the walles of Ramoth Gillead. Here I stayed all the daye'.[6] 'Ramoth Gillead' as a name is wrong. Ramoth Gilead (Deut. 4:43; Josh 20:8, etc.) is, understandably, in Gilead, a region in present-day Jordan east of the River Jordan between the Sea of Galilee and the Dead Sea, and is securely identified as a site called Tell Ramuth.[7] A large town called Ramle, north-west of Jerusalem, was often called 'Ramoth Gilead' mistakenly by western travellers, but Timberlake was near Hebron, a long way away. On nineteenth-century maps of the region around Hebron, however, you can find a site called 'Rama' or 'er-Rameh', on the right of the road leading to Bethlehem, two miles north of Hebron. Rama means 'rise' or 'hill' in Arabic; it is not really a place name. The full name is 'Ramat al-Khalil', and it would have sounded like 'Ramoth Gilead' to Timberlake.

It is possible to be even more specific about where the caravan for Damascus parked in this area, because Timberlake later mentions a 'fountain' – a spring – and in the valley beside Ramat al-Khalil there was indeed a spring at the time of the Survey of Western Palestine, completed 1882–88. 'Ain al-Mezrûk was a natural spring west of the roadway. The walls mentioned by Timberlake were perhaps the old walls around the sacred precinct of Ramat al-Khalil, built by Herod the Great in the first century BC, enclosing an area 157.5 x 216 ft.

In understanding 'al-Khalil' as 'Gilead' Timberlake managed to miss the site's very important association. Hebron in Arabic is called al-Khalil, 'the Friend', because of the town's association with Abraham, who is in Arabic Khalil Allah, 'the Friend of God' (as in Isa. 41:8; James 2:23). Hebron is so named because it contains a sacred site whose veneration stretches back thousands of years, to the Bronze Age. This sacred site is the burial place of Abraham.

Abraham is held to be the common ancestor of Arabs, Jews and Christians. His tomb has therefore been deeply significant to the many groups populating this country over time. Jews trace their ethnicity to Abraham, via his second-born son Isaac, his son Jacob (renamed Israel), and his son Judah; those who convert to Judaism gain this ethnicity by adoption. Muslims send peace and salutation to the Prophet Ibrahim five times a day during prayers, and all Arabs trace their ethnicity to Abraham by his first-born son Ishmael. Christians hold themselves to be the true children of Abraham being, as the apostle Paul wrote, 'people of faith' who are 'clothed in Christ' and therefore 'progeny of Abraham, the heirs named in the promise' (Gal. 3).

In Hebron, at the site of Haram al-Khalil ('the sacred place of the Friend'), the ancient Cave of Machpelah (see Gen. 13), where he is buried, was enclosed in a mosque. This contained not only the remains of Abraham but also, purportedly, other Biblical patriarchs and matriarchs. There are seven tombs, believed to contain Abraham, Sarah, Isaac, Leah, Rebecca and Jacob and Joseph. A large temple here was built by the first-century BC King of the Jews, Herod the Great (son of an Idumaean convert to Judaism and a Nabataean princess), though in Arab legend the huge stones came to be associated with the ancient King Solomon, who constructed the building with the aid of *jinn*. It became a mosque after the Arabs conquered the region in the seventh century AD. The Crusaders converted the structure (*c*.1115) into a church, but the Mamluks restored it as a mosque and closed the entrance to the crypt in the fourteenth century.

Abraham is also considered to be the fundamental example of a man of faith in the religions of Judaism, Christianity and Islam, with all their many variants. He is a uniting figure for all. His story is told somewhat differently in each one, and yet the central core remains the same. Abraham was a traveller, a wanderer, who departed from his home to be a stranger in a strange land, searching for a new place. God promised him a new home, in the land of Canaan, where his descendants would be many nations. This Land of Canaan was the Promised Land. Claims to this area by Jews, Muslims and Christians all rest on this original promise to Abraham.

Abraham was the prototypical man on the move, a nomad chief moving cautiously through alien, often hostile, territory, with only his indefatigable trust in God to guide him, but a trust in God that would accommodate dialogue, as in the Bible when he negotiates with God about the destruction of Sodom, asking for clemency (Gen. 18), or in the Qur'an asks God for proof he could raise the dead (Sura 2). God tests Abraham by asking him to sacrifice his son (Isaac, in Gen. 22, in the Qur'an unidentified, though usually thought to be Ishmael, from Sura 37) and he makes ready to do so, surrendering to God's will, halting only when God stops him. In Islam, it was Abraham, with his son Ishmael, who established the holy Ka`ba in Mecca, the focus of all pilgrimage. In Islam Abraham's religion is believed to have been revived by Mohammed, not invented by him; it is simply God's way of righteousness, that Abraham intuitively knew, a way that is not correctly followed within Judaism and Christianity.

The Biblical story presents Abraham as the paragon of virtue. Abraham shows hospitality to the strangers who appear at his encampment, offering them water and bread, behaving as their servant, in complete humility, with the utmost generosity of spirit, not knowing that the strangers were messengers from God (Gen. 18). In this way he reflects the ideal of offering help to the stranger that is found all over the Middle East, an ideal found also in the New Testament: 'Be not forgetful to entertain strangers: for thereby some have entertained angels unawares' (Heb. 13:2). In the Qur'an Abraham (here Ibrahim) offers great hospitality to strangers who simply come to him saying, 'Peace' (Sura 51). He asks no questions about who they are, whether they were friends or foe, whether they deserve his hospitality or not. In Abraham's understanding when someone comes to you and says, 'Peace', *Salaam*, then you respond by saying, 'Peace', back to them, and you mean it. 'You are a people unknown to me,' says Abraham, and then he lays before them a sumptuous feast. He looks after the strangers in the strange land; it is the will of God that this is what you should do.

Ramat al-Khalil ('hill of the Friend'), north of Hebron, was where this incident of humble hospitality traditionally occurred, the old name of the site being Mamre (or Terebinthus). At Mamre, the story goes, Abraham planted a terebinth – a kind of oak tree – and dug a well. The site became, like his tomb in Hebron, a locality of great devotion for many peoples living in the region: Jews (Judaeans/Judahites),

Idumaeans (Edomites), Nabataeans, Arabs and so on. When the Christians took charge of Palestine in the fourth century AD under the newly converted Roman Emperor Constantine, he ensured that the site was appropriated by the Church, though, despite the rhetoric, archaeological excavations have shown that the pre-Christian altar here continued in use until the seventh century.

For thousands of years, Mamre was venerated by people who did not have the same religious beliefs, and yet held the same man to be their great ancestor, and each took this shrine to be deeply holy. They shared it. The trouble starts when people feel that a holy place has to be exclusively in the hands of those who 'correctly' revere it, because it might be desecrated by those who do not have the same beliefs, who might be 'unclean', or blasphemous, with it, because they will contaminate it, or break it in some way. Or else the holy place becomes a commodity of power.

Once the fear starts of the 'others', then the claims begin, like with the Emperor Constantine. He could not bear to think that this site, associated with the holy patriarch Abraham, might be in the hands of wrong-thinking Semitic tribes and Jews. After receiving the report of his agent – his mother-in-law Eutropia – who had visited Mamre in the year 326, he wrote a furious letter to the Bishops of Palestine, fuming that the imperial lady 'has made known to us by letter that abandoned foolishness of impious men which had escaped detection by you' was taking place there. Such 'criminal conduct' at a holy site was reprehensible: it was 'a grave impiety indeed' that it should be 'defiled by some of the slaves of superstition in every possible way', for 'impure sacrifices are performed there continually' that are 'unworthy of the sanctity of the place' (Eusebius, *The Life of Constantine* 3: 52).[8] Constantine's indignation reflects exactly the same sentiments that many people have today, when they see others, not of their religion or ethnicity, coming to a place they deem holy, without the same kind of respect, or the same beliefs. The truth is it is very difficult to share holiness, because recognising something as holy strikes at the very depths of your soul, so that you seem to be connected with it in some way, or so that you feel you are somehow protecting God from being violated. Anyone who has a different sentiment about it feels like an enemy, or a vandal, or a thief.

Despite the Emperor's vituperations and the Christian takeover of the site, the Bishops tried initially to fit Christianity into the formula rather than ram Christianity down everyone's throats, and it worked, for hundreds of years, like this, until in the end the Christians triumphed. But that triumph was short-lived.

The ruins that Timberlake saw testify to the fact that sometimes the claim to exclusivity can result in a kind of all-or-nothing scenario. Christianity triumphed here just decades before the Arab Muslim invasion. Afterwards the fortunes of the church at the site gradually diminished. Muslim rulers developed the old shrine of Abraham's tomb as the main focus of sanctity in the region, a site that had been less revered by Christians. People gradually converted to Islam, and many abandoned veneration at the Christian site. The village of Mamre, and its holy place, slowly fell to ruin. But some of the locals (who had been pagan or Jewish, Christian and then Muslim in the course of only a few hundred years) still venerated the site, and, when the old tree there died, the identification of Abraham's oak seems to have moved around to different places nearby, until it found its present spot a mile and a half north-west of Hebron, at `Ain Sebta.[9] The Spanish Franciscan Juan Perrara, visiting in 1565, reported seeing the place where Abraham met the angels beneath an ilex tree, a mighty stump from which three shoots had sprung. This ilex is now the property of the Russian Church. The original enclosure was still venerated by a few as Beit al-Khalil, the 'house of the Friend', the site where Abraham pitched his tents.[10]

And this is where the caravan pitched its tents.

Muslims like al-Fessi could pray in the mosque of al-Khalil, close to the burial place of Ibrahim/Abraham. It is said that even Adam prayed here; there is a rock with his footprint in it. Visitors looked at the enormous hewn stones of the mosque. All this must have been even more striking given that the Muslim travellers of the caravan were fasting during the day because of Ramadan. In a fasting state, you are so much more vulnerable to awe.

What thoughts did al-Fessi carry away with him from his visit to the mosque? Perhaps he thought of Abraham, and his hospitality to strangers.

Meanwhile, at Ramat el-Khalil, Timberlake and Burrell would have surveyed the scenery: the ruin of the old church, the hills covered with orchards, the extraordinary prettiness of their surroundings. In spring this place is verdant, flowery, and full of birds. Almond trees blossom, and everything seems washed and alive. At this time of year there are masses of red poppies growing in fields, and daisies dripping with water.

Perhaps all this freshness and beauty made Timberlake want to be clean after the rigours of travel, and the dusty sand of the desert. He gathered up various dirty items of clothing. He took his soap, and departed for the spring.

When he reached the water he started on his laundry. He could have asked some women in the caravan to wash his linen for a fee, but perhaps he felt it was wiser to keep out of their way. If there was one thing he would have known about Muslim women (apart from prostitutes) it was that a foreign man should never talk to them, without talking first to their brothers or fathers, or you were liable to offend someone. He would wash his own laundry.

And then something happened that gave him a tremendous shock. Timberlake writes (though, as usual, I supply the punctuation):

> I went downe to a fountayne to wash my fowle lynninge, in which tyme there came
> to me a Moore and tooke my lynninge clothes out of my hand sayinge that he would

helpe me, and called me by my name – I beinge in a maze to heare [him] name me in that place, being so farr from my cuntry, and in a strange land.[11]

So there he was, at the spring washing his laundry, and the Moor, al-Fessi, came up to him, saying, in the lingua franca: 'Let me help you Captain Henry Timberlake,' taking the shirts from his hand.

Timberlake was stunned to be addressed by name at such a place, so far away from home, by a Moor speaking Frank, and stared, astonished, at the man.

For many days al-Fessi must have known that someone appearing remarkably like Henry Timberlake rode with the caravan. Even with so many people, two Franks would have stood out, and there would have been talk of the skirmish they had had with the Bedouin, Burrell's near escape and perhaps Timberlake's valour. For many days, however, al-Fessi had held back, possibly because he was not sure that this Frank could really be the Captain of the *Trojan*.

Unless he purposely followed Henry Timberlake, al-Fessi must have come himself to the fountain, to refill his water bottle to rinse his mouth, and seen Timberlake washing his clothing. Now, finally, he had a chance to look intently from close quarters, while the Captain busied himself with soap, water, scrubbing and rinsing. Was this the same man?

Something decided it. What was it? Did he have a distinctive tattoo, as sailors often do, now exposed? Did he sing a sea shanty? Did he bring out that chronometrical device to fix the time by the sun before he began? Had he done that exactly on board ship? There was something, anyway, that made al-Fessi certain, finally, that this was the Captain, and not someone else with a remarkable resemblance to him.

With that realisation also, al-Fessi felt a discomfort too strong to shrug off. It made him completely change course.

To wash one's own clothes, as a man, could be seen as a kind of shame in a world in which honour and shame were part of the fabric of society. Men of honour should always act with honour. To see the esteemed Captain of the *Trojan* doing menial women's work – washing laundry – at a spring would have jarred terribly. Timberlake, a wealthy and honourable man, had no servant, no slave, no woman, nobody to do this job for him. Al-Fessi would have known that the women of the caravan could wash laundry for a fee. If they were there at the spring it would have been an option for him to organise their labour, paying the charge himself if he wanted to. But he does not do this.

Who else was at the spring? Surely anyone seeing this Frank washing his clothing would have found it a little amusing. It is quite likely there were others around here: women washing clothing, in particular, or gathering water for cooking. The Christian had no shame! Was there a comment made about Timberlake? No one but al-Fessi and his friend knew that this Christian was master of a great ship, an affluent trader, brave and skilled. To them he would have been just another infidel pilgrim, misguided and low.

Al-Fessi acted. Here, pointedly, rather than advising Timberlake to get the women to wash his clothing, he offers to do it for the Captain himself, subverting his own honour as a man in the process. It is a kind of sign. It is not just a case of a job that needs to be done, for a fee, because the rules have suddenly gone by the wayside: all the established norms of what men would do.

Here they are: two men on pilgrimage, one on the *hajj,* and the other on some kind of Protestant quasi-pilgrimage he should never have been on in the first place. It is as if al-Fessi could outdo Timberlake in humility and take on a mantle of shame for a higher purpose. Where Timberlake the Captain would wash his own clothes, al-Fessi would wash the clothes of another, those of a Christian!

There was also all the background of friendly dealings between the Moroccans and the English, and the ruling from the Sultan of Morocco that Englishmen should be looked after in his lands. Here they were far away from Barbary; but perhaps he felt it was in keeping with the Sultan's orders that he should act to protect and help the English Captain. There was no obligation on the part of al-Fessi to behave with any concern whatsoever for him otherwise. Surely al-Fessi would have known that Timberlake had taken the pilgrims from Algiers to Alexandria for money, not out of pious duty. There was no obligation to repay that service.

Something of the aura of Abraham's hospitality was in the air.

Nowhere in Timberlake's account is there any indication that al-Fessi acted out of a wish to make money. There were many people Timberlake could have hired en route if he had wanted to, but his donning of pilgrim clothes indicates that he adopted a certain pilgrim piety and mode of autonomy, that he was determined to be self-sufficient and humble. Surely that was what caused the dissonance for al-Fessi: he could not bear to see the Captain be so humiliated. A ship's captain, in those days, to many people was a kind of hero, someone of very high status and a certain glamour.

Timberlake was completely taken aback. The Captain did not even recognise this Moor who knew his name, and wished to render him service. He was amazed, and looked with bafflement at this stranger. He goes on:

> He presently sayd unto me in the Franck tongue, 'Why Captaine, I hope you have not forgotten me. It is not yeat 40 dayes since you landed me at Alexandria amonge the rest of your passengers which you brought from Argier in the shipp the Troyan. And here is another in the cara[van] that you brought likewise, which would be right glade to see you.'[12]

Timberlake, surprised, tried to wrack his brains to place this man in his memory. He asked questions to find out more about this Moor by his side.

> I asked yf he dwelt there, but he said no, but that he and his fellowe were going in the caravan [to] Damasco, which they called Sham, and from thence to Bagdatz, which

we call Babellon, and to Mecha to make [themselves] a hadgee – for soe they are
called when they have bin at Mecha. Alsoe he told me that he dwelt in the cittye of
Fess in Barbarie.

For Timberlake too, al-Fessi was completely out of context. The world of the ship
from Algiers to Alexandria must have seemed distant in his mind. He was now
completely wrapped up in the world of the caravan, and the dangers of the road,
the direction of travel on land, and the sights. His mind had to shift, remember,
return to the deck, the waves and winds, the sails, the conversations with passengers. At last, this face fell into place.

After I had heard and veywed him well I remembered that I had such a one in my
shipp, but it is much to remember one man amongst 300.

So there was this moment of recognition, remembering, and astonishment. But
the offer had been made. Al-Fessi wanted to wash Henry Timberlake's linen: to
do a menial job for this foreign Christian in a strange land. He didn't have to do it.
He didn't have to show such humility himself. Christians were sometimes called
'dogs' in Muslim lands, a word reflecting the derision many Muslims felt. Here
the Muslim would have none of that. He would make an example of himself.
If Henry Timberlake was prepared to be so humble as to wash his own clothing, then he could go one step further. Perhaps that would show Timberlake
something else that needed to be demonstrated: he would bear witness to God's
compassion.

On the *hajj*, he was supposed to submit completely to God's will. Did he interpret the coincidence of Timberlake's appearance in his travels as God's act: God
had placed Timberlake in his path for a reason? He too would have known that
the way they travelled was very dangerous. Did he read this coincidence as meaning that God wanted him to protect this stranger, to offer him hospitality, in this
place where Abraham had offered hospitality? He would be fulfilling the wishes
of the Sultan as well, broadening them out to encompass the entire Dar es-Islam.
The Englishman and the Moroccan were to be friends.

While al-Fessi too was a foreigner, the ways of Egypt and Palestine were more
familiar to him, simply because to some degree they were the ways of Islam and
Arab cultures. The language, though different in terms of its form, was still Arabic.
He knew how to operate here. Timberlake clearly did not. His action of washing
his own clothes was an advertisement of his difference. He was brave, and humble,
and completely naive. How was he going to survive this place?

There is a kind of charity in Islam known as *sadakat*: the charitable works shown
voluntarily to strangers, to anyone, Muslim or non-Muslim. It is part of what you
may be called upon to do. You have to be alert to the opportunities that present
themselves. It goes back to Abraham. Strangers came to him, saying 'Peace' and he

replied saying 'Peace.' Then he brought out a fattened calf and laid it before them, asking them to eat (Qur'an 51, 'The Scatterers' 20–27). Abraham trusted God. He went out and did what he had to do, unwavering. He surrendered.

Whatever it was that motivated al-Fessi it was a deep feeling, for what follows bears this out. It was nothing weak and whimsical, and the act by which he demonstrated his service was also nothing shallow, and would have caused astonishment to anyone who saw it. And it is interesting that Timberlake allowed him to wash his clothing, as if there was no arguing against it. The Moor insisted – taking the clothing from his hands – and Timberlake held back and let him do it, amazed.

If anyone today made up a story like this it would seem unbelievable. When you write a historical novel, it has to conform to the kinds of things people did, and how they thought, or it does not 'ring true'. But here is a true story, written down by one of the participants in it, which does not conform to how we generally think people of this time should have behaved. Timberlake, for a start, should not have gone on a pilgrimage to Jerusalem, as a Protestant English sea captain and merchant with stock in Cairo and a ship full of sailors waiting for him in Alexandria. The Maghrebi, al-Fessi, should not have taken the Captain's clothing from his hands and washed it, offering to protect this Christian in Palestine, when he was bound for Mecca on a pilgrimage. That is what is so wonderful about real history rather than any imagined version. It is so much more varied and complex than we assume. Human emotions, beliefs, motivations and actions can be totally surprising. It is our great forté, as human beings, to listen to our hearts and act on gut feelings that fly in the face of what we 'should' do.

They talked, and Timberlake asked him to take him to his companion, the one he had spoken with more on the voyage from Algiers.

> Soe I desired him to bringe me to sight of the other man, which – when he had washed my lynnynge – he did. And that man I knew well, soe these ii concluded that one of them should goe in the carravan and the other should goe with me to Jheru[salem]. Soe the fyrst man accompanied me and had such care of me that he would not leave me in a strange land.

'Captain, I will not leave you in a strange land.'

The Englishman was to be looked after by al-Fessi. It was the true spirit of Abraham.

9

Heaps of Stones

From Ramat al-Khalil, Timberlake and John Burrell decided to go off on their own, with twenty-two Greek Orthodox and Armenian pilgrims from Egypt, and al-Fessi, since they were bound for Jerusalem. They would have hired donkeys and a donkey-driver. It does seem a little odd to me that they parted company, since the natural route from Hebron to Damascus was through Jerusalem, but it may have been a case of timing. The caravan might have rested here, since it would soon be the Muslim feast of 'Idh al-Fitr at the end of Ramadan.

Before departure, Timberlake deposited with the leader of the caravan eight letters that he had written the previous afternoon. These were all to be conveyed, somehow, to Constantinople, to the Levant Company ambassador there, who would ship them back to England along with Company correspondence. Timberlake and his party then travelled northwards.

It was Tuesday 24 March, or at least Timberlake and Burrell thought it was 24 March, but one of the things that changed when you left England was time. The English way of reckoning the days of the year was not followed by many other nations.

As Timberlake went up the road towards Jerusalem from Ramat al-Khalil, having departed from the caravan, he believed it was the year 1600, but to a Spaniard, Italian or Portuguese, or for us today, it was the year 1601. This is because England retained an old system in which the year began on 25 March, which is Our Lady's Day, the Feast of the Annunciation of the Virgin Mary (i.e. Christ's conception day).

But the difference was worse than that. Your calendar defined you in terms of your religion. Very recently, in 1582, as a result of extensive astronomical investigations, the Catholic Church had made a decree that ten days should be dropped from the calendar, during the month of October, to bring the time of the spring (vernal) equinox in line with what it appeared to have been at the time of the seminal (for Christian dogma) Council of Nicaea (AD 325), viz. 20 March. The spring equinox had been getting rather early in the year under the old – Julian – calendar, which meant that Easter – which occurs on the first Sunday after the first full moon after the spring equinox – was also, it appeared, getting earlier. Something was clearly wrong, and before long Easter would be in February. The dropping of 10 days took place under the authority of Pope Gregory XIII, and hence the system we use now has the name of the 'Gregorian' calendar. Catholic countries immediately adopted it once orders were made for the day-cutting to occur; other countries could see the astronomical sense of it and likewise followed suit, but not so islanded England, and its eventual colonies, which saw the change of the calendar of no import whatsoever. Doggedly asserting its independence against the continental innovation, England resisted, no matter what astronomical sense dictated. To accept a Papist calendar was just not considered right, and in fact it was rejected until the middle of the eighteenth century, when England relented, leaving only the Orthodox churches to continue it to this day. In other words, while Timberlake was content to think of the date as 24 March 1600, most other Europeans thought it was 3 April 1601.

But differences between Catholics and Protestants paled into insignificance when it came to the differences between Christians and Muslims, because 24 March 1600 in the Julian calendar of England and 3 April 1601 in the Gregorian calendar was 29 Ramadan 1009 in the Muslim world, where the calendar was worked out from the date of the Prophet Mohammed's *Hijra* (flight to Mecca) in AD 622.[1] In the case of Galilee, there is literary confirmation of the date that Ramadan ended, in that the Aleppo parson William Biddulph (to whom we will return) says his caravan stayed at Engannim all of the day of 26 March because the feast of the Idh al-Fitr (or Biram) began that day, and no one wished to travel. This means the feast in Palestine began on the evening of 25 March, so that most of the day of 25 March, until sunset, was 30 Ramadan.[2]

In his book, *The Crescent and the Rose*, Samuel C. Chew noted regarding Timberlake that 'it was of course to a Christian's advantage to win the good-will of a Mohammedan fellow-traveller.'[3] This makes it sound as if Timberlake actively tried to win his goodwill. In fact, this Mohammedan positively went out of his way for Timberlake; he was more than a friendly fellow traveller. While Timberlake would have seen his assistance as advantageous, it must have seemed a little bizarre to him as well. Timberlake was not paying this Muslim; there was no contract between them. The Moor's assistance had been offered very unexpectedly, inexplicably. It is indicative of Timberlake's character that he would accept the offer without great deliberation. He trusted al-Fessi.

What did John Burrell think? The allegiance of the Moor was to Timberlake, not to him, though it benefited him also, as along as he remained with the Captain. But did he really see the benefits? How would Burrell have interpreted al-Fessi's motivations? How could he know whether this Moroccan was to be trusted or not? You can imagine his doubts. What if the Moor intended to slit their throats while they slept and abscond with their saddle-bags and valuables? How could Henry Timberlake invite an infidel into their party, trustingly, as if this was not a problem at all? Was sex involved? What was the Captain thinking?

Actually, the Captain was thinking of measurements.

Timberlake would write that, assuming Jerusalem to be in the position of London, Gaza is Salisbury, Beersheba is Alton, and the plain of Mamre (adjacent to the city of Hebron) is Guildford. This estimation of distances indicates that Timberlake had already travelled around southern England, and had an interest in precise distances, but it also requires his readers to undertake curious mental gymnastics, in which pictures of rural England are juxtaposed with Palestine. Given that any estimation of distances here was not a piece of cake, with only a few Roman milestones occasionally visible to give some guidance (and a Roman mile was shorter than an English mile), Timberlake was not completely wide of the mark. Gaza is seventy-five English miles from Jerusalem (via Beersheba), but Salisbury is eighty-four from London; Hebron is about nineteen miles from Jerusalem, but Guildford is twenty-seven. Timberlake was trying to give a rough impression of the layout.

They do not camp until they reach a place Timberlake names Cudi che Leneb. He defines it quite precisely as being sixteen miles from Hebron and '5 litle miles from Jerusalem'. No such place can now be found.

This site was perhaps a village named al-Khudr, if 'Cudi' is right as a transcription of a local sound. This name is actually that of a Muslim saint (St George) usually spelt al-Khadr, but in the pronunciation of this district, the 'a' becomes 'u' in sound, so al-Khalil (for Hebron) is pronounced 'eal-Khulil' locally. However, the village of al-Khudr lies seven miles from Jerusalem, off the main road. It was also quite a major site for the veneration of the saint, whose powers of healing (especially from mental illness) were famous, and there was (and still is) a Greek Orthodox church at the sanctuary, which Timberlake would have mentioned if he had been there. Later (on 30 May, 1669), an Englishman named Thomas Bodington was taken to al-Khudr with his party, rather circuitously, via Solomon's Cisterns, and he states that there was 'St. George's Church, where the Fathers say the Chains remain, wherewith St. George was bound, which will presently cure a mad Man, if bound therewith'.[4]

Timberlake is, furthermore, too careful with his distances to be wrong about '5 little miles' from Jerusalem. Simply to plot his position sixteen miles from Hebron and five little miles out of Jerusalem would place him, more correctly, outside Beit Jala.

Here they camped. What did an Englishman and a Moor speak about sitting by a fire, just outside Jerusalem, in the year 1601/1009? At least Timberlake and al-Fessi could use Frank. They were both equalised by having to employ a second language. They could talk seriously about their respective work in Mediterranean trade, asking one another questions. They could joke. A conversation can be a dance, a turning over of each other this way and that, until, at the end, you have got to know a person, so that a stranger is no longer a stranger, and has begun to be a friend. You can imagine them speaking softly, sleepily now, after hours of talk, in a language that was hardly written down, and is now a lost speech from a lost world. We hover on the edge, as ghosts from the future, and try to hear.

But their words have flown into the past, and gone.

Daylight. It was customary with any caravan that hawkers would move through and offer people provisions to buy, most importantly bread, though many of the Muslims fasted during the day, because of Ramadan. Here they were isolated, and not one of the locals had come to disturb them. After his prayers, perhaps it was al-Fessi who suggested to Timberlake that the people of a house nearby might have food enough for them to buy some bread and cheese, and he would go there and ask.

Timberlake wrote:

> 'It channced myselfe, Mr. John Burel, and my _____ Moore, being within 5 miles of it [Jerusalem] lodginge in the fields all night [to require food, so] I sent my Moore to a house to buy us some breade, for we had nothinge to eate. And commine to us he brought us word that the master of this house nor his children did never eate bread in all theire lyves. Such is the poore estate of the cuntry that in 10 miles you shall not see a plot of ground to feed a horse or cowe. But the cuntries that ar round about it [Jerusalem], as Palestine on the one side, and Gallila on the other side, and Sirria to the west [= east?] of it, are all most good and plentifull cuntryes. And Jerusalem [is] the most barrenest place that ever I saw in all my travelles (the desarts excepted). Theire is not any place in England so barren, but the barrenest place in Cornwall, where there is nothinge but stones and rockes. But by the reporte of the inhabitants the stones doe growe dayly more and more. Whosoever hath travelled thither or shall travaile thither hereafter will say with me that when 15 miles round about it [Jerusalem] it is no other than a heape of stones and the most barrenest place in all Mesopotamia.[5]

In the manuscript quoted here there is an underline showing a word missed out before 'Moore', 'my _____ Moore'. 'Good'? 'Kind?', 'Helpful?' How strange the copyist did not write the adjective. It is in none of the printed editions either.

We can see al-Fessi then with a basket of dried dates in his arms, offering it to Timberlake. The hungry Christian company look at him suspiciously. No bread. Can this be true?

The lack of bread in this house may have had something to do with the fact that the house does not seem to have been part of a village, where there would have been bakers, and perhaps this lone family somewhere outside Beit Jala had a secret history that made them shunned in the community, hence no bread. Or perhaps the fact that there was famine further north, around Aleppo, had a knock-on effect. But the observation that the area was rocky and the fertility of the soil was not good is valid, then as now.

Timberlake thought that the barrenness of the area immediately around Jerusalem was some kind of Divine vengeance: 'the most noteable thinge of all is to see how the Scriptures ar fulfilled in that Citty (which is) that it should be made a heape of stones, which thinge I deeply considered and did find that theire

is noe ground within 15 or 16 miles neere to the cittye (the playn of Jhericho
excepted) but it is all a heap of stones and that in such exceedinge quantitie that I
doe marveile how they lyve in it.'.

The area around Jerusalem is the Judaean hill country, not a fertile plain, and
it is very rocky, made of limestone. Conifers grow wild here, and it is sometimes
cultivated with olive, almond and fig orchards, especially around villages. White
limestone nestles in beds of grass, herbs, shrubs and thorns (Plate 1). It is good
country for grazing sheep and goats, but it does not constitute fertile farmland,
and cultivations require sophisticated agricultural skills. Farming here always
relied on terracing, soil-building and irrigation, with much stone-removal work
needed to form the walls and terraces. As the author of the Book of Ecclesiastes
said: there is 'a time to cast away stones, a time to gather stones together'
(Eccles. 3:5).

The population was not as great as it had been as a result of invasions. People
concentrated their agricultural efforts on the areas with richer soils, which were
additionally not such a focus for invading armies.

But Timberlake had perhaps imagined Jerusalem and the area of ancient Judaea
as being the most fertile place in the whole region. The Promised Land as a whole,
shown to the Israelites after they crossed the desert from Egypt, was supposed to
be 'flowing with milk and honey' (Josh. 5:6) and, given Jerusalem's extraordinary
significance over time, Timberlake had probably thought it would be lush and
verdant. It was a shock that this was not the case. He connected its present rocki-
ness with the prophecy of Jeremiah: 'And I wil make Jerusalem an heape and a
den of dragons, & I will make the cities of Judah waste, without an inhabitant' (Jer.
9:11, Geneva Bible).

Timberlake was not the only one to notice, with disappointment, that the
nearer one came to Jerusalem the worse the conditions were in terms of fertility and agricultural abundance. At the end of the seventeenth century, Henry
Maundrell would write, going up through the hill country north of Jerusalem:

> The country discover'd quite a different face from what it had before, presenting
> nothing to the view in most places, but naked rocks, mountains and precipices. At
> sight of which, pilgrims are apt to be much astonished and baulked in their expec-
> tations; finding that country in such an inhospitable condition, concerning whose
> pleasantness and plenty they had before form'd in their minds such high ideas.

That was the point. Israel/Palestine as a whole is a fruitful land, but as you ascend
to the hills it gets rocky, and Jerusalem is a city of the hills rather than the fertile
plains. In Hebrew you always 'go up' to Jerusalem. You ascend to a holy city closer
to the heavens than others around about. Only when the population was denser
and more wealthy were the villages and towns around Jerusalem well inhabited
and the land intensively farmed. Maundrell in fact sees behind the desolate present

to the past, and notes that it is obvious that the rocks and hills must have been once covered with earth, noting the many terraces that still existed, uncultivated, testifying to agriculture in former times, even though now it was 'a rude stony country, which yet yielded us the sight of several old ruin'd villages'.[6]

Natural geology aside, the conditions of sporadic cultivation and reduced population in the hill country around Jerusalem were understandable in the light of the history of the land for the preceding millennium, during which time successive empires had claimed the holy city. From the seventh century onwards, after the Arab Muslims defeated the Christian Byzantines in Palestine in 638, many people, who had widely already swapped their diverse religions (Nabataean, Ituraean, Idumaean, Hellenistic, Samaritan and Jewish) for Christian, converted to Islam and became Arabised, though various Christian, Jewish and Samaritan communities still retained their religious faith, resisting conversion, living together with Muslims in many parts of the land. Palestinian Islam always retained various indigenous, local features and ancient local shrines.

Conversion to Islam and adoption into an Arab tribe had some advantages under the Muslim empires, but the population as a whole had to endure heavy taxation and exploitation. The Palestinians around Jerusalem occasionally rose up in revolt to claim independence, for example in 841, but Jerusalem was too great a treasure to the empire-builders for the population of the holy city to have any chance.

Stability was short-lived. Jerusalem was governed successively by the Umayyads (638–750), the Shi'ite Abbasids of Baghdad (750–878), the Egyptian Tulunids (878–915), the Ikhshidids (91–969), and the North African Fatimids (915–1071/3).[7] The invasion of the Seljuk Turks in 1071 or 1073 was followed by widespread burning and evictions. In 1098 the Fatimids reconquered Jerusalem. In other words, prior to the Christian Crusaders invading, there had been seven Muslim invasions in less than 500 years. The Crusaders from Europe defeated the Fatimids in 1099, brutally massacred the non-Christian population, and held Palestine, as the Kingdom of Jerusalem, from 1099–1187. Salah edh-Din (Saladin), a Kurd from modern-day northern Iraq, then took Egypt in 1171 and successfully evicted the Crusaders from the holy city on 2 October 1187. The Ayyubid dynasty he founded held Jerusalem to 1243, not only tolerating Christians and Jews but allowing some degree of Christian control, but then came the Mongols, from far away in Asia, who sacked Jerusalem, massacred the Christians there, and destroyed churches.

The Mamluks rose to power in the wake of the Ayyubids, staging a coup in Egypt and defeating the Mongols in Palestine in the Battle of Ain Jalut (1260), thereafter seeing off the Crusaders from Acre in 1291. After gaining Jerusalem, they set about rebuilding it as a very strongly Islamic holy city. Under a succession of powerful emirs (= governors), Muslim immigration and pilgrimage were encouraged, seminaries and hostels built. But, understandably, little could revive the confidence of Palestinians – whether Jews, Christians or Muslims – to live in the region surrounding Jerusalem, since it was generally Jerusalem and its territory that suffered most at the hands of all invaders. At the point that the Mamluks took Jerusalem in the mid-thirteenth century, Jerusalem had been conquered or reconquered six times beforehand in the past 200 years alone.

Along with the conquering of the city, the farms about it were frequently ravished to feed the invading army. Villages could be torched, and the population coerced into service duties or enslaved. Both agriculture and industry had declined in the region around Jerusalem, and only the most devout and resilient people – whose ancestors had managed to survive multiple horrors, or people who had recently migrated there – dared to live in the city itself. The people of Jerusalem at this time relied upon food to be brought in from further away, such was the lack of agriculture in its immediate environment.[8]

Finally, there came the Ottomans from what is now north-west Turkey, the greatest Muslim empire of them all. After taking the Balkans they captured, in 1453, the great Byzantine city Constantinople, and then went on to Armenia, Syria, Palestine and Egypt under Selim I (1512–20). At its fullest extent Ottoman rule stretched into Hungary, and through North Africa to Algiers. Jerusalem was one *sanjak* (administrative district) in a larger province with its headquarters in Damascus (al-Shams), the largest commercial city of the region. Under the Sultan Suleiman the Magnificent the walls of Jerusalem were built, completed in 1540, the water system greatly improved and endowments were made for Muslim institutions. The Dome of the Rock was beautified with blue and turquoise tiles. But despite this interest in the holy city, Jerusalem's surrounding territory of hills continued to be sparsely populated. The need for food to be brought into Jerusalem from further afield in Palestine remained during Ottoman times. Given the history of the region, there seems still to have been a crisis of confidence among those living around Jerusalem. To live in the city meant you were ultra-religious and committed, and the population, comprised of Muslims, Christians and Jews, appears to have been only about 15,000.

One should be careful, however, with European sources that stress the bad conditions of the area around Jerusalem. You cannot apply it to the whole of Palestine. As noted above, it seems that the inhabitants of Palestine were afraid of looking wealthy or engaging in unnecessary agriculture for fear of attracting unwelcome attention of the sipahis, the elite cavalry, or the taxmen. It was a case of keeping your head down and trying to be secure: a common experience for people subject to imperialism. Some European writers, however, condemn the local population for 'laziness', without taking into account these circumstances. While they decry Ottoman oppression, they also characterise both the rulers and the ruled as feeble. This characterisation may look like incipient 'Orientalism', as defined by Said,[9] but actually owes more to a Christian theology current at this time that would see Jews and old Judaea as needing to be humiliated on account of the sins of the ancestors. All Palestinians, whether Jewish, Muslim, Samaritan or Christian, therefore participated in this humiliation by living in the Holy Land. For example, the Dutch botanist Leonhart Rauwolf, visiting Palestine in 1573, provides a succinct summary of the view:

> This Holy Land (which, according to the promise made to the Patriarchs, was for many years in the possession of the Israelites) was, as you read in Deuteronomy chap. viii. a most fruitful and rich country, abounding with corn, fruits, wine, and all that is required to the maintenance of a man's life... For it hath rich valleys, hills, fields and gardens, richly adorned with fountains and trees, so that it was very well chosen to be the worldly Paradise... Now as the land in it's goodness surpassed other lands, so did Jerusalem excel all other cities in building, glory, fortification, and number of inhabitants... But when they would not acknowledge [Jesus Christ's] merciful visitation, nor receive his messengers, but did rather abuse, ridicule, and kill them, rejected the Lord of Glory himself,... God did reject and disperse them among the heathens, burnt and destroyed their city and temple, and reduced their fruitful country into barren desarts and a desolate wilderness, and so the punishment came upon them, which the holy Prophet Esaiah did foretel... in the twenty-fifth chapter, and second verse, *Thou hast made of a city a heap; of a defenced city a ruin; a place of strangers to be no city, it shall never be built*... This ought to serve us and all men as an example of the fervent anger of God, to be a warning to us for ever.

With this kind of understanding, not that many European writers were going to record happily that anyone in Palestine was doing very well. The Europeans had grand visions of the Biblical past, confirmed by hundreds of years of imaginative paintings that depicted Biblical events against backdrops of wondrous cities and lush vegetation. Loaded with these images, Europeans could not help but find contemporary Palestine far less glorious. European visitors compared the state of the Holy Land they saw with a grand past of magnificent Renaissance edifices and abundance depicted in the paintings that had never in fact existed, and found it wanting.

But it would not have suited their theology to be corrected. Rauwolf, imagining 'the glorious city of Jerusalem, which God had chosen before others,... [with] vast buildings' finds himself disappointed that, of these 'there is at this day nothing at all to be seen' and states that 'the gardens... are surrounded by mud walls, not above four foot high, so that one may climb over them without any difficulty... [and] want mending continually' while 'their habitations are also little and low, have clay walls, and many of them are decayed', not knowing that this kind of housing was much the same in Biblical periods, apart from the palace-temple complex of Solomon and other major buildings. The Second Jewish Temple was indeed one of the world's architectural masterpieces, but only the most blinkered visitor could fail to be impressed by the Dome of the Rock, and Jerusalem of 1601 was not without its palaces and madrasas and fine architecture. It is as if Rauwolf just will not see them. Even the imposing walls, built by Suleiman the Magnificent, do not impress him: 'although they are very high, yet they are so thin and slight, that they are not able to withstand the least violence'.[10] He may be comparing them with the thick walls of a castle, perhaps, but he overstates the case. He does so even more when he says that the old steep valleys around Jerusalem 'are now quite filled up... so that one may go into the town, as into an open village, without any hinderance or pain'. The walls are several metres thick and have a pathway along the top, and the Kidron and Gehinnom Valleys are as deep as ever.

In terms of the wider environs, says Rauwolf, the land of Judaea is now 'occupied by Turks, Moors, and Arabians, that do not love to till or cultivate the ground, but will rather starve than take pains to get a good livelihood by their hand-labour'. Really? Rauwolf himself has just noted in passing that Palestine produced 'great quantities of corn' which were sent to Joppa and then by sea to Constantinople, and that around Ramle 'these fields are very fruitful and very well till'd and sown with corn, cotton and Indian millet', as well as amazing watermelons.[11] Rauwolf seems to insist on a degenerate reality even when it has been smashed with the evidence he has seen with his own eyes. The same productivity is noted by Sandys, even as they near Jerusalem: 'Some six miles beyond Rama [Ramle] the hils grew bigger and bigger, mixed with fruitfull vallies. About two miles farther we ascended the higher mountains... but at severall places [there was a] passage exceeding difficult... on each side are round hills, with ruines on their tops; and vallies such as are figured in the most beautfiull land-skips. The soile though stony, not altogether barren; producing both corne and olives about inhabited places.'[12]

This kind of abundance where cultivation takes place is actually noted by several observers. Take, for example, Rawdon, who writes that 'the lande liing aboutte the cytty doth seem to be very barone, but is rather excedinge rich' because once you break the rocks you get good earth, and here you can grow good wheat at an astonishing speed. He ate bread grown locally 'being as goode as ever I did eatt'. There was also 'good & plenty fruitte as oringes, lemondes, figges, poumgarnets of most & best sortes that be'. At Christmas time the earth was green 'the grasse not being longe, yet thicke & sweett & feedeth sheepe & goattes exceedinge fatt, & on the higher groundes a worlde of partriges. They ar very greatte & will runne up & downe the highe wayes as they wer hennes growen halfe wilde & call not much unlike. Ther is greatt store of wilde swine. Ther is also aboute the cytty many wells & fountaines of fresh water being verye goode. It doth drincke not much unlike to milke being so sweett & delicatt a taste.' Rawdon here seems to enthuse about the place he saw without a thought for the dominant Christian theology.[13]

So invading armies, cruel sipahis, genocide, famine and plague apart, the Palestinians were still busily cultivating Palestine, apart from swathes of the rocky hills around Jerusalem and elsewhere where many were afraid to live.

Timberlake, however, reads the geology of the stony hill-country as evidence for God's judgement on Jerusalem, here keeping to what he believed. The area they went through was barren, and he did not see past it to the past, or divert his attention to an alternative reality in the present. Apart from this observation, Timberlake's concerns were with measuring.

They were, nevertheless, about to encounter a problem. As they would reach Jerusalem on this day, they would need to declare who they were at the entrance gate and, being Christian, surrender their weapons. Word was that the Ottoman authorities of Jerusalem accepted two types of Christians: the Orthodox and the Catholics. The Armenian hostel was small and only accepted Armenians. The Greeks must have assured the Franks that the Greek Orthodox Patriarchate would grant all Protestants the freedom to worship in whatever way they saw fit, though their hostel was also impoverished. They would have warned Burrell that the Catholics – given the current animosities – would show no tolerance for people they deemed to be heretics. Whatever, Burrell had decided that at the gate of Jerusalem he would call himself a Greek. He could bluff his way well enough with the language. But Timberlake had apparently scoffed at such deceit. The Captain remained resistant to Burrell's suggestion that he should join the Greek party, and to say he was Greek when asked for his identity at the gates of the city. He would declare himself to be what he was: an Englishman and a Protestant.

Burrell resolved that whatever Timberlake chose to do, he would save his own skin and lie.

Right: 1. Frontispiece from Nathaniel Crouch
(1683).

Below: 2. Section of Jan Visscher's view of
London (1616).

3. A merchant ship, frontispiece from Anon. (1603).

1600

ABDVLGVAHID.

LEGATVS REGIS BARBARIÆ IN ANGLIAM.

ÆTATIS:42.

4. Portrait of 'Abdul Guahid', or 'Abd al-Wahid.

5. European visitors to the pyramids from Sandys (1615/1673).

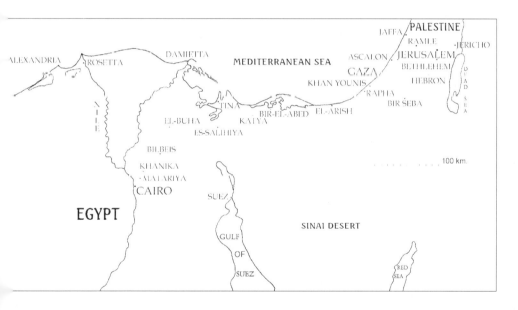

Above: 6. Henry Timberlake's route through Egypt to Jerusalem.

Right: 7. The Palace of Pilate from Amico (1609/1620).

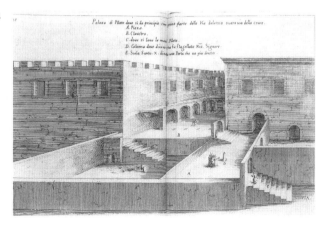

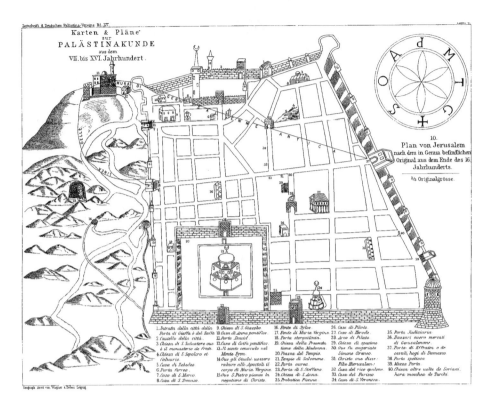

Karten & Pläne
zur
PALÄSTINAKUNDE
aus dem
VII. bis XVI. Jahrhundert.

10.
Plan von Jerusalem
nach dem in Genua befindlichen
Original aus dem Ende des 16.
Jahrhunderts.

⅔ Originalgrösse.

1. Intrata della città della Porta di Giaffa ò del Zaffo.
2. Castello della città.
3. Chiesa di S. Salvatore ouе è il monasterio de frati.
4. Chiesa di S. Sepolcro et Caluario.
5. Casa di Zebedeo.
6. Porta ferrea.
7. Casa di S. Marco.
8. Casa di S. Tomaso.
9. Chiesa di S. Giacobo.
10. Casa di Anna pontifice.
11. Porta Dauid.
12. Casa di Caifa pontifice.
13. Il santo cenaculo nel Monte Syon.
14. Oue gli Giudei uoserо rabure alli Apostoli il corpo di Maria Vergine.
15. Oue S. Pietro pianse la negatione di Christo.
16. Porte di Syloe.
17. Ponte di Maria Vergine.
18. Porta sterquilinia.
19. Chiesa della Presenta- tione della Madonna.
20. Piazza del Tempio.
21. Tempio di Salomone.
22. Porta aurea.
23. Porta di S. Stefano.
24. Chiesa di S. Anna.
25. Probatica Piscina.
26. Casa di Pilato.
27. Casa di Herode.
28. Arco di Pilato.
29. Chiesa di spasino di Gerusalemme.
30. Oue fu angariato Simone Cireneo.
31. Christo oue disse: Filie Hierusalem.
32. Casa del rico epulone.
33. Casa del Farisеo.
34. Casa di S. Veronica.
35. Porta Judiciaria.
36. Bazzari ouero mercati di Gerusalemme.
37. Porta di S. Efraim o de cauali, hogi di Damasco.
38. Porta speziosa.
39. Mezza Porta.
40. Chiesa altre uolte de Soriani, hora moschea de Turchi.

8. A sixteenth-century pilgrim's map.

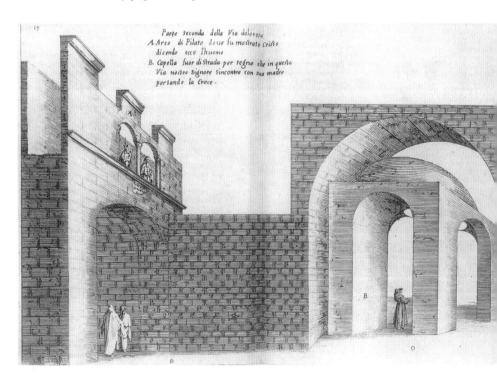

Parte seconda della Via dolorosa
A. Arco di Pilato doue fu mostrato Cristo dicendo ecco l'huomo
B. Capella fuor di strada per segno che in questa Via nostro signore s'incontrò con sua madre portando la Croce.

9. The Ecce Homo Arch from Amico (1609/1620).

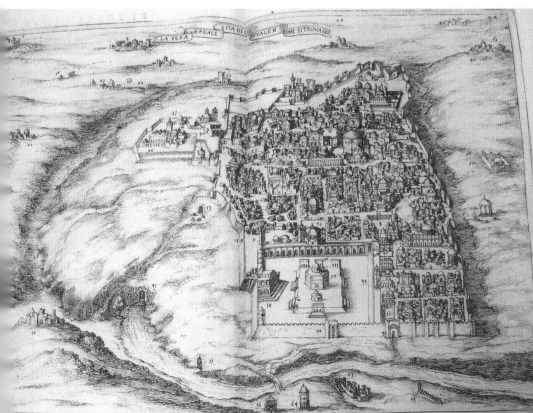

Right: 10. The plan of Jerusalem that appeared in Crouch (1683).

Below: 11. Antonio d'Angioli's view of Jerusalem from Amico (1609).

12. Aceldama from Sandys (1615/1673).

13. The House of Annas and the House of Caiaphas from Amico (1609/1620).

14. Holy places en route to Bethlehem from Sandys (1615/1673).

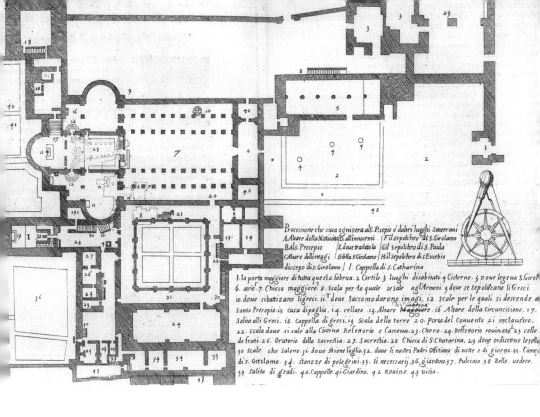

Above: 15. Bethlehem. Plan of the church and monastery from Amico (1609/1620).

Below: 16. Plan of the Church of the Holy Sepulchre from Amico (1609/1620).

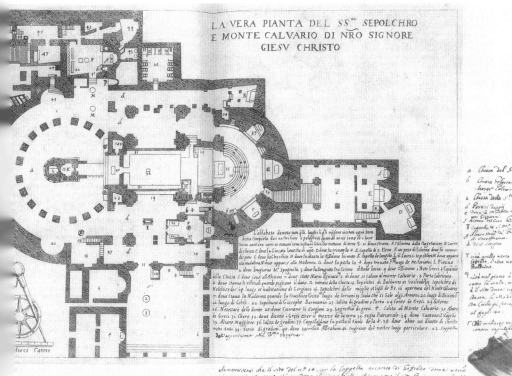

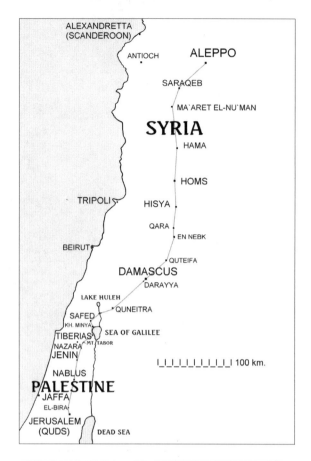

Top: 17. The route taken from Aleppo by William Biddulph and his companions.

Above left: 18. Title page picture from *A Relation of the Travells of Two English Pilgrimes* printed by John Norton for Hugh Perry (London, 1611).

Above right: 19. Manuscript page.

10

Jerusalem

Arriving from the south, you round a bend, and find the city of Jerusalem boxed up above you. You have some time to contemplate it before you reach Jaffa Gate (Bab al-Khalil) on the western side, the gate adjacent to the strong Citadel (al-Qal'a), originally constructed by the Umayyads in the seventh century. It looks particularly imposing from this direction.

Timberlake, al-Fessi, Burrell and the others arrived in Jerusalem on Our Lady Day in Lent, 25 March 1601, the last day of Ramadan, and the first day of the Protestant new year. Timberlake writes:

> And 9 of the clocke before noone, I sawe the cyttye of Jheru[salem], beinge within a furlonge of the gates. I and my companie [John Burrell] went to the west gatt of the cittye and then we stayed, for it is not lawfull for a Christian to goe in before he be admitted.[1]

This is the manuscript version, as usual. The 1603 edition of Timberlake's account has a section in which, seeing Jerusalem, Timberlake and Burrell kneel down, say the Lord's Prayer, thank God for conducting them there and approach Jerusalem singing and praising God.[2] Purchas' version has: 'at nine of the clocke I saw Hierusalem, kneeling said the Lords Prayer, singing we went to the West Gate, and then stayed.'[3] I think the manuscript here misses out a line, because the fact that Purchas and Archer both independently have Timberlake and Burrell praying and singing probably means this was in their source material. It would have been appropriate too for them to sing, or recite, Psalm 103, as William Lithgow did.[4]

The Moor likewise would have felt grateful to God for bringing him to the sight of al-Quds, the Holy. Greeks, Protestants, Armenians and Muslim would have been united in wonder, praise, thankfulness and joy.

But the singing would have ceased as the warlike battlements of the big western gate drew near. The Ottoman janissary guards there were tough. It was Ottoman policy to leave Christians alone as much as possible, but they were also considered a source of both revenue and disturbance. All kinds of additional charges fell on them, both on visitors and on Christian inhabitants, and these could at times be exploited by local officials.[5] The main protector of non-Orthodox Christian pilgrims was the head of the Franciscan order, the Padre Guardiano (or Custos), who negotiated a careful path between obedience to the Ottomans and protection of Christian sacred sites and travellers. A Padre Guardiano told William Lithgow's group in 1610: 'All you travellers must in generall bee indued with these 3. worthy gifts: Faith, Patience, and Money; Faith, to beleeve these things you shall see heere at Jerusalem; Patience, to indure the apparent injuries of Infidells; and Money, to discharge all tributes, and costs, which heere... and about this citty must be defrayed.'[6]

The Franciscans themselves, based as now at San Salvatore monastery, in the north-western part of the city, were not always able to keep passionate feelings for the city and anger at Muslims at bay, let alone soften the feelings of pilgrims. Nineteen months prior to the arrival of Timberlake's party, on 15 August 1599, a Spanish friar named Cosmas of St Damian, from Andalusia, had walked up to the Dome of the Rock holding a crucifix and proclaimed to Muslims there (in Arabic, apparently, taught to him by an interpreter named 'Issa, 'Jesus') that if they wanted to attain salvation they must abandon Islam and become baptised as Christians. For a Christian to enter the sacred area of the Haram esh-Sharif was forbidden, punishable by death;[7] that he would additionally try to convert the Muslim faithful there made the outrage even worse.

After being lynched, and surviving, Cosmas was condemned by the authorities to death by fire in front of the doorway of the Church of the Holy Sepulchre, Christianity's most sacred shrine. The Qadi (= judge) also ordered the arrest of the then Padre Guardiano, named Evangelista da Gabbiano, but, not finding him, soldiers seized three other Franciscan friars, who were bound up, and ordered to witness the grim execution.[8] Some years earlier, in 1582, a Spanish nun named Mary had been burnt, also just outside the entrance to the Church, and in 1557 a Sicilian friar suffered the same fate.

Burning, however, seems preferable to some of the other types of Ottoman executions. John Sanderson, in his writings, made a detailed list of them for everyone's edification; gaunching, i.e. being thrown down from a height to be impaled on metal spike or having the spike driven through you from your anus upwards to your neck, was probably the worst. Gaunching was the penalty for treason and serious offences. There are Ottoman records of Bedouin being gaunched. The more humane practice of strangling was reserved for notables.[9] Nevertheless, it seems a little hypocritical of the English to bewail the cruelty of Ottoman executions given the popularity in England of the 'hung-drawn-and-quartered' method, something particularly used on Catholics and traitors.

This was an age of grotesque punishments for relatively small offences. One example from Jerusalem is the case of a Jewish woman, Manuha bint Musa, who was accused by a Jewish man Shmu'il ibn Shihaba for publicly calling him the 'son of a whore'. The woman was convicted and sentenced to immediate flogging.[10] Beating the soles of the feet – what Europeans call 'bastinadoes' – was common, and could result in the victim being made lame. They could also bastinado kneecaps. John Sanderson tells a story of a Genoan merchant in Cairo who was 'bastinadoed upon the kneepanns' by order of the Pasha who accused him of holding on to the goods of a deceased Christian merchant, when the belongings of a foreigner dying in 'Turkie' should have been handed to the authorities.[11]

At the gate, Timberlake had to surrender any weapon he carried. Christians and Jews had to unbuckle their swords and hold them in their hands, and to pay entrance charges levied for non-Muslims. He would enter weaponless.

Then there was the declaration of identity. Burrell had decided to pretend to be a Greek, to gain entry without any problem as a classifiable type, outside the jurisdiction of the Padre Guardiano and exempt from Mass, but Timberlake had no such intention. He was going to declare himself to be exactly what he was. He would hope for the acceptance of the Ottoman authorities. That was a very reckless decision.

How was Burrell feeling, knowing that Timberlake would not allow himself to be untruthful about his religious affiliations or national identity? Having just had the wondrous experience of seeing Jerusalem with his own eyes, knowing that it was so much wiser to be Greek Orthodox than a Protestant, what ferment must have been going on in his mind, as they drew up to Jaffa Gate, where the guards stood with javelins, swords and pistols, with up to 100 of them stationed in the Citadel ready to rush out to the streets and deal with any difficulties? He must have known his companion was making a terrible mistake. He had to say he was a Greek or he would be forced in with the Catholics, and then have to go to Mass. As a last attempt he tried desperately once again to convince the Captain he was wrong, arguing that he had to say he was a Greek, to gain admission to the city and avoid Mass. It was the only way. He had to lie.

> My companie [Mr. Burrell] requested me to say I was a Greek, only to avoyd goeinge to masse. But I, not havinge the Greek tongue, refused absolutly so to do, tellinge him even at the gatt that I would neither deny my cuntry nor religion.[12]

At the gate, Timberlake insisted again that he could not pretend. He did not speak any Greek. Many of the janissaries were Greek-speaking, having been Christian children taken to be military servants of the Sublime Porte. They would find him out. It was better to tell the truth, and at any rate he would not deny his religion or his country. That would have stung Burrell. There, in the holy city, this is exactly what Burrell would do.

As for al-Fessi, what did he make of the dispute between the Englishmen? Timberlake's determination to speak the truth no matter what the Greeks and Armenians advised must surely have seemed admirable.

At the gate travellers had to wait for admission by officials in the Citadel who eventually came down to examine the party. Timberlake tells the tale of what happened next:

> Soe when they asked what we were Mr. Burrell answered in the greeke tongue that he was a Greeke and I an Englishman. Soe he was admitted to the Greeke Patriarche, and I was taken, and cast into prison, after I had stayed an hower at the gatt. For the Turks did all deny that ever they had hard eyther of my Queene, or Cuntry, or that she payd them any trybute.[13]

It is hard to imagine how dumbfounding this must have been to Henry Timberlake, despite Burrell's warnings. In the holy city of Jerusalem, they had not heard of Queen Elizabeth, Gloriana! They had not heard of England. This, after all the efforts on behalf of the Queen and the Levant Company to pay respect to the Sublime Porte! That the guards in Jerusalem denied she paid any tribute to the Sultan seems to have followed an assertion that she had, hence the denial. Timberlake was perhaps thinking of the organ sent in 1599 and all kinds of other presents.[14] What about all the English ships and merchants? They had made no impact on this part of the Ottoman empire whatsoever. In one fell swoop, Timberlake's confidence was crushed by ignorance, and all his pride in his nation, with her sea-going ships, trading, adventure, exploration, products, traditions, culture, literature, theatre, science, history and naval prowess was trampled underfoot. These guards had never heard of *England*?

Henry Timberlake had arrived at the gates of Jerusalem with no letters of introduction, explanation or recommendation. To the guards he would have been a very weird man wishing not to be placed in any category at all. He did not look as if he was wealthy. He did not look of any repute. He seemed to be some kind of Frank, but of what kind could not be ascertained. The Ottomans had not exactly forgotten their defeat at the Battle of Lepanto, in 1571. A free-range Frank was about as welcome as an incendiary device.

In the *New Dictionary of National Biography*, Richard Raiswell states: 'When he reached the west gate, though, Timberlake loudly proclaimed that he was English and was promptly gaoled.'[15] But in Timberlake's account Burrell did the talking, though not much talking apart from a simple declaration. Al-Fessi must have been separated out, and ushered away. At any rate, it does not seem that the Captain managed to declare his own position in his own words, or through an interpreter other than Burrell.

Along with the affirmation that Timberlake was an Englishman, Burrell additionally supplied the information that the Captain did not wish to be placed under the protection of either the Greek Orthodox Patriarch or the Padre Guardiano of the Latins, being a Protestant, but under the protection of the Ottoman authorities alone. One has to remember here that the original meaning of 'Protestant' was 'one who protests (against the Catholic Church)', specifically originally against the Diet of Spires (1529), but thereafter in general. Whatever way it was translated into Greek or Arabic, the 'protester' aspect of the designation would have been obvious. Burrell might have avoided using the term, thinking it would sound as if Timberlake wanted to start a protest in the middle of the holy city, but whatever way he described Timberlake's persuasions would only have succeeded in making Timberlake sound totally anomalous. To be anomalous, in a city – and empire – where everyone had to be categorised in terms of known, long-established labels, where there was a strict dress code designed to define instantly who men were by the colour of their turbans, was extremely dangerous. Essentially, Timberlake was condemned for eschewing categorisation.

Burrell, at the sight of Timberlake being seized and dragged off to an unknown fate inside the city surely resisted thinking 'I told you so!' This was too tragic and dreadful a result for any smugness about being proven right. The reality was that Timberlake's future at that point was bleak. It was generally supposed by Europeans that the Ottoman authorities did not need any major excuse to execute Christians in the city: a statement challenging Ottoman authority or disturbing the general peace would suffice as a crime worthy of death, or at least a heavy fine. For example, resisting the attempt of soldiers to extort money or objects was never a good idea. George Sandys tells the story of a soldier 'being denied by a Frier of some trifle he requested; gave himself such a blow on the nose that blood gushed forth; and presently exclaiming as if beaten by the other, complained to the Sanziacke (= Sanjakbey, governor): for which Avania (= insult) they were compelled to part with eight hundred dollars.'[16]

Being accused of being a spy was very grim. Five years earlier in Cairo the Ottoman authorities had allegedly hanged the highly popular and clever French consul – Paul Mariani (a Venetian by birth) – for the crime of espionage, without a trial, and without a care in the world for relations with European powers. According to Sanderson, 'he hanged by the necke in his redd velvett gowne under the chiefeste gate of Cairo; being privatly by force fetched out of his house in the eveninge'.[17]

Added to that, Fynes Moryson indicates how jumpy the Jerusalem authorities were about Christians. When he was looking at the view from the flat roof of the monastery of San Salvatore he was seen by the soldiers of the Citadel and immediately a messenger was despatched from the Agha (= military commander) ordering him and his companions to desist 'from beholding the Castle, or otherwise he would discharge a peece of ordinance (= cannon shot) at us'.[18] Moryson also noted how the authorities would invent accusations against the Franciscans by secretly burying bodies in their monastery grounds – when it was forbidden to have burials there – only to 'discover' them later and order the friars to pay 'large ransomes for redeeming of their lives'.[19] There was a story that in 1537 Suleiman the Magnificent, angry at the destruction of his fleet by the Genoans, imprisoned all the Franciscans of Jerusalem and Bethlehem in the Citadel, and then deported them to Damascus, where they were incarcerated for three years. The Franciscans were seen by the Ottomans, in many ways, as the permanent European-Christian embassy, and if parts of Europe and the Ottoman empire fell out badly, their position became very vulnerable.

As everywhere, money could be a remedy for a capital sentence, unless the crime was deemed too heinous. If Timberlake was lucky, he might expect to languish in jail for months before pleas for clemency were heard and a sufficient ransom was paid. But a summary execution for spying was not an unlikely prospect. To be seized by people who did not know either your country, your monarch or your religion was really no joke. There was no English ambassador to call upon for help.

Timberlake was cast into prison in a dungeon located not far from the entrance to the Church of the Holy Sepulchre, just metres away from where Father Cosmas' body had been consumed by flames. 'The dungeon wherein I was' is 'right against the Sepulcher of Jesus Christ,' writes Timberlake, with some irony. And whom did he blame?

He blamed the Padre Guardiano of the Franciscans, not the Ottoman authorities. It was all the Custos' fault, somehow. It was he who was 'the defender of all the Christiane pilgrimes', but here he was 'the principall actor of my imprisonment, because I would not offer my selfe under his protection, but stoode fully in it that I would rather be protected by the Turkes then by the Papists.' Somewhere along the line, those at the gate had decreed that Timberlake should place himself under the protection of the Catholic representative in Jerusalem, who could argue his case before the Sanjakbey. If he was a Frank then he was appropriately the responsibility of the Franciscan Custos. Timberlake refused, and said he would rather be protected by the Turks than the Papists. John Burrell must surely have felt some awkwardness translating this assertion.[20]

Hours passed, in which Timberlake (falsely) surmised that the Padre Guardiano had 'made the Turke soe much my foe that they were incensed against me that I was a spie, and soe would not let me out of the dungeon by any meanes.' Timberlake clearly had no idea about the delicate diplomacy required by the Custos. It is possible that the Padre Guardiano, who considered himself the representative of all Europeans no matter what their religious perversions might be, did indeed quickly speed to the Agha and the Qadi before any hasty decision was made on this uncategorisable Englishman.

As for Timberlake, if he put himself under the protection of the 'Turk', he would have wanted an Ottoman legal advisor. However, the Qadi does not feature in this story at all, as if he was absent completely. It has to be remembered that this was the last day of Ramadan and the evening would be a feast. It was not really the right time to fall foul of the authorities; it was eerily like the day before Passover, the day on which Jesus was traditionally brought before Pilate. How desperate Timberlake must have felt.

For many hours, Timberlake stood alone in the dark, reeking space of his prison cell, with no lawyer there to represent him, and no idea about what kind of fate he would endure. There was no other Englishman in Jerusalem apart from John Burrell; no other Protestant, as far as he knew, for hundreds of miles; and no one who would necessarily want to stick his neck out with the Ottoman authorities to rescue him from this grievous predicament, with the threat of rather nasty punishments in store.

How many ways did he have of getting free? How could he plead his case? What money did he have to promise to the officials? Whom could he write to? Whom could he bribe? How could he make himself understood? Would they torture him to get information? What might he confess to in great pain? How many days, weeks, months would he be here? Or would they give him a speedy execution to make him an example to anyone who would threaten the Sublime Porte? Such are the thoughts of people imprisoned without trial in a foreign land, when they have to prove their innocence rather than their guilt.

Did he think of home, his ship and his men, the stock he had not sold? Did he worry about his wife and children? Did he chastise himself for ever thinking of travelling with John Burrell to Jerusalem? Did he tremble, and lose his nerve?

But then there was a voice outside the door. Someone had been allowed to speak to the prisoner. Someone had paid the necessary fee.

Al-Fessi called him to a small hole in the door. Timberlake saw that the Moor was much distressed by this turn of events. The Maghrebi's emotion indicates what great regard he had for the Captain, and the deep importance he placed on his mission to give him protection in this 'strange land'.

> He wept, but bade me be of good cheare, and went awaye to the Basha of the Cittye and to the Sanjack...[21]

Al-Fessi wept.

He had made a commitment to protect the English Captain, and already he had not managed to keep him safe. Clearly, from his words to Timberlake at the prison door, he had determined now that it was his responsibility alone to secure the Captain's release, and that God would help him. He would succeed, despite the obstacles. Whatever the Padre Guardiano was doing, it does not seem to have been as effective as what al-Fessi did.

Al-Fessi assured Henry Timberlake that he would go to the governor of Jerusalem, and that he should be confident of a good outcome.

Al-Fessi went immediately to the top and acted with complete appropriateness. He set his course for government house, in the Jawiliyya, on the outside corner of the Haram esh-Sharif. There he would have met guards at the bottom of a long flight of steps. It was up to him then to beg for an audience with the governor. Ironically, he would have been completely unaware that Christians identified this place as the exact spot where Christ first took up his cross on the way to Golgotha (see Figure 7).

There he would have asked to see the Sanjakbey: no slight request for a man who, fasting all day, had only recently set foot in the holy city. He must have been feeling very fragile himself, hence his tears. It had torn his heart that his protection of Timberlake had been so easily devastated. And how to remedy it? Fervent imploring and money: that was what could work.

He would have been ushered through the entrance, into a courtyard. There were the remains of a column believed by Christians to be that to which Christ was tied when he was scourged by the Romans. There was then another courtyard, and here the place where, Christians believed, Pontius Pilate washed his hands of the guilt of condemning Jesus to death.

Then, at last, he would have been told to sit at the southern end of the courtyard, where there were sundry others, to wait until, finally, it was his turn. He was ushered through a gate, up stairs into a cloister dominated by the judgement room, the *qibla iwan*, at its far end, behind a huge pointed arch. There he would have stepped up, and noted that through one of the three great grilled windows he was seeing the Dome of the Rock for the first time (Plate 3), at the very moment he had to bow to the ground before the Sanjakbey, Nasuh Jawish. Along with him was another man, identified in Timberlake's account as 'the Basha of the cittye'. The Pasha and Sanjakbey could be the same person, but it reads as if the two are distinct. Interestingly, the wealthy governor of Gaza, Ahmad Pasha's endowments for the North-West and North-East prayer cells on the Haram esh-Sharif were made in March–April 1009 A.H., or 1601, which means that he was in Jerusalem precisely at this time.[22]

What words passed between Jawish and al-Fessi at this time, on the subject of the peculiar Englishman, Henry Timberlake? How did al-Fessi make his plea? How much money did he pay? Somewhere in the Jerusalem records that still survive, a scholar who reads Turkish may find the answer. Or perhaps it was *sub judice*, unrecorded and private, and nothing will be found of this conversation.

The Sanjakbey would have been reluctant to overturn the decisions of his guards and Agha at the gate. There was no proof that Timberlake was not a spy, only now the good word of a Muslim who claimed to know him. From the point of view of the Sanjakbey, this Muslim from the Farthest West himself could have been suspected of some kind of collusion with the Englishman. Morocco was not Ottoman. Al-Fessi too was a stranger in a strange land, even if he spoke the Arabic language (with a different accent), knew many of the customs, and was a Muslim. He was brave to venture into the heart of Ottoman administration, to the highest authority of the *sanjak*. It was a terrible risk: it could be a success, but he himself could find himself a co-conspirator with Timberlake. To beg for the life of an unclassifiable Christian in a land not your own took courage.

He first had to take an oath that he would tell the truth. Then he had to explain the whole story of where he first met Henry Timberlake, and what kind of man he was: a merchant and Captain of the ship, the *Trojan*. He would have made his plea on his knees. His strategy was to insist on Timberlake's help to Muslims going on the *hajj*, even though the Captain himself was probably only thinking of remuneration from so many passengers. It could neverthless be configured for this purpose as a good action.

> [he] tooke his oath that I was a mariner of a shipp that had brought 300 Turcks and Moores into Egypt from Argier and Tunnis which came to goe for Mecha. [23]

There was someone else there also, despite Timberlake's suspicions: the Padre Guardiano, Francesco Manerba. He insisted to the Sanjakbey that Timberlake would be welcome to stay in the monastery of San Salvatore, as long as he participated in a simple candle ceremony. He had come to the Sanjakbey, despite Timberlake's refusal of his protection, because he believed it was his duty. There would have been payments made, from both al-Fessi and Manerba. Nothing came free.

But it was the plea of al-Fessi as a Muslim that made the Sanjakbey change his mind. He saved Timberlake's life.

Strangely, when al-Fessi, with the janissaries, rushed back to the prison where Timberlake was incarcerated, after his audience with the governor of Jerusalem in the Jawiliyya, he would have taken the route of the Via Dolorosa, the 'sorrowful way' that traditionally marks the route Jesus took, carrying his cross from the Praetorium of Pontius Pilate – where Jesus was sentenced to death – to his crucifixion place at Golgotha. Al-Fessi would not have thought anything of it, because for a Muslim the events of Christ's crucifixion are bogus. The Prophet 'Issa, Jesus, was a homeless wanderer, *Imam al-Sa'ihin*, a constant traveller speaking the truth. He was not the Son of God, but a man, the son of Mary, and he did not die on the cross. His crucifixion was some kind of illusion. Some local Muslims called the Church of the Resurrection (i.e. the Church of the Holy Sepulchre) – *Kanîsah al-Kayâmah* in Arabic – the 'Church of the Dunghill' – *Kanîsah al-Kumânah*. [24] There is no salvific death of the Son of God, and no Easter, only the Ascension, whereby Jesus is taken bodily up into Heaven (Sura 4: 157–8).

So the fact that al-Fessi pleaded for Timberlake in the room believed by local Christians to be on the site of Jesus' interview with Pontius Pilate would have meant nothing to him. [25] The Ottoman seat of government happened to be on the site of the first-century BC Fortress Antonia, built into the north-west corner of the Jewish Temple platform, and identified as the Praetorium of Pilate by the Knights Templars in the twelfth century, at which point various architectural items were taken to Rome for veneration. A massive retaining wall, four metres thick, can be distinguished here, and the room where al-Fessi went is actually one of three excavated into this ancient wall.[26]

In the early seventeenth century the route of the Via Dolorosa went from the Ottoman governor's residence to a gate close to the Church of the Holy Sepulchre, recalling the painful events of Jesus' Passion, both Biblical and apocryphal. The commemorative stations had been developed by the Franciscans in the fourteenth century, and in due course there was some dispute about what exactly should be commemorated and where, a matter that would not be settled until the eighteenth century, when fourteen stations became the agreed standard. By 1601 Franciscans seem to have accepted eight stations of the cross, the first being Pilate's palace, identified with the Ottoman government house, or more particularly the audience chamber where Pilate condemned Jesus to death (Mark 15: 6–20), and the second being the column where Jesus was scourged on Pilate's order (Mark 15:15).

Al-Fessi would have then gone past the roadway leading to the third station, the Palace of Herod, and walked under the fourth, the Ecce Homo arch, where Pontius Pilate reputedly stated 'Behold the man!' (*Ecce homo*, in Latin; John 19:5). He would then have passed on his left the fifth station, a Christian chapel, the Church of the Spasm, where Jesus encountered his mother Mary and she collapsed with grief, and turned a corner at the sixth station, where Simon of Cyrene took the cross of Jesus, when he stumbled (Mark 1:21), and then asked the women of Jerusalem not to weep for him, but for themselves in view of coming disasters (Luke 23:27–31). A little further on, al-Fessi would have passed the house of Veronica on his left, who (extra-Biblically) wiped Jesus' face with a cloth, and gone through the eighth station, the Judgement Gate, where Christians believed the city gate of Jesus' time was located, from which he would then have zig-zagged to the courtyard of the Church of the Holy Sepulchre,[27] near Golgotha/Calvary, where Timberlake's prison was located. These sites are plotted on a pilgrim's map of the sixteenth century (Figure 8).

Timberlake must have waited anxiously. The Muslim was his only hope. As far as he knew, there was no one else who could plead his case. All day he was stuck in a dark, smelly cell, with no one he could rely on to help him but al-Fessi, whose hope for success with the Sanjakbey cannot have seemed too definite as far as Timberlake was concerned, despite his reassurance.

But a miracle happened. As the evening neared, footsteps sounded on the steps of the courtyard. There was al-Fessi's voice again, calling Timberlake to the hole in the door. He told Timberlake what had happened. And there was the curious condition, set by the Padre Guardiano. Al-Fessi gave him the choice: to stay in the prison with execution hanging over his head or to accept that he could carry a candle in a ceremony and lodge with the Padre Guardiano. It was up to him.[28]

Perhaps Timberlake pondered for a minute. Could it be some Papist trick? But how could he know? Better to risk it, and spurn trickery at the time it occurred than stay in this hell-hole. Al-Fessi had accomplished all this for him.

Timberlake had been full of resolute determination in the morning, but a day in a dungeon had made him far less keen to uphold his absolute devotion to Queen and religion. He would compromise. He agreed.

A key in the lock. The door opened. A rush of light. Space. Air. Freedom. Al-Fessi, relieved. *Il ham du lila*, he would have said, 'Praise God', to Timberlake's thanks.

Timberlake wrote:

This Moore, because he was a Mussellman, so much prevayled that before night he came to the prison doore with 6 Turkes, [and] called me to the doore. And there [he[29]] told me that if I would goe to the house of the Pater Guardian and rest under his protection I should be forced to noe religion but myne owne, except the holding of a waxe candle in my hand, to which I consented. And soe payinge the charge of the prison I was straight way delyvered, and brought to the Pater Guardian's monastary.

11

San Salvatore

Timberlake consented to holding a wax candle in his hand. That may seem like nothing much. However, Henry Timberlake, as a Protestant, was supposed to have rejected the use of candles in any kind of Christian ceremony. In this age, actions could speak volumes. Lighting a candle had meaning.

Protestants spurned many aspects of established worship and belief, from the significant to the insignificant, from the deeply theological to the practical and trivial: holy shrines, priestly celibacy, monasteries, various sacraments, holy water, Latin in church services, confession to a priest, crossing, images, statues of the saints (and saints themselves as mediators), chantries, relics, rosaries, transubstantiation of the bread and wine into the body and blood of Christ in Mass, purgatory, the Virgin Mary as special mediator, indulgences, the authority of the Pope, the use of candles in religious rites.

I think something happened to Timberlake in that cell in Jerusalem, and, as the hours wore on, it made him somehow a changed man. It did not, unfortunately, suddenly rid him of his anti-Catholic prejudice, but it rocked him at a profound level, leaving him vulnerable in a way he was not vulnerable before, leaving him with a loss of confidence when lack of confidence had not been one of his problems. It would have been in character if he had rejected carrying a candle at the hospice of San Salvatore, no matter what the consequences were, but the horror of the cell had shaken his nerve. He was simply not a man to be shut into a dark hole.

If Timberlake's anti-Catholic prejudice seems abhorrent and slightly absurd now, it is probably well to remember the times in which he lived. When the English King Henry VIII cut ties with the Pope – prompted by his desire to divorce his first (Spanish) wife, Catherine of Aragon – and proclaimed himself head of the Church of England in 1534, he was still fundamentally a Catholic in what he believed. Even with the brutal dissolution of the monasteries and the accompanying hideous executions, Henry himself was not a great reformer of fundamental belief. It was not until the Archbishop of Canterbury, Thomas Cranmer, and his associates had their theological way with Henry and his son

Edward VI (1547–53) that Protestantism of the more Calvinist kind really began in England, with all the above rejections, but it started off more of a reforming movement from above than a groundswelling popular uprising in the pews.

Edward's short reign was followed by a complete reversal, when Henry's eldest surviving child, Mary, daughter of Catherine of Aragon, became Queen (1553–58). Mary sought to stamp out Protestantism in England, burning at the stake about 200 of the Protestant elite (clergy, scholars, other leaders), including Cranmer, and driving many to flee to the Continent. The bodies of notable Protestants who had died prior to Mary's reign were exhumed and burned. She probably would have been largely successful had it not been for her early death. The reign of Queen Elizabeth (1558–1603) reversed the trend, but English Protestant hatred of Catholics and a kind of consolidation of English Protestantism stems partly from the experience of this Catholic backlash at home under Spanish-friendly Mary. It was fired also by tales of Catholic atrocities elsewhere, such as in France, where Protestants were massacred on St Bartholemew's Day in 1572, and in the Netherlands, under the rule of Spain, where the Duke of Alva killed thousands of Protestants between 1567 and 1573. In 1601 the fight for Dutch independence was still fierce. The French Wars of Religion between the Huguenots (Calvinists) and Catholics raged off and on from 1562 until 1598. These were fuel to the fire of hatred.

The Pope made matters worse by encouraging English Catholics to overthrow Elizabeth: not a very good move in terms of finding a peaceable settlement. This gave Elizabeth further justification to torture and execute Catholics as traitors and plotters, including – appallingly – Mary, Queen of Scots, in 1587. The animosity between England and Spain was seen in many ways as religious, since Spain backed efforts to depose Elizabeth in 1571. In the famous painting in the National Maritime Museum, Greenwich, which depicts the defeat of the Spanish Armada, tiny figures of friars fall from the Spanish galleons into the churning water.

Many in England also despised the Spanish for the Inquisition, begun in 1542. This programme to root out heretics spread to Italy and France and greatly deterred Protestantism by its use of heavy propaganda, coercion, torture and executions. The Inquisition was influential on the last session of the Council of Trent, where, in 1564, Pope Pius IV prohibited about 75% of all books printed in Europe.[1] If Elizabeth's England was itself horrific in its treatment of Catholics and in its anti-Catholic prejudice, it must be seen against this backdrop of war.

In accepting he had to stay at San Salvatore and carry a candle if he was to survive his Jerusalem sojourn, Timberlake must have felt like he was in danger of becoming a traitor to Queen and country. It was to prevent such a taint of betrayal that he had been particularly determined to resist this fate at all costs. But as he went to San Salvatore from the prison outside the Church of the Holy Sepulchre, he walked down a path of compromise, a path necessary for all peaceful solutions to conflict, and a path very hard, at times, to take.

The Franciscans in Jerusalem, isolated from the mainstream of Catholic politicking in Europe, were masters of compromise, the treading of a fine line between upholding fundamental principles and allowing the enemy to feel some sense of success. Rome ensured that the turnover of Franciscans in Jerusalem was fairly swift, not only to keep its people in Jerusalem up-to-date and politically correct, but also presumably to prevent any burn-out in what would have been considered a posting involving a significant hardship factor.

The Franciscans in Jerusalem had to be very careful to keep the appropriate humility no matter what circumstances prevailed in regard to the Ottoman administration and military. Furthermore, they did not have a significant local Christian community to support them. The Christians of Palestine were usually Greek Orthodox or, less so, Armenian Orthodox, and relations between the two main wings of the Church, East (Orthodox) and West (Catholic), were not exactly warm. Besides that, in Jerusalem, there were Georgians, Copts, Abyssinians and various other smaller Christian denominations who guarded their ownership of certain Christian sites with dogged determination. The Christians did not really provide a strong united front against the Muslims. In fact, they squabbled. In 1595 – when additional fees were introduced – the squabbling led to tittle tattle, exposing Christian tax dodgers: Christians and Jews were subject to a special poll tax, the *jizya* (and, by 1601, also a wine tithe) and the authorities were always on the look-out for evasion. The Ottoman authorities could exploit the Christian dissension to this cause.[2]

Soon after their seizure of Jerusalem the Ottomans decided to evict the Franciscans from their monastery on Mount Sion, where they had lived since the fourteenth century. Because it was also here that Jews and Muslims believed the tomb of King David lay, the Ottoman authorities decreed that it should be under their direct administration as a mosque. The Franciscans asked the Georgian Orthodox Church if they could have their 'Convent of the Column' in the north-west of the city, but the Georgians were resistant, and sold it only under pressure from the authorities, in 1558. The Georgians, however, wished to recover their lost property and continued to petition the authorities for its return. In 1595, the Qadi was favourable to the Georgian claim, and the Franciscans had to go all the way to the top, to Constantinople, to obtain a *firman* (= decree) that the Franciscans legitimately owned what was now the monastery of San Salvatore. Nevertheless, the fear of expulsion by the authorities and the animosity from the Georgians remained.[3]

That the Franciscans came to be the chief representative of Catholicism in the Holy Land is in some ways quite surprising. Franciscans are named after St Francis of Assisi (1182–1226). According to the fourteenth-century collection of stories about the saint, entitled the 'Little Flowers of St Francis', he was the dissolute son of a rich merchant before he dedicated his life to God. He renounced his fortune to live a life of prayer, preaching, poverty and helping the poor and the sick, following the example of Jesus. He saw all animals, plants, heavenly bodies and forces of Nature as pointing to God, being brothers and sisters of human beings ('brother sun', 'sister moon', 'brother wind', 'sister Mother Earth'), and established an order – a rule of life – followed by all those who would seek to live as he lived. They were to be the 'Friars Minor', the 'lesser brothers', for everything they did would be service in true humility. This order was associated with the order of nuns, the Poor Clares. St Francis travelled to Moorish Spain, sent friars to North Africa, and then later went himself to the Middle East.

The story goes that Francis of Assisi sailed from Ancona in June 1219 and arrived on an island at the mouth of the Nile, against the port of Damietta, to find himself stuck in a Crusader siege, which he found repugnant. He was disgusted by the behaviour of the soldiers. He went to the Muslim camp in peace and was accepted. So impressive was he as a man of wisdom and compassion that the Ayyubid Sultan of Egypt, Malik al-Kamil, let him stay and discuss spiritual matters for several days. Then, however, feeling a failure, unable to move the Muslims to convert or the Crusaders to reform, Francis left Damietta – rife with starvation and disease (it would fall that November) – to go to Acre in Palestine, held at this time by the Crusaders.

On the basis of his example, Franciscans, more than any other monastic order of the Middle Ages, set themselves the task of preaching the Gospel to non-believers, establishing missionary centres in North Africa and the Middle East, as well as in Orthodox Christian countries, and as far as the Buddhist world of Tibet. The secure position of the Franciscans in the Holy Land was thanks to the involvement of the royal family of Naples, King Robert of Anjou and Queen Sancia, who, about 1333, enabled the Franciscan friar Ruggero Garini to buy what remained of the great Crusader Church of St Mary of Mount Sion from the Mamluk Sultan of Egypt, to build the aforementioned monastery and church and to gain the rights to be sanctioned as regular officiants at the Church of the Holy Sepulchre. In 1347 the Sultan authorised them to live in Bethlehem. The Naples initiative was backed up by Pope Clement IV on 21 November 1342, with papal bulls confirming administrative details. Statutes of 1377 established that twenty friars, under the authority of the Padre Guardiano, were to ensure worship in the holy places and give spiritual assistance to pilgrims. But their position in Jerusalem was often precarious. As late as 1623, Pope Urban VII would issue a papal bull declaring it was the duty of all Catholic Princes and also Popes to protect the Franciscans in the Holy Land.

Identifying the fractured nature of Christianity in Jerusalem in the seventeenth century is not meant to imply that Muslims and Jews had united fronts with only the Christians engaging in insecure bickering. Jerusalem was a mosaic of different interest groups founded on different religious beliefs and national affiliations (since, among Muslims as well as among Christians and Jews there were many different incomers who had decided to live in the city, for religious reasons, from the farthest corners of the world). It was in many ways an international multi-faith centre. The Ottomans favoured Hanafi legal interpretations and the Hanafi Qadi was the Ottoman choice for official chief judge, but there was also a Shafi`i Qadi, and those following Maliki and Hanbali schools of thought, who could decide legal cases in Jerusalem, and the Jewish *dayyan* could judge in cases between Jews. The different legal schools of Sunni Islam do not make for such differences as one finds with Christian denominations, but they do make differences.

Jews likewise were not a unified whole. In various streets in the south of the city there were both Rabbinite Jews and Karaites (who spurned the tradition of the rabbis), with separate religious trusts, and also subgroups of Ashkenazis (European Jews), *Musta`riba* Jews (speaking Arabic), and Sephardis (Southern European and North African Jews).[4] Unlike with the Christian denominations, which the Ottoman authorities differentiated between, however, the Jews were treated administratively as an undivided whole, partly because the numbers were small. A list of male Jews between fifteen and sixty (inclusive) liable to tax in 1587 numbered only fifty-one names, most of whom were 'very poor':[5] women, children and the elderly were not included. Including these missing persons and allowing for certain omissions, it has been estimated that the Jewish community numbered between 816 and 980 persons.[6]

In this game of interested parties all aiming to throw their own aspirations for survival and success in the faces of anyone who might threaten them, the Franciscans had to dodge between the authorities and the other Christian and non-Christian groups of the city and surrounding territory as well as deal with the wild-card sensitivities and fanaticisms of pilgrims. It was not easy. It required diplomacy.

Timberlake would have entered the monastery of San Salvatore through a low, narrow gateway rather than the large, main door. The gate, made of strong iron bars, was swung shut behind him and locked. He would have proceeded down a dark corridor, through a doorway and into a central courtyard, where a friar approached. It was the Padre Guardiano, Francesco Manerba.

Some of the conversation that passed between the Custos and Henry Timberlake is recorded in the Captain's account, and it is necessary to fill in only a few lines of dialogue, mainly Timberlake's replies, to reconstruct it in its entirety. It is an extraordinary conversation between an Italian Catholic and an English Protestant, both men of influence and prestige in their own spheres, in the year 1601.

It was necessary for Timberlake initially to identify himself and ask to rest under the Padre Guardian's protection. 'Signor, Padre Guardiano, my name is Captain Henry Timberlake, Master of the good ship *Trojan*, from England.' His words may have been Frank or Italian. Whatever the case, the two men were able to understand each other.

The Custos took Timberlake by the hand.

That he did so speaks volumes. For a Catholic to reach out and shake the hand of a Protestant at this time was a remarkable action.

'You are welcome, Captain Timberlake,' he said, in his northern Italian dialect. Franciscan records show that he came from the province of Brescia, near Milan, and had been in post in Jerusalem with his team for only five months. He was still learning how to operate in this strange city, with the various difficult parties to negotiate with, and with the constant pressure of the Ottoman administration.

'You know, Signor, that I come not of my own will,' Timberlake surely replied. From his account, it does not sound as if he tried to be pleasant. How did he feel about the handshake? That he reported Manerba taking him by the hand indicates its impact.

'I know, Captain Timberlake,' said Manerba, 'and I marvel that you would so much err from Christianity that you would rather put yourself under the protection of the Turk than of myself.' These are words reported by Timberlake.

'You must then also understand why I did so. I will not go to Mass. I follow that form of prayer which is used in English law,' replied Timberlake.[7]

But the Padre Guardiano, as we shall discover, was by no means a coercive and superior-minded man. The Franciscans were masters of careful compromise, and Francesco Manerba was the master of the Franciscans. Perhaps he considered Timberlake something of a test case, an interesting experiment. If Manerba could deal with the Turks, he would also accommodate the heretics. And this heretic had already shown himself to be prepared to compromise himself, in agreeing to hold a candle in a Catholic ceremony. So much for Timberlake's blustery show of defiance at the gate. There was a chink in his resolve. This man would not die for his religion. After all, he was a merchant: trading, striking a good deal, always needed a bit of give and take.

'Captain Timberlake, there have been many Englishmen here, but – of course, being Catholic in their religion – they have come to Mass. When questioned at the gate they have told the Turks that they were French, for indeed, as you have discovered, the Turks do not know what you mean by the word 'English'. On your return to your native land you would kindly instruct your fellow countrymen that if they come to the holy city they should term themselves Frenchmen – or even Britons perhaps – but do not call yourself 'English'. It means nothing here.'

Timberlake would have been irritated by that. To call himself a 'Briton' would be like a Frenchman declaring himself a 'Gaul'. The Padre Guardiano might have read the historical works of Julius Caesar and Tacitus, in which Britons fight the Romans, but why would a 'Briton' make more sense to the Turks than 'Englishman'? At any rate, 'Britons' to Tacitus and the ancient Romans were a bunch of uncouth savages. Perhaps that was Manerba's subtle point, as an Italian, whose legacy was with the Roman conquerors of Britannia.

'This and such like conference passed betweene us,' Timberlake wrote.

What 'such like conference'?

Perhaps Manerba dropped his voice, and spoke quietly, to tell Timberlake of a current predicament. Venice and France had been given capitulary rights by the Ottoman empire from 1569, which gave them a protected legal status. Other Italian states had no such status, and nor did Catholic Europe as a whole. Manerba was no Venetian. Had he lied to the Ottoman authorities? Speaking the truth, here in Jerusalem, was not always the wisest course of action.

'Tell me, what is the age of your Queen now?'

'Nearing seventy.'

'A grand age for a prince.' Then Manerba fired another question. 'And what is the reason that Queen Elizabeth of England gives nothing to maintain the Holy Sepulchre, the sacred place of Our Lord's burial and resurrection, when other Christian kings and princes willingly contribute to the expenses?'[8]

What did Timberlake say to that? He does not give his reply. Perhaps he simply said he did not know. A justification of Queen Elizabeth's neglect would, after all, have been deeply insulting. 'She will not pay money to servants of the Pope, who has excommunicated her'? How could Timberlake say that? Perhaps Manerba wanted to provoke, to make him have to be offensive, in order to rub in the meaning of what he had planned to follow this initial interview.

Here you have a Catholic and Protestant facing each other in a Muslim land, engaging in a kind of deft battle of wits, a verbal equivalent to a sword duel. Timberlake was not grateful to Manerba; he was suspicious. Manerba was equally suspicious. But both men resisted a sharp thrust of aggression. As swordsmen could play with the tips of their swords striking, moving around each other, eyeing each other like two cats in a spat, so Timberlake and Manerba faced each other, and used words, yet held back.

They were interrupted by a commotion. There were people coming. There emerged in the twilight of the courtyard the woebegone figure of John Burrell.

The unfortunate and rather cowardly Burrell had apparently not made any pleas with the Jerusalem authorities for the release of his companion. He had now been found out and ejected from the Greek Orthodox Patriarchate, possibly at the request of the Padre Guardiano. The last thing those in charge there wanted was another reason for animosity between themselves and the Catholics. His ruse of entering the city of Jerusalem under false pretences was itself not successful. Now both men were, in the eyes of the authorities, in their rightful place: with the Padre Guardiano. Timberlake comments that Burrell 'was yet inbued to come to this monastary or els he must not stay in the cittye, such sway doth the Papist beare there that noe Christian strannger canne come there but he must be protected under them or els not enter the cittye.'[9]

What must Francesco Manerba have thought of these new visitors? It must be remembered that Father Francesco had probably never knowingly had to deal with a Protestant visitor before; 'knowingly' because there were some Protestant visitors to Jerusalem who pretended they were Catholics, lodging at San Salvatore without taking Mass, by means of various deceits. For example, the English Protestant Fynes Moryson, who visited Jerusalem in the summer of 1596 with his brother, lists a catalogue of excuses they made so as not to attend Mass the entire time, which reads like a schoolboy diary on how to skive Maths. He even made much use of the 'I don't feel well' ruse. His account indicates also that he was not the only Protestant to play Catholic for the sake of an easy visit to the holy city, though his particular success he puts down to a prior familiarity with friars, so that clearly he knew the lingo and Catholic rituals, and the time he and his brother spent in Jerusalem was short. However, it seems fairly clear that his accompanying French Franciscan guide knew the game he was playing very well, and chose a path of silence. Moryson admits this friar had a 'sharpe wit, joined with the wisdom of experience', and outlines how the Protestants made a special effort to manipulate him to be a friend, for fear they may be found out 'yet I perceived by many and cleere arguments, that he thought us to differ from him in religion.' Once, the French friar simply stated outright, alluding to Fynes Moryson's name: '*En verité vous êtes fin*' – 'In truth you are sharp', or 'crafty', as Moryson easily understood, interpreting the comment: 'In truth you are as crafty as your name imports, but I will endeavour to make the Guardian interpret your excuse to the best.'[10]

The botanist Rauwolf recorded that the Padre Guardiano who greeted his party, Father Jeremy of Brixen, announced that all who came to Jerusalem without a certificate of proof that they had been to Rome first to be absolved by him were in the Pope's excommunication, much to the horror of many Catholics who had no idea that this was the case. The Padre Guardiano then announced that he had authority to absolve those who did not bring certificates, but these shock tactics seem to have been designed to weed out Protestants from any company.[11]

Then there was the candle ceremony. After recording his conversation with the Padre Guardiano and Burrell's entrance, Timberlake tells of the ritual that took place in the courtyard once darkness had fallen.

From inside the buildings a procession of twelve friars came, silently, each holding a burning wax candle, with two extra candles for the visitors. Timberlake's discomfort is shown by the fact that he calls them 'some 12 fatt fryers': an indication of his critical eye in regard to the ceremony. Noting the well-fed bodies of supposedly ascetic friars was a common ruse to poke fun at them in English tradition: from 'Friar Tuck' in the tales of Robin Hood and Chaucer's avaricious and greedy friar in *The Summoner's Tale*.

Then another friar appeared with a great basin[12] of hot water in which there were roses and other flowers to make a lovely scent. Further friars came with a carpet and two chairs with cushions. The Padre Guardiano beckoned the visitors to sit down on these chairs, which they did. He passed them both a candle.

There was a pause, and then another friar came forward. He took off their dusty shoes, and stockings, so that the two Englishmen were sitting there now with their pungent-smelling, travel-worn feet exposed. They had no idea what would happen next. The friar took the basin of hot water and put it down in front of them on the rug. The procedure that was usually followed at this point was that a friar knelt down in front of them, took his subject's right foot in his hands, and began to wash and dry it. During this action the others sang hymns. The friar proceeded carefully to his left foot. The same would have been done for both of them. After the friar finished the Padre Guardiano would have come forward, knelt down before them, and kissed their feet, reciting formulaic phrases, in Latin, in which he had to call the English Protestants his sons. Then the other friars had to come forward, one at a time, kneel down, and kiss the Englishmen's feet.

This ritual of foot-washing would have been particularly poignant when the Franciscan monastery was located at the place where the Upper Room was supposed to have been, where Christians believed the Last Supper had been celebrated. This had been reconstructed as the Cenacle on Mount Sion by the Crusaders. This place was also considered to be the site where Thomas doubted and Christ appeared (John 20:24–29) and where the Holy Spirit descended at Pentecost (Acts 2:1–4).

The foot-washing command comes from Jesus himself. It is stated in the Gospel of John that on the night Jesus was betrayed, he took a basin of water and washed the feet of his disciples (a lowly duty normally done by household slaves). After washing the feet of his disciples, he commanded his disciples to do likewise for each other:

> So after he had washed their feet, and had taken his garments, and was set down again, he said unto them, 'Know ye what I have done to you? Ye call me Master and Lord: and ye say well; for so I am. If I then, your Lord and Master, have washed your feet; ye also ought to wash one another's feet. For I have given you an example, that ye should do as I have done to you.' (John 13:12–14)

Imitating Jesus, the Franciscans of Jerusalem washed the feet of pilgrims who came to them. They continued the ceremony even when the associations of the location could no longer be drawn upon, after their eviction from the Cenacle.[13]

The foot-washing ceremony is described by other visitors who came to San Salvatore, both Catholic and Protestant (once the idea that Protestants could stay there became more accepted).[14] Thomas Bodington, in 1669, described the ritual in detail. A large basin of water was placed beside a chair. Certain friars sprinkled roses and herbs into the water while the others stood in a row singing hymns. Bodington and his party (of fourteen in all) had to sit down on the chair, one at a time. The Padre Guardiano put a towel on their laps to save their clothes. Bodington writes of the process that: 'having first dry'd the left Foot, the Fryer kisses it, and puts on our Slipper, then he does the right Foot, and wraps the Towel about the Sole of the Foot, and setting it on his knee, covers the Toes with his Hand, and then come all the Fraters, and kiss it.'[15]

The fervently Protestant Timberlake sat there while the friars kissed his newly washed feet. That he felt excruciating embarrassment is reflected in the fact that, while he describes everything else in the ceremony, he does not specifically mention this action. Kissing was an important part of the ritual. Instead, Timberlake writes only: 'Then came a fryer and pulled off our hose and putt the bason upon the carpett and he washed our feete, and as soone as he began to wash the 12 fryers began to singe, and so contynewed till our feete were washed.'[16]

How did the friars feel at having to kiss the feet of a heretic? It was done at the Padre Guardiano's command. He could have waived this entire ritual if he had wanted to, as we shall see. The Custos, Francesco Manerba, perhaps aimed to make a symbolic statement to the troublesome Timberlake: it was his job to welcome *all* pilgrims, even those who had initially rejected him.

Had Manerba been touched by the humility of the Moor, in begging for the Captain's life in front of the Sanjakbey? Who knows. But he would respond to Timberlake's hate with an action of love, despite his suspicions, despite his own fears.

The San Salvatore monastery courtyard in Jerusalem (Plate 4) today is not quite as it was, since the monastery as a whole is much expanded, and straddles St Francis Street. The lower part of the eastern wall of the present courtyard was part of the old monastery. A more modern building has been built to the south with large arches that have been filled in time, and this has cut into part of the old courtyard. There were two doorways in the eastern wall, and a window in the middle of the wall; the southern one of the doorways is where a newer window is now located, near the newer wall that has reduced the size of the courtyard. Behind the original two doorways was a bakery on the left, and a flour mill on the right, and above them friars cells.[17] The original building on the south was also double-storeyed, and had two domes in a flat roof. There were work rooms on the ground floor, including a forge and a wheat store. Beyond, further to the south, was a wood store, piggery and gardens. On the north was the refectory. The monastery was a place of active work, not just of contemplation.

It was customary to follow the foot-washing with a procession into the dark, little church[18] for Mass and Confession.[19] The Service that Timberlake and Burrell attended, singing, with candles in hand, seems to have been in lieu of Mass. The chapel service contained a short sermon, said in Latin, and Timberlake appears familiar enough with the language he would have learnt as a schoolboy to get the gist of it. The sermon was the usual one given by the Padre Guardiano in welcoming pilgrims, but here he is not the one who gives it. Timberlake says 'one of them', one of the friars, was 'making an Oration'. This was usually recited while pilgrims were kneeling before the altar. The standard address concerned the importance of visiting the holy places, for at these sites they could with sincere hearts and devout intent pray to God, and praise his holy name, that had brought them to this place where his Son was born and crucified for humanity's salvation. Let them not think further of the rigours of travel, he said, for Christ in coming to the world suffered reproach, shame, punishment and death to become our mediator and saviour.[20] Given that the Padre Guardiano did not give this address to the visiting Englishmen, but had someone else do it, perhaps he was deliberately hanging back, watching, observing their reactions.

The importance of visiting the holy places was stressed. The Franciscans were in the habit of handing out indulgences at holy places. The idea was that you had to pay for your sins, either on Earth, or in Purgatory, even after you have been reconciled to God through penance and absolution. However, if you did certain good and difficult things — like going on pilgrimage to holy places — the Church would grant you indulgences that guaranteed a minimisation of the amount of time you would spend in Purgatory, and each holy place attracted different 'bonus points' in that regard. Protestants completely spurned this practice. But the importance of the holy places could be stressed in a sermon without any mention of this troublesome bone of contention.

That first night, after the service, Timberlake and Burrell were given supper by the friars in a chamber. The manuscript reads:

> The sermon beinge ended they brought us to a chamber and brought us super and afterward we went to beade, this beinge the 25th March 1601.[21]

Interestingly, in the first edition of 1603, the text reads:

> there [in the chamber] we ate somwhat fearefully, in regard the strange cates (= delicacies) have as strange qualities: but committing our selves to God & their outward-appearing Christian kindnesse we fell to [eating] hartily, supt very bountifully, & afterward (praysing God) were lodged decently.[22]

In the short version of Timberlake's letter that appears in Samuel Purchas, *Purchas his Pilgrimes*, there is:

> Hence they brought us into a chamber to supper which we for feare of poyson doubted to eat. Thence to bed.[23]

It might be a case in which the manuscript has missed out an original line, for there is nothing about fearing poisoning here. Timberlake and Burrell have a sudden flash of paranoia, even after all this overwhelming washing, kissing, singing, praying, holding of candles.

Furthermore, the friars, even at this early stage, were known for their skills in preparing medicines. As time went on, a large pharmacy was developed, and the monastery commissioned the firm of Giacomo Boselli in Savona to produce an array of gorgeous apothecary jars, now on display in the Franciscan museum in Jerusalem. Mysterious jars of medications could easily be interpreted as dangerous poisons, if you were suspicious.

The Englishmen did not pause to fear for very long though. They were too hungry.

Meanwhile, what of al-Fessi? He would have left Timberlake at the monastery, once he had passed him over to the care of the friars. He would not have been permitted to enter. A heretic was one thing but an infidel was another. It was up to him to find his own accommodation on this festival night.

Al-Fessi would have found a Muslim pilgrim hospice, with a bed and a well-earned meal.

They had arrived in Jerusalem.

12

The Pilgrim Trail

So the Protestant Englishman, Captain Henry Timberlake, awoke early on Thursday, 26 March 1601[1] in the Franciscan monastery, San Salvatore, of the holy city, Jerusalem. During the last twenty-four hours Timberlake had been arrested by Ottoman guards at the city gate who did not know what or where England was; imprisoned by the authorities as a spy; forsaken by his Protestant countryman, who was pretending to be a Greek Orthodox pilgrim; rescued from prison by a Moroccan Muslim, and, to top it all off, he had participated in a sacred ritual in which he held a candle while his feet were washed and kissed by a group of Catholic friars whom he despised. He was in a topsy-turvy world where none of the old rules applied.

Timberlake writes in his account that his first act after arising 'early in the morninge' (and eating the usual breakfast of 'milk' – yoghurt – and fruit) was to salute the Padre Guardiano, who then appointed seven friars and an interpreter to accompany Burrell and Timberlake around the holy places. The appointment of seven friars and an interpreter ('trudge man') was not as ridiculous as it sounds, as pilgrims tended to go in a kind of mini-procession, but it was quite a big procession for two men, and I think he was being exceptionally careful. Perhaps the Pasha had asked for the Custos to be especially vigilant, and make a report.

The pilgrim trail was ritualised. A procession acted as a barrier between the sacred and the profane, meaning that the participants would not be so disturbed; they were clearly not interested in haggling over merchandise, but had their minds on holy business.

There are a number of maps of Jerusalem dating to the sixteenth and seventeenth centuries, none of which is very accurate (e.g. Figure 8), but they enable us to get some understanding of pilgrim routes and sacred places, though they do not show mosques, madrasas or synagogues. The routes and the places had become standard, and just about every Christian pilgrim going to Jerusalem went on the same tours and got the same information.

So on 26 March 1601, Day 2 of his visit to Jerusalem, Timberlake, Burrell, an interpreter and seven Franciscans set off on foot from San Salvatore, soon after breakfast, to walk the Via Dolorosa – as was usual – in reverse, viz. (according to Timberlake) first going to the Gate of Judgement, the last stop before the Church of the Holy Sepulchre at Golgotha; then to the house of St Veronica; the house of the rich glutton, where Lazarus lay; the spot where Simon of Cyrene carried the cross; the site of the 'daughters of Jerusalem' meeting; the Church of the Spasm, where the Virgin Mary fainted; the Ecce Homo arch; and Pilate's Palace. They then went to the Church of St Anne (Virgin Mary's house), the Bethesda Pool and St Stephen's Gate, where, just outside and to the left, they were shown a rock upon which St Stephen was stoned to death.

Timberlake seems to have accepted everything as possible, adding 'as they say' to a few sites to indicate he was not completely incredulous. But he was no scholar. He had no way of determining what was true and what was false.

It is interesting that Timberlake and Burrell had never heard of St Veronica and the story of the wiping of Christ's face as he paused on his way to execution. 'I asked what saint she was,' he writes. This story is not in the New Testament, but is a later legend. Still, it is amazing that England could so easily have wiped out the memory of this important saint, within a generation anyway. Veronica was supposed to have given Christ her headcloth as he made his way to Golgotha, where he would be crucified. The idea is that it was pressed to his face, and the cloth thereafter carried an impression of his features, formed from the sweat and blood.

Timberlake records what the friars told him without any feeling of awe or sentiment. The place that most impressed him was the Ecce Homo Arch:

> there is an old arche of stone, which is still mayntained by the Christians. It is in the
> high waye, so that we passed under it, much like to the way that passeth under Mr.
> Hamonds house in the Bulwarke, but that the arche is higher, for upon that arche is
> a gallery [which] goeth over our heads from one side of the streete to the other, for
> that Pilates pallace was one bothe sides of the high way, and had great windowes soe
> that he might see both wayes in the broad streete, as Mr. Hamond cann doe well att
> bothe his windowes.[2]

As Timberlake could situate the towns of Palestine in accordance with what he knew of English towns, so he would understand the Ecce Homo arch in accordance with what he knew of the arch at the Bulwark around the Tower of London. His template was England.

The Ecce Homo arch in Jerusalem is actually part of a Roman triumphal arch probably built by the Emperor Hadrian around AD 135 for the northern forum of the city. It has nothing whatsoever to do with Pilate's palace or Praetorium, which in the first century was located in the south-western part of the city. Today, you can see that the arch still has (later) rooms constructed at the top of it, with windows looking down at the street below. It makes rather a strange image, to imagine Pilate standing at a window on top of the arch, instructing people on the street below: '*Ecce Homo*!', 'Behold the man!' But that was the image sixteenth and seventeenth-century European visitors to Jerusalem must have had when faced with the reality they were shown. The present window is not that big, but in 1601 it was larger: a double arch with a column in the middle. Bernadino Amico's drawing of the arch, with the window, in fact shows Pilate, dressed as an Ottoman governor, and Christ. (Figure 9).[3]

There was an inscription underneath which apparently once read, '*Tolle, tolle, crucifige eum*', 'Take, take, crucify him', (now only 'TOL'). These are the words the anti-Jesus crowd supposedly shouted at Pilate. Perhaps pilgrims of former times then tended to imagine a less massive interaction between Prefect and Jerusalemites than is common in contemporary films of the life of Christ. It must, surely, subliminally, have struck some of them that only a few hundred Jews could have crowded below this window in the narrow street, a fairly small number given the ramifications. According to the Gospel of Matthew, the crowd shouted that Jesus' blood would be 'upon us, and on our children' (27:25). Christians came to interpret this to mean that the guilt for Christ's death would rest on all Jews everywhere for all time, regardless of whether they were in the anti-Jesus Jerusalemite crowd or not. Standing there looking at the window above the Ecce Homo arch, did any pilgrim wonder that such a huge consequence would follow from the clamouring of some throng in this little narrow street? How would they have staged things in their imaginations?

The scene imagined by Timberlake must have been more intimate than we might imagine it, with Pilate thrusting Christ to the window so he could be seen by the group gathered below, and then taking him back to the 'judgement hall' (John 19:9), where the judgements of the Ottoman authorities were still taking place, where Timberlake's fate was itself judged, intimately, with al-Fessi pleading his case.

The point about the pilgrim trail is and was that it is not necessarily about historical authenticity, of working out what is definitely the place that Jesus did or said something. Pilgrimage is about memory, and organising memory. It is a case of laying out a course of triggers to memory, for every time you get to a place the stories you have learnt since childhood, and perhaps might not remember very well, burst out vividly. A sacred place opens a holy story, a story about the nature of God and humanity, about the nature of power, truth and love. The experience of having that story triggered in your mind is so powerful it is almost as if you are there, not hearing the story, but experiencing the story. It is immediate.

Dinner at the monastery of San Salvatore in 1601 took place around noon, and is described at times by visitors.[4] Two or three Palestinian lay-brothers attended at the door to the courtyard, holding a basin and jug of water, and asked visitors to wash before entering the refectory. Inside, the friars all stood on one side, and recited Grace in Latin, going on to sing the Lord's Prayer. They then bowed to a picture hanging on the wall, which depicted Christ at the Last Supper, with his disciples, in a frame adorned with silver crosses. This picture hung above the chair reserved for the Padre Guardiano.

There were three long tables, one for the friars, one for pilgrims, and one for the Padre Guardiano and his personal guests. Everyone went to sit down after the friars had stooped to kiss the ground.

This first part of the meal was called *altum silentium*, or 'deep silence', and consisted of the ritual of saying Grace, but also a reading from the *Golden Legend* in Latin by one of the friars. The *Golden Legend* was spurned by Protestants. It was a summary of Biblical and apocryphal stories, especially concerning the lives of the saints, compiled by one Jacobus de Voragine, Archbishop of Genoa, in 1275, and in the late fifteenth and early sixteenth centuries it was the most frequently printed book in Europe. Protestants thought of it as a bastardisation of the true Word of God found in Scripture, and a repository of Papist propaganda. It was nevertheless an important basis for Christian tradition, though it seems to be designed for the kind of monotonous, rhythmic oral recitation that would test even the most devout person's powers of concentration.

Food was served. Each man was given an allotment in a little dish, or rather several little dishes containing different sorts of food, as well as fruit, water and wine. Halfway through a friar came to change the water, so it would be fresh. The period of eating was called *stridor dentium*, for the process of chewing, after which, at an appropriate time, was *rumor gentium*, when people could talk.[5]

Eating in silence is a very strange thing when you are not used to it. You have to stop yourself mentioning the things you are thinking, or from making some idle remark. Eating suddenly seems very loud.

Given that there were few pilgrims at this time and the refectory was not large, they might not have been at a separate table. They were probably sitting with the Padre Guardiano, underneath the picture of Christ and his disciples, as his special guests. That would have been appropriate. They were accompanied by Jesuits, whose presence is indicated by other sources. Among them was, most notably, a Father Benedictus from Seville.[6] Jesuits and Protestants at one table?

Dressed in black, Jesuits of this age were a very different kettle of fish to the gentle Franciscans. They were a new order, begun less than seventy years earlier, and at the vanguard in the battle against Protestants. By this time they were scholarly, austere, and had vowed an unquestioning obedience to the Pope. Their order, known as the Society of Jesus, was conceptualised as a band of soldiers, with the Pope as commander-in-chief. They were holy warriors, on a holy war. Like the Franciscans, they were interested in missionary work, particularly in America and other far-flung places, but compromise was the last thing on their minds. They were the instruments of the Inquisition, fiercely loyal to Pope Clement VIII.

Conversation cannot have been entirely cordial, especially given that Father Benedictus was a Spaniard, and therefore an enemy of England.

The Franciscans and the Jesuits would surely have discussed the curious events of Timberlake's imprisonment, and delivery, thanks to the intercession of a Muslim. In doing so, how could they not have thought of the story of the Good Samaritan, as told by Jesus to those who questioned him about love?

This story is worth remembering. Jesus here plays on the animosities of his time, and overturns stereotypes. Jews and Samaritans in the first century AD utterly despised each other, each seeing the other as perverting the true religion of Moses and Israel. The Samaritans claimed to be the descendants of the nine northern tribes, and the Jews the descendants the tribe of Judah (and Benjamin), with the tribe of Levi – from which Moses came – found within both groups. While Jews had evolved a religion that had adapted and expanded – with Jews going to live all over the Roman and Parthian worlds and by making numerous converts – the Samaritans had tended to be more introverted, concentrating on their old cultic centre of Mount Gerizim and the letter of the Law. But still they were a sizeable religious population of the area defined by Jews as Eretz-Israel, the Land of Israel, a term that harks back to nomenclature from the time of David and Solomon. The Samaritans of the first century occupied much of the region now known as the West Bank: Nablus, Sebastiya, Jenin.

Jews disliked Samaritans because of their terrorist acts and claims which they considered partly false. They were heretics and saboteurs. Jesus, as a Jewish teacher, told the story of the 'good Samaritan' to other Jews loaded with this dislike. When you read the story, for 'Samaritan' you can substitute whatever person you feel an innate predisposition to fear and hate – the terrorists, the enemy, the heretic – and the victim someone you would feel a comradeship with, one of your own kind. The priest and the Levite are the respected members of your own community, people you look to for authority, justice and decency: the mayor, the priest, the judge, the professor. Now see how it all plays out, according to the Geneva Version of the Bible that Timberlake and Burrell would have known.

> Then behold, a certain expounder of the law stood up, and tempted him saying, Master, what shall I doe to inherit eternall life?
>
> And he said unto him, What is written in the Lawe? how readest thou? And he answered, & said, thou shalt love thy Lord God with al thine heart, and with all thy soule, and with al thy strength, and with all thy thought, and thy neighbour as thy selfe.
>
> Then he said unto him, Thou hast answered right: this doe, and thou shalt live.
>
> But hee willing to justifie himselfe sayd unto Jesus, Who is then my neighbour?
>
> And Jesus answered, and said, A certaine man went downe frome Jerusalem to Jericho, and fell among theeves, and they robbed him of his raiment, & wounded him,

and departed, leaving him halfe dead.

And by chance there came downe a certaine Priest that same way, and when he sawe him, he passed by on the other side.

And likewise also a Levite, when hee was come neere to the place, went and looked on him, and passed by on the other side.

Then a certaine Samaritane as he journeied, came neere unto him, and when he sawe him, he had compassion on him. And went to him, and bounde up his woundes, and poured oyle and wine, and put him on his owne beast, and brought him to an Inne, and made provision for him.

And on the morowe when he departed, hee tooke out two pence, and gave them to the host, and said unto him, Take care of him, and whatsoever thou spendest more, when I come againe, I will recompense thee.

Which nowe of these three, thinkest thou, was neighbour unto him that fell among the theeves?

And he sayd, He that shewed mercie on him.

Then sayde Jesus unto him, Goe, and doe thou likewise.

For Jews in the first century the story would have been shocking because there was not supposed to be a good Samaritan. In the sixteenth and seventeenth centuries, there was not supposed to be a good infidel. There was not supposed to be a good heretic. Such was the thinking of the Jesuits. Such was the thinking of the Protestants and Catholics. Such was the thinking of the Muslims. Such was the thinking of nearly everyone in the world, or so you might believe. But historical reality is never quite as simple as you think.

13

The Hammam

Jerusalem, in the year 1601, was a centre for Sufism.[1]
Sufism is defined a little differently by different people, but it is basically
a tradition that heavily emphasises the mystical path to God. It is currently, in
today's Muslim world, rather unfashionable, but in other periods of Islamic history it flourished. In Jerusalem there were a number of Sufi *madrasas* (= teaching
academies), each led by a spiritual master, the charismatic sheikh, who would
share his wisdom with groups of devoted disciples who saw themselves as brothers (and women could be included here). They were bound together by a spiritual
discipline (*tariqa*) that would enable them to experience God, using methods like
the recitation of the 99 names of God (the *dhikr*) and poetry.

On a basic level, Islam requires its devout adherents to accept the 'five pillars': say
with belief the creed (*shahadah*), 'There is no God but God, and Mohammed is his
messenger'; pray five times a day at the designated times (*salat*); give to the poor and
needy (*zakat*); fast during the month of Ramadan (*sawm*); and go on pilgrimage to
Mecca (*hajj*). But the Sufis realised it was possible for people to do all these and yet still
not engage their hearts and souls. You could totally miss the point of Islam. The highest aspiration of the Sufis was to meet God face to face, like Mohammed himself.

One night, it was said, Mohammed had travelled on the back of the winged horse
Buraq to Jerusalem, and ascended from the great rock that stood exposed there – the
Stone of Foundation – through the seven levels of Heaven, meeting the greatest
Prophets.[2] It was the journey into Heaven that opened the door of truth, and it was
not only a true event but a potent symbol. For it was the opening of the door in the
soul to God that mattered. Everything turned together, but the heart of it all was this
one thing. You had to purge yourself – fight the Great Holy War, *al-Jihad al-Akbar*
– against the infidels of the soul: all that was evil in yourself. You had to fight those
infidels off, and destroy them, in order to ascend, to keep the door open. And that
is what the Prophet Mohammed had done. The Dome of the Rock – built in AD
691 over a once naked rock that lay in the wide, abandoned space of the old Jewish
Temple precincts – symbolised to the Sufis the heart of Islam, the heart of humanity's
ideal relationship with God. It was truly the Noble Sanctuary, the jewel of Jerusalem.

From their experience of God the devoted Sufis would glow with mercy, love and compassion: these were the fruits of their discipline. In the Qur'an, God is always invoked as 'the merciful and the compassionate'. Ultimately, thought the Sufis, all Islam is directed to realising these aspects of God in the world. Everything could be a dance to heavenly rhythms, to the strings of mercy, wisdom and love.

Given the importance of the rock from which Mohammed ascended into heaven, located in Jerusalem, this explains why so many Sufis were there, and their presence must have imbued the city with an extraordinary quality. Muslim visitors to Jerusalem might stay in pilgrim hospices run by Sufi brotherhoods. They would have been touched by their understandings. Some people said that at the end of time Mecca and Jerusalem would merge into one, for the holy Ka`ba in Mecca would transport itself to Jerusalem to perform the *hajj* and embrace the holy rock.

I cannot help but see al-Fessi at the Haram esh-Sharif, in the Dome of the Rock and the vast al-Aqsa Mosque, in the company of Sufis. His action to help Henry Timberlake itself seems to reflect the Sufi passion for mercy and love, widely given. Perhaps he had met Sufis in Morocco. Perhaps his *hajj* was motivated by them.

He would have moved around the wide sacred precincts, answering calls to prayer, praying first with one imam, and then with another, though mainly with the Maliki imam in the Dome of the Rock itself, who followed the tradition of Morocco. The timings and the patterns were choreographed by the sun and the moon, and the powers of Heaven.

Visitors to the Haram esh-Sharif were usually amazed by the sheer beauty of the buildings, all the gold and colour of the interiors, the mosaics, the lead-covered dome, and how many smaller mosques there were all over plateau, so that you travelled around it being astonished by one thing, and then another: the small mosque east of al-Aqsa where on a stone there is God's announcement to Zakariyya that he would have a son named Yahya (John – the Baptist), and the mosque of 'Issa (Jesus), where his cradle is kept. The place was so beautiful: paved with white marble, dotted with sacred buildings, date palms and orange trees. You could be impressed by the age of the buildings, nearly 1,000 years old, but even more so by the great antiquity of the sacredness: for Adam, the Prophet of God, had reputedly built a sacred edifice here forty years after he had built the Ka'ba in Mecca.

It remains as beautiful today, even more so with the dome being gold now, and the peaceful view to the Mount of Olives is hardly changed (Plates 5 and 6). In 1601 non-Muslims were not allowed on the Haram esh-Sharif. It was then reserved in its entirety for those who understood the spiritual significance of it. There was nothing built without significance. In the al-Aqsa mosque guides of that time explained that the seventeen rows of marble colours represented something: the two green sides signify the daybreak prayer; the eight white sides were the number of prostrations at the noon and afternoon prayers; the four red sides signify the prayer at sunset; the three black sides signify the prayer at evening darkness. Everywhere you looked in the seven-aisled building there were symbols of the universe, and of the faith. Everything pointed beyond itself.[3]

While Timberlake and Burrell had walked the Via Dolorosa, al-Fessi would have been here, on the day of the Idh al-Fitr. Finally, he had peace.

Along with Sufism, Jerusalem was also a city of bath-houses (hammams). To some extent, the baths were where Christians, Muslims and Jews met, though in practice there were preferences for each faith to go to one or the other of the multiple bath-houses all over the city. They were used for personal hygiene, but also as a place to meet, eat and talk. Men had certain times, and women had certain times. There were pre-marriage bath rituals, and all kinds of other reasons to turn up and spend hours in cleaning and massaging. For a city that spent so much time thinking about the soul, it is remarkable how much time was also spent tending to the body.

If you wanted news, or to meet people, the baths were a very good place to go, especially if you were new to the city. The most appropriate ones for Timberlake and Burrell to have visited were near where an important Sufi *madrasa* was located, and also proximate to the monastery of San Salvatore. The Baths of the Patriarch, as they were called, were mainly frequented by local Jerusalem Christians, who usually belonged to Eastern rites (Greek Orthodox, Armenian Orthodox).

The Baths of the Patriarch (Hammam al-Batrak) were old, no one knows how old, and located on a main market street, Harat al-Nasarah, 'Christian Street', not far from the pool of the Patriarch (Birkat al-Batrak), west of the Church of the Holy Sepulchre. The 'Patriarch' in question refers to the Greek Patriarch of Jerusalem, whose origins stretched back to the second century, for the 'Greeks' (Hellenised Palestinians) continued the ancient traditions of the first Jewish Church in Jerusalem, when all Jews were evicted from the city by order of the Roman emperor Hadrian in AD 135. The Greek Patriarch lasted until the time of the Crusaders in 1099, who removed him in favour of a Latin (Western) leader, and, when Salah edh-Din reconquered Jerusalem for Islam in 1171, he turned the Patriarchate into a *khanqah*, a hospice, which became a convent of Sufi mystics (1187–9). The names remained the same, even when the Pool of the Patriarch became a *waqf*, endowment, for the *khanqah*. So it goes, in Jerusalem, with things turning over.

Visitors went inside through an L-shaped entrance, and came into the summer undressing room. They were given red and black cotton bath-coverings, and went behind wooden screens hung with cloths to undress and wrap these around their lower halves. They had to put on special bath shoes, leaving their own shoes under a bench. The floor was finely constructed with inlaid coloured stone in geometric designs. A marble font was in the centre, where water splashed.[4] They passed their belongings to the attendant, and proceeded through two small rooms to the main hot room. It was stifling, and steamy. Water bubbled in a huge brass cauldron, built into the furnace, tended by men on the other side, in a different room. Visitors were careful of the fire slab in the floor where, underneath, the smoke from the furnace passed on its way to a chimney. The floor here was also beautifully inlaid with coloured, polished stone, with drains in the corners.

The bathers then placed themselves on stone benches, on which towels were spread out, on either side of a basin with hot and cold water. Daylight came in muted, diffracted, through the domed ceiling, where there was a constellation of small, glassed holes arranged in a pattern.

Timberlake had surely visited baths like this in Algiers and other places. Perhaps Burrell also knew the routine. The Captain would have known that you could strike good deals in such places. But a good deal was not his concern in Jerusalem. After the pain of travel, and his incarceration in a dungeon, cleanliness and relaxation would have been on his mind. The first day he had of pilgrimage in Jerusalem also was brief, allowing time for other things.

It is in this setting it is possible that a meeting between Timberlake and local Palestinian Christians took place, since this was a common place for meeting people. It is clear from his account that he talked to them in Frank, which means they were probably themselves traders, perhaps soap merchants. Soap was one of the most lucrative exports of the region, and the soap made from the potassium-rich plants around the Dead Sea was particularly prized.

As they talked, an attendant would have entered with hummous, falafel, bread, a bean dip, salad, water and coffee, arranged on a large brass tray. At some point another attendant would have given them all a robust massage. There were attendants also to help with washing and drying.

Wherever it happened, Timberlake's conversation with Palestinian Christians supplied him with information about the abuses of the Ottoman authorities that would colour his attitude to Jerusalem strongly. He was horrified by what he learnt. He writes that in Jerusalem there are 'three Christians for one Turke, and many Christians in the countrey round about, but they all live poorly under the Turke'.[5] This ratio of 3:1 in Jerusalem indicates that here Timberlake is talking about the Ottoman ruling class as 'Turkes', an elite that could be readily identified: the administrators, local dynasties, sipahis and their retinues.[6] He could not be referring to Palestinian Muslims as a whole, for in Jerusalem Muslims greatly outnumbered Christians. Elsewhere, his words are more ambiguous. He writes that the region of Jerusalem was:

I thinke quitt forsaken of the Lord, for the maior parte of the Turkes that inhabitt theire doe use all manner of filthines in soe much that all the Christian inhabitants ar forced to mary theire children very younge, at ten yeres old, for feare least the

Turks should defile them and cause them to turne. They keep boyes openly, and ar
not ashamed to keep them at theire doores, for a show which of them hath the fair-
est. And as the better sorte of the Christians have told me, theire is not that sin in
the world, but it raigneth theire in Jheru[salem]. And therefore they use these words
often; *Terra Sancta, a. c. no mais*, that is that name of the holy land, and no more.[7]

In the 1603 printed publication the words of the local Christians are given as
'Terra Sancta è no mais' – 'Holy Land is not but [in name]'.[8]

Later on, in the revised edition of 1609, the whole passage has been changed
to read: 'for that they use the sinne of Sodom and Gomorrah very much in that
Country, whereby the poore Christians that inhabite therein, are glad to marry
their daughters at twelve yeeres of age, unto Christians, least the Turkes should
ravish them.'[9] Here the publisher has removed the ambiguity of the word 'Turks'
so that the reference is to all Palestinian Muslims. Additionally, it is not so direct to
talk of the sin of Sodom and Gomorrah, or to say it is the daughters who are mar-
ried at twelve, rather all the Christian children at ten, and actually that statement
does not follow. In the first version, the concern is to protect the young boys,
who are taken by the 'Turks'. Marrying daughters at twelve was very common in
many parts of the Mediterranean and Middle East at this time – and it was legal in
England. That would not have been as shocking to Timberlake as the custom of
arranging marriages for both girls and boys at age ten, to protect the *boys*.

This later edition of 1609 also played with other things Timberlake wrote in his
letter as found in the manuscript. It reads: 'for all holinesse is cleane banished from
thence [the Holy Land] by those Theeves, filthie Turks and Infidels that inhabite
there'. Timberlake actually never wrote that. He himself was a merchant whose
frequent dealings with Muslims seem to have led him to a much more open view
of Islam than most Europeans had. He was a man who would trust Ottoman
law and accept the good companionship of a Moor. The publisher altered the
manuscript which has Timberlake writing about highwaymen on the roads. In
his original letter he wrote that certain 'wild Arabians' who are 'theyves' are those
who 'make prize of Christians, Turks, Moores and alother sorts of people, them
selves excepted.'[10] Out of this statement the publisher, Thomas Archer, created
anti-Muslim vitriol, when Muslims are in the original the *victims* rather than the
aggressors. The blanket disparagement of 'Turks and infidels' is reflective of the
prejudice of England, not Timberlake. In those days the printed page did not
always reflect what the writer wrote.

The Ottoman authorities were imperial occupiers of Palestine. Following the
ways of the Mamluks, they configured administrative borders to ensure it had no
integrity, as with Greece, which no longer existed. If you wanted to erase revolt,
you erased the country, conceptually. People were left with a sense of belonging
to a village, town, or a region, but 'Palestine', Arabic Filastin, remained a geographical concept.[11] The Ottomans were interested, as with all empire-builders, in

keeping the people docile, loyal to their rule, and dutiful in declaring what they owed to the empire in revenue. Did the ruling class sexually abuse children also? Did Muslims in Palestine join with them in taking Christian boys, sodomising them, converting them to Islam, and so on? Whatever the story told to Timberlake by the Palestinian Christians, their claim is more interesting than a simple case of true or false. That the Jerusalem Christians who spoke to Timberlake chose to give, as an expression of their subjugation, the story of their boys being taken away by the 'Turks' to be sodomised and exhibited as prizes in a boy beauty contest represents their own powerlessness and sense of abuse, regardless of whether the story is true.

The notion that people have a right to self-determination is a very recent concept, but people of the past, under an empire, could nevertheless know that they were oppressed and wish for something better: the throwing off of foreign domination, the right to freely cultivate land and earn money without harsh taxation or pillage or destruction, the maintenance of traditions, religion, customs and laws, the protection of their children.

14

Echoes

On 27 March 1601, Timberlake and Burrell, 'saluted the Pater Gaurdina and hired asses for the fryers and the trudgmen'.[1] They then embarked on a vigorous plan of seeing a large number of Christian holy places outside the walls of Jerusalem, which meant they would not be back for lunch (with the Jesuits) at the monastery. They set off towards Bethany, located about two miles from Jerusalem. En route, skirting the Mount of Olives, they passed a fig tree which the friars pointed out as being the very one cursed by Christ (Matt. 21:18–22), and then went on to the House of Lazarus, Jesus' friend – where only one wall remained – a House of Mary Magdalene – which had pieces of a wall (today covered by the Greek Orthodox church of Bourdh al-Hammar) – and the stone where Jesus sat when the sisters Mary and Martha told him that Lazarus was dead (John 11:20, 30–35).

Timberlake and Burrell then back-tracked to Lazarus' tomb (John 11:1–31), a site that dates at least from the beginning of the fourth century and the location of a succession of churches dating from around 380. In Timberlake's day it was a deep, square vault, accessed by many steps, with two small chapels above.[2] Timberlake thought it 'poore and bare'.

This circuit allowed pilgrims to remember the stories associating Jesus with the sisters Mary and Martha, and their brother Lazarus, who lived in Bethany.

The Spanish Franciscan Juan Perrara described Bethany as being inhabited by 'a few Moors'.[3] It was only a tiny place. From the Tomb of Lazarus the party climbed up the Mount of Olives via a village identified as ancient Bethphage, where Jesus placed himself on a donkey on the day of his triumphal entry into Jerusalem (Mark 11:1–10).

A re-enactment of Jesus' procession into Jerusalem was undertaken by the Franciscans each year on Palm Sunday, as it is to this day. The Padre Guardiano of the Franciscans would sit upon a donkey at Bethphage, and act as Jesus entering Jerusalem. Christians who were so inclined would become the crowd of Jesus' day, shouting, 'Hosanna to the Son of David: Blessed is he that cometh in the name of the Lord; Hosanna in the highest' (Matt. 21:9). People would take off some of their clothes, cut down branches from the (palm) trees and spread these in the way of the donkey, as they did for Jesus. Historical re-enactments like this are one step beyond the usual pilgrimage experience, and allow the participant to engage very deeply in the holy story.

A story was told at Timberlake's time of an incident in which a Christian woman, carried away by the experience, took off some of her clothing, 'as in modesty she might', to spread on the pathway of the ass. A Muslim guard, equally overcome with derision, 'tooke a cudgel and all to belabored her therewith saying, Thou foole, art thou so mad to thinke that this is Christ?'[4] On another occasion the Padre Guardiano himself was dragged from the donkey and beaten by 'Turks'.[5]

Muslims were not the only ones to be derisive. Regarding the Padre Guardiano riding on an ass, Protestants liked to make a joke about 'the greater Asse riding upon the lesser',[6] and generally scoff at the whole thing, so that a later – rather liberal-minded – Padre Guardiano named Guadentius Saybantus is recorded as making a speech to the visiting Protestants, saying:

> You Pilgrimes, who refuse to be participant with us in the Sacraments, nor will not adhere to the Processions and Ceremonies, which wee follow of the Roman church, I would therfore intreate you (your liberty being here as much as mine, whereby you may do whatsoever seeme good in your owne eies) only to abstaine from scandalizing and mocking our rites and ordinarie customes, which at this great feast wee must performe.[7]

The village of Bethphage identified to Timberlake was south of the foot of the Mount of Olives. It was where Simon the Pharisee's house was pointed out.[8] Going due north, the party came to the place of the Benedictus (Luke 1:68–79), before the party ascended the mount and arrived at the site of Christ's ascension (Luke 24:50–1). The site of Christ's Ascension was (and is) a mosque, not a church. A Christian church had been built on the site around AD 390, and this was rebuilt by the Crusaders, where note was taken of the mark of Jesus' miraculous footprints there on a stone, but in 1198 Salah edh-Din claimed the site for two of his followers. One of the footprints was taken to the al-Aqsa mosque, while the other remains. The Mosque of the Ascension is an octagonal structure, with white marble pillars at each corner 'frequented by Christians, possest by Mahometans; yet free to both their devotions' (Plate 7).[9]

That is quite an important point. Mosques could be open to both Jews and Christians for their worship. Jews would visit a mosque for worship at a holy site when they would not set foot in a church (loaded as it tended to be – in the East – with icons and sacra). As long as you took off your shoes and – if you were a woman – covered your head and body, then there was no problem.

Travellers often did not even distinguish between what was a church and a mosque, using the same word 'church', for each. For example, when Timberlake earlier considered the Haram esh-Sharif and Dome of the Rock, from St Stephen's gate, he wrote: 'in that place is a goodley church built of (= by) the Turkes (= Muslims)'.

At the place of the Ascension Timberlake was distracted. He was amazed by the view. This was something he clearly loved: to stand at a height and see for miles and miles. From the top of the Mount of Olives, he could get a view of the city, and see the dry, hilly landscape full of rocks, drizzled with budding olive, almond and fig trees, little villages, and antiquities. In Nathaniel Crouch's edition of Timberlake's account, there is a map, a sketch plan in someone's notebook, from this very point on the Mount of Olives. Perhaps it is Timberlake's, but perhaps not (Figure 10). There are several much more sophisticated, roughly contemporary pictures depicting the city from the same spot, the best one being that of Antonino d'Angioli, drawn with the help of the then Padre Guardiano Francesca della Salandra, dating to the end of the sixteenth century (Figure 11).[10] Many other pictures of Jerusalem at this time drawn by Christians concentrate on Christian monuments, so that these are exaggerated at the expense of the Muslim and domestic buildings. While d'Angioli's picture suffers slightly from the same tendency, it is not nearly so extreme. It even includes a reference to the Jewish quarter, in the south of the city. Though it is not to scale, it provides an excellent overall image of how Jerusalem looked in the early Ottoman period.

Timberlake was thrilled at what he could see. He writes:

> This is the highest parte of the hill. From hence you may see manye notable places: as fyrst west from it you shall see the prospecte of the newe cittye of Jherus[alem], and southwest from it you may see Mounte Sion, which joyneth to newe Jheru[salem], and in the vally betweene Syon and the mount where I stoode I sawe the brooke Cedron, the poole Silo, the garden wherein Christ prayed, and the place where he was betrayed, and mane other notable places which is in this vally of Gethsemena... South from the Mounte I could see the places that [we] came fro[m], Bethania and Bethphage: alsoe east north east from this mounte you may see the ryver Jordane, which is 15 miles of, and Jericho, but it is note so farre, because it is to the westward of Jordan. And fro[m] mounte Olyvett east and southeast lyeth the lake of Sodome and Gomara (= the Dead Sea), which is one 100 miles in length and 8 miles over.[11]

He was clearly elated at being so high, asking questions of the friars, scribbling away on his 'table books', notebooks. Like the good sea-captain he was, he carried his compass with him, and held up his party – geared to the veneration of sacred places – by a much more scientific investigation. 'I sett all these places with the compasse when I was upon mount Olyvett, for I stayed there two howers and did [work] upon the top, havinge alitle compasse aboute me.'[12]

Later on in his account, he returns to the description of what he noted that day
when he had 'a little Compasse about me, to set such places as I could easily come
by', but this is not available in the manuscript, only in the 1603 printed text. He
writes of 'new Jerusalem', because it was explained to him that old Jerusalem was
on the Haram esh-Sharif and Mount Sion, and 'now I finde this newe citie scitu-
ated so farre to the North part, that is almost quite off of mount Sion, but yet not
off mount Moriah'.[13] The city had been exactly in this place since the earthquake
of 1033, when the old walls had been destroyed, and new walls were built in the
southern part of the city along the present alignment, leaving any buildings on
Mount Sion outside.

Timberlake was very interested in the walls and the gates, dangerously interested, in fact, for someone who had recently been accused of spying. He had
noted perhaps already the day before that at St Stephen's gate 'I saw but five
pieces of ordinance there, and they were betweene the gate and the relique of
port Aurea'. The port Aurea, or the Golden Gate, is a gate probably built by the
Caliph 'Abd al-Malik (685–705), but had long been blocked up. From his vantage
point on the Mount of Olives he noted that the city was impregnable to attack
in the east, 'by reason of the edge of the hill which it standeth on, which is five
times as high as the wall'. As he continued, and went around the city as a pilgrim,
he would take note of all the walls, gates and mounted cannon, and in the letter
to his English friends he would include an assessment of the impregnability of
the city of Jerusalem that is unique in a pilgrim account. This is not to say that
Timberlake really was a spy, but he was remarkably and quite unwisely interested
in the subject of military logistics. Perhaps he was led to speculate because of the
stories he had heard about the abuse of Christians in the city. Perhaps he could
not shake off the thought that a Christian recapture of Jerusalem might not be
an altogether bad idea under these circumstances. As he stood on the Mount of
Olives drawing a plan and taking notes, he was clearly not only concerned with
getting a sense of the layout of the city for the sake of a better understanding of
the Bible, but also thinking about the logistics of making an attack to vanquish
the oppressive Turks. He was doing exactly what the Ottoman authorities did not
want him to do, and the friars (and Burrell), waited patiently for two hours.

After all of his investigations, he arrived at a complete assessment, and we get
a detailed piece of Tudor intelligence reporting buried in his letter. It seems that
this passage has been drawn from his notebook, written in Jerusalem:

From the North-east angle of the citie, to the North-west, is the shortest way of the
citie, and from the North-west angle to the South-west, is as farre as from the South-
east to the North-east: but from the South-west to the South-east, which is the fou[r]th
wall that standeth on the foote of mount Sion, I measured, and found it to be 3777.
foote, which is about three-quarters of a mile. Upon this south-side of the citie, is a
great Iron gate, about which gate are laid seaventeene pieces of brasse ordinance: this

gate is as great as the west gate of the Tower of London, and exceeding strong, the walls being very thicke, and on the south-side 50. or 60. foote high: so much for the south wall and side of the citie. The North wall is not altogither so long, but much stronger: for on the Northside it hath beene often surprized, but on the southside never: and on the East side it is impregnable by reason of the edge of the hill which is standeth on, which is five times as high as the wall. On the north side also are 25. pieces of brasse ordinance neere to the gate, which is of Iron also: but what is in other places, as at the corners or angles, I could not come to see, and demaund I durst not. The east wall, containing the gate where saint Stephen was stoned a little without, and to this day called saint Stephens gate: I saw but five pieces of ordinance there, and they were between the gate and the relique of port Aurea, which is to the southward: and concerning the west side of the citie, at the gate whereof I entred at my first arrivall, it is verie strong likewise, and hath fifteene pieces of ordinance lying neere togither, and all of brasse. This gate is also made of Iron, and this West wall is altogither as long as the East wall, but it standeth upon the higher ground: so that comming from the west to the west wall, you can see nothing within the cities but the bare wall; but upon mount Olivet, comming towards the citie from the East, you have a verie goodly prospect of the citie, by reason the citie standeth al on the edge of the hill. To conclude, this citie of Jerusalem is the strongest of all the cities, that I have yet seene in my journey, since I departed from the Grand Cayro: but the rest of the countrey is very easie to be intreated.[14]

As for Burrell, did he ask the enthused Captain Timberlake what on earth he thought he was doing? Did the friars start to get a little uncomfortable, seeing the Englishman observe and take notes carefully, using his compass? The recent accusation that he was a spy rather than a pilgrim seems to have enflamed Timberlake's interests rather than muted them. He was a navigator. He liked measuring, and setting his position. In this case, the measurements and observations he made might have a definite use in England, if ever the Crown turned to thoughts of regaining the Holy Land for Christendom. It was as if he was thinking: 'well, if they think I am a spy, then so be it!'[15]

Eventually Timberlake completed his studies, to his satisfaction, and as the party moved down the hill 'towardes the foote of the hill westward' they came to a place where – according to the friars – 'a woman called Sancta Pelagia did penance in the habite of a fryer'. Timberlake burst out laughing, much to the friar's consternation.

And I laughinge att it they asked me whie I did soe. I answered that to belyve Pelagia was a sainte did not stand in my creede. But they told me when they came home they could shewe me authors for it.

In the 1603 edition, there is the addition: 'but when I came home I had so much to doo, in writing my notes out of my table bookes, that I had no leysure to urge their Authours for S. Pelagia.'[16] Perhaps Archer did not wish to convey the impression that Timberlake had been studying the lives of the saints with Franciscans.

Timberlake and Burrell might have found the story of Pelagia funny because, to begin with, they found friars themselves slightly ridiculous ('fatt fryers'), and then the idea of a woman pretending to be a friar seemed the last straw. Timberlake's image of Pelagia what probably more the image of a comedic dame of the theatre than a holy woman. Penance, in addition, was not something that Protestants did. But it is always illuminating to see what makes people laugh, in different cultures and times.

The cell of Pelagia – who purportedly lived sometime in the fourth century – was already mentioned by a pilgrim from Piacenza in AD 570, and she is described in the important collection, *Lives of the Fathers*, from the same century, which gives biographies of a great many exemplary ascetics. Pelagia was apparently a famous courtesan in Antioch who converted to Christianity and lived a frugal, reclusive life on the Mount of Olives, dressed like a man. No one knew she was a woman until her death. She was buried in a cave south of the site of the Ascension. Or so the story goes. The cell of Pelagia became one of those sites that Muslims, Christians and Jews interpreted differently. Muslims honoured it as the shrine of er-Rabah, and Jews as the shrine of the prophetess Huldah. Three claims, one tiny cave.

After this, according to the manuscript (though Archer in the 1603 edition adds some other places, possibly from another source), they went to 'a church of our Lady, where her sepulcher is', also the tombs of Joseph, Anna, and others. The Tomb of the Virgin, as it is now called, is a Byzantine church right at the foot of the Mount of Olives, close to Gethsemane. You descend down a huge flight of steps to subterranean depths. There is a *mihrab* next to the tomb, showing the direction of Mecca; Mary's tomb is holy to Muslims because, according to tradition, Mohammed saw a light over the tomb of his 'sister Mary' when he was brought to Jerusalem. As mosques could accommodate Christians, churches also could accommodate Muslims.

The church is cruciform, dark and quiet. For a couple of Protestants, however, whose esteem for Mary was not as great as Catholics or Muslims, it appears not to have been that interesting. The friars of the party went into the little square tomb, cut out of the rock and faced with white marble, where inside eighteen lamps, maintained by Christians and Muslims, burned constantly 'and said prayers or masse'. The Englishmen, however, took the experience very lightly. While waiting, they had lunch.

We went to dyn... In this Church is a fountaine of exceedinge fine water, and because we went down as it were into a vault it giveth an exceedinge great eccho.

The poor friars, then, had to concentrate on prayers in the small tomb chapel itself, while hearing the noises of Protestants outside, in the main part of the church, who, after drinking water from the well in front of the Abyssinian altar, were enjoying playing with echoes.

After the friars had completed their prayers, the party then moved off to the adjacent Gethsemane Cave, the site where Judas betrayed Christ, one of the oldest Christian venerated sites of Jerusalem and one of the likeliest to be genuine. They then walked over to the Garden (of Gethsemane), a medieval construction in which there was, and still is, an assemblage of old olive trees (Plate 8).

The group went on to the supposed tombs of Absalom and Jehoshaphat, in the Kidron Valley (Plate 9): two out of three funerary monuments from the first–second centuries BC (now usually called the tombs of Absalom and Zachariah). At the tomb of Absalom Jews and Muslims threw stones to execrate Absalom for his rebellion against David, so that there was a pile of stones in front of it.[17] They followed the route of the River Kidron, which runs between Jerusalem and the Mount of Olives. Timberlake notes that this brook had 'not on drop of water in it', and is a 'ditch' to convey water from the Mount of Olives or Mount Sion when it rained. This characteristic of the Kidron was more interesting to Timberlake than holy sites. He does not comment on the valley's beauty. There are still old olive groves and almond trees. Bright red poppies burst through lush green grass. Birds dip and sing around you.

Timberlake's mind was definitely not focused on holy thoughts with unflagging concentration, but rather – given his notes – the construction of the walls of Jerusalem, high above. When they came to the Pool of Siloam (Plate 11), however, the two Englishman were pleased to get off their donkeys and splash themselves with water, as instructed, in imitation of the blind man whom Jesus heals in John 9:6. Timberlake's record of the Pool does not concern the healing, but only their washing. They were thereafter shown the place where, extra-biblically, the prophet Isaiah was sawn in pieces and close by, 'an exceedinge deepe well, where they said the Jewes did hide the holy fyre[18] in the tyme of Nabuchadnezer'. The friars said this; the friars said that.

But then something happened, unexpected.

They had gone some way south, into the steep valley that in the New Testament is called Gehenna, often used synonymously with 'Hades', or Hell, since it was once the rubbish dump in the city of Jesus' day. As they climbed up the southern side of the valley, they were shown where – traditionally – the apostles hid themselves in a cave after Jesus' arrest.

Then, further up, 'they brought me to the feild or rather the rocke where is the comon buriall for stranngers, bought with 30 peices of silver that Judas hade to betray our Saviour. This place is called Acheldama.'

Aceldama was a great underground vault built by the Crusaders in the twelfth century as a charnel house. Here the bodies of knights and pilgrims were lowered down and left exposed to rot, their remains mixing with the soil of the Holy Land.

This sad structure is in a strange position on the edge of the valley of Hinnom – there is something isolated about it – something a little eerie. The valley is full of trees, as it has been for hundreds of years, and is visually serene. The city of Jerusalem is obscured. It is quiet. Sound from the city above does not reach in, not even traffic. Additionally, the meeting of the deep valleys makes a natural sonic chamber for any little sound within it, and it is funnelled strangely, so that you can suddenly hear someone speaking a long way off, in the village of Silwan, from the wrong direction. You hear the clanging of a stones being broken with a huge axe. Perhaps this effect of sound has always seemed eerie down here, and that is why the association was made between Jesus' betrayer, Judas, and this locality.

In the Gospels, the story is told of Judas' death, that he returned the thirty pieces of silver he had been paid by the chief priests, and hanged himself. The chief priests then bought the field of Aceldama in which to bury strangers (Matt. 27:3–8). The Acts of the Apostles also associates the field with Judas, but more gruesomely. Peter, speaking to the assembly of disciples, states that Judas 'purchased a field with the reward of iniquity; and falling headlong, he burst asunder in the midst, and all his bowels gushed out. And it was known unto all the dwellers at Jerusalem; insomuch as that field is called in their proper tongue, Aceldama, that is to say, the field of blood' (Acts. 1:18–19; *haqel dama,* in Aramaic).

The field of blood. The remains of the Crusader vaulted structure are visible outside the Greek Orthodox monastery of St Onuphrius to this day. It was actually largely cut into the rock on three sides, with the fourth side on the slope constructed out of stone blocks (see Figure 21). Of the superstructure, Timberlake describes it as follows:

> It is made in this manner. There is 3 holes above and one the side there is a vente. Att the uper hole they use to lett downe the bodyes 50 foote deepe.

George Sandys described the building as being flat-topped, with 'certaine little cupolos open in the midst to let down the dead bodies'. You could look through these to see the bottom of the vault covered with bones: 'A greedy grave; and great enough to devoure the dead of a whole Nation. For they say, (and I beleeve it) that the earth thereof within the space of eight and forty houres, will consume the flesh that is laid thereon.'[19]

Timberlake writes:

> In this place I sawe two bodyes that hade bine buried but 4 or 5 dayes before, and lookinge upon them (for where the dead bodyes doe lye it is very light by reason of

the 3 greate holes above) I did take such a scent into my stomacke that I was very sicke, and soe intreated the fryers to returne home into the cittye for that tyme.[20]

Now, anyone can feel extremely nauseated from the sight or smell of something alone, but Timberlake was a ship's captain, who had presumably seen many, many nauseating sights and experienced a large number of unpleasant sickening odours; he was not some closeted, genteel person who walked around with a lavender pouch under his nose. He says himself it was the smell of putrefying flesh that – evocatively – went into his stomach, but perhaps it was more than the smell that hit him.

Other pilgrims looked into the vault as a matter of course without any severe reaction, at least none that they record. The Scottish pilgrim William Lithgow, for example, writes: 'As I looked downe, I beheld a great number of dead corpses; some whereof had white winding sheetes, and newly dead, lying one above another in a lumpe' and that these 'yeelded a pestilent smell, by reason they were not covered with earth, save onely the architecture of a high vault.'[21] The white sheets were knotted at the head and the feet, but would have slowly decomposed along with the bodies they covered.

Seeing the gruesome sight, and smelling the odour, the sea captain was incapacitated. He was 'very sicke'. It was not simply a passing moment of nausea. He entreated the friars to go no further, to return 'home' to the city, to San Salvatore. They led him off, still nauseated, through the Hinnom Valley, away from Aceldama, and stopped at the foot of Mount Sion where he drank the water he had brought in a bottle from Siloam, and rested there an hour – an *hour* – eating a few raisins and olives which they had brought with them from Jerusalem in the morning. This all indicates that he experienced a very strong, powerful reaction when he looked down into the great vault of the charnel house, saw the bones and decaying bodies, and smelt the odour of death.

Not so long ago he and Burrell had happily been making echoes in the Tomb of the Virgin, unworried by the number of burials all around, and here he was retching over thorns, as if the hand of death had reached from below and pulled him down: here, of all places, in Gehenna.

The miserable Biblical associations must have had something to do with it. Perhaps this experience was too close to the horror of his incarceration, which he had tried to push aside by force of reason, and which now jumped out to scare him unexpectedly. Perhaps he was not quite himself yet. He had wanted to be robust, go through with the pilgrim trail of Jerusalem and see the sights, and gather himself together instantly, organise his homeward travel, head back to Egypt, without much of a pause. He could handle this.

But already that day Timberlake and Burrell had walked or ridden on donkeys a long way: out to Bethany, up the Mount of Olives, down through the Kidron Valley, and up the side of Gehenna. Around Jerusalem you are always walking up and down, and it is wearing. Exhausted, you are much more vulnerable emotionally and physically. At some point, you just want to sit down.

From action adventure novels you expect a strong man always to go on, never flagging. But in real life even strong men can crumble, often at unexpected things. We all have a breaking point, and Timberlake had lost two of his children by this time. Death must have stared him in the face in the prison cell. No one likes to think of one's own mortality. So there it was, for Timberlake, with its stench, finality and ugliness. Strong man that he was, he was not immune to the power of death, or the claustrophobic entrapment of it.

After Timberlake had 'rested there and refreshed my selfe' for an hour, the friars, probably equally as baffled as Burrell, took the Englishmen up Mount Sion, towards the site of the former Franciscan headquarters. They showed the visitors where Peter went after he had denied Christ and heard the cock crow three times, and then to a couple of places associated with the Virgin Mary; the house of Caiaphas (Christ's prison), in an Armenian church, which had also the chapel containing the stone which lay on Christ's sepulchre and was the actual place where Peter denied Christ. Then they went to the Cenacle, newly made into a mosque; a place where Christ came to the disciples and Thomas doubted, and the site of death of the Virgin. In other words, they went back on to the pilgrim trail, with the accompanying commentary, and Timberlake could concentrate on taking notes and settling his mind.

The friars then showed the Englishmen a burial ground for European Christians which the Pope bought off the Turks, for 'he will not have them cast into Acheldama'. The burial ground was once attached to the Franciscan monastery on Mount Sion, but now existed independently. Timberlake writes: 'they [the friars] told us that yeare last past theire were buryed in this place 5 Englishmen'.[22]

Five Englishmen buried in Jerusalem? Fynes Moryson, who visited Jerusalem in 1596, pretending to be Catholic, tells a similar tale. Indeed, Timberlake must have misheard. It was not the year before that the deaths of the visitors took place, but six years before, in 1595, and Moryson is the one who tells the whole story, though it may not all be true.

When Moryson and his brother stayed in the same hospice in the San Salvatore monastery in 1596 they noted the names of English and Flemish pilgrims recorded together in the graffiti on the wall. He writes: 'we beheld upon the wall in the chamber where we were lodged, the names written of Henry Bacon, and Andrew Verseline (two English Gentlemen), of Abraham Serwenterb Frederichson, and Henry Vonwildt, Peterson Von Narden (two Flemmings), whose names were written there upon the fourteenth of August, 1595'. These four, coming together to Jerusalem, stayed in the Monastery, and, after seeing the sights of the city, went to Bethlehem. On the way, the Flemish visitors drank the health of the King of Spain, which the English refused to do with them, and the ensuing argument developed into a physical fight, so that the Flemish visitors returned to Jerusalem badly wounded. Apparently, according to Moryson, it was customary for the friars in Jerusalem to ask the sick first to make confession and take communion prior to a physician being called or medicine administered. At any rate, the Franciscans asked for confession and communion in this particular instance, but since the wounded men refused it became clear that 'they were of the reformed Religion, (whom they terme heretikes)'. Moryson claims the friars then neglected to heal them. The two Englishmen likewise eventually returned, and one of them, Verseline, soon died. Within eight days the Flemish men had also died. Moryson lists 'poison' as one of the possible causes of their deaths, given that the friars 'have one of their order, who is skilfull in physicke, and hath a chamber furnished with cooling waters, sirops, and other medicines most fit for that Countrey'. Bacon died soon after, having promised a young friar his armbands of gold, and the friars – according to this tale – secretly buried him in the monastery so that the armbands went to their coffers rather than to the Ottoman authorities, who claimed all the possessions of any visitor who died in their domains.[23]

This story of Moryson's probably has some truth to it, but it is overlaid with anti-Catholic rumination. I have to wonder who told the tale. It could not have been one of the friars, for the order comes out so badly. It must have been someone else. Timberlake reports that his guides pointed out the graves of five Englishmen, and Moryson has two English and two Flemish, noting their names on the wall. I would opt for Moryson's testimony, based on the graffiti, except that I think he recorded the names wrongly, and made two names out of an original five Flemish. He has 'Henry Vonwilt, Peterson Von Narden' as a single name, when it could possibly have been 'Henry Vonwilt' and, secondly, 'Peter Von Narden', misread. As for the story told to Timberlake and Burrell of 'five Englishmen', the difference between the Flemish and the English may not have been very great to the latest batch of Italian friars, and so they mentioned five English. I have no doubt that the tale about the gold armbands and the burial in the monastery to secure their seizure is bogus. It sounds exactly the kind of story that led the authorities to try to find illicit burials within the monastery grounds, and Timberlake's guides indicate that all five were in fact buried on Mount Sion, Protestant or not. The fight between the Flemish and the English on account of a toast to the health of the King of Spain – well, I cannot think of anything much more absurd than angry fisticuffs on the road to or from Bethlehem on this account, but it does at least serve to show the strong feelings involved. The tourists would have been accompanied by friars and an interpreter, who would have been able to report the incident. It is such a bizarre and disreputable story for everyone concerned that it seems quite possibly, at core, true. No one comes out of this looking good.

The deaths of five men in the space of about a week, who have all eaten the same food, might not in fact be tremendously mysterious. Food-poisoning was usually not intentional. According to Moryson, he did not eat with the Franciscans in the refectory as a rule, but ate the 'mutton, hennes and sallets, and good wine'[24] separately. Visitors could therefore partake of a meal that the friars did not eat, and we are talking about meals prepared without any fridges or understanding of basic hygiene.

Interestingly, by the time of George Sandys' visit in 1611, the story had changed a little. Sandys, coming with his party to the same burial ground on Mount Sion, noted that it contained the remains of six Englishmen who killed their translator.[25] So much for benign pilgrims.

They went on. At this point in his account, Timberlake makes a mistake and writes about the House of Annas, as if it was located outside the city walls, on Mount Sion, but it was actually inside. This mistake is unlike him and suggests that he was still not feeling completely well. The party first had to go through Sion Gate. Perhaps Timberlake was at this point scribbling in margins in his notebook, and wrote things fully later out of order.

Timberlake was interested in the gate. He and Burrell got off their donkeys and 'I noted it very well, for now I hade seene three of the gates.' He wanted to see the north gate, so the Friars took him all the way to Damascus Gate through the city. Gates and walls are, of course, extremely important for a dossier of espionage.

From Sion Gate they went through the Armenian quarter, stopping firstly at the aforementioned House of Annas, 'where is nothing but to old wales to be seene and an old olyve tree joyninge to one of the wales'. These older walls were built into a church called the Church of the Angels, belonging to the Armenian Orthodox, built of stone and earth.[26] Here the friars pointed out an olive tree at the side of one of the walls to which Christ was tied. Timberlake and Burrell queried this, to which the friars replied that when Christ was brought into Annas' house, the priest was asleep and his servants would not wake him, so they tied Jesus to an olive tree and, when Annas woke up, he was brought in to be examined (Figure 13). Here there was a stone that apparently would have cried out if the people had not shouted 'Hosanna' when Jesus came riding on a donkey into the city.

Timberlake's party then proceeded to the Church of St Thomas (actually a mosque), and then followed present St James' Street to the small and ancient Syrian Orthodox Church of St Mark. From here they followed quiet streets around towards the Pool of the Patriarch, in order to avoid some of the hurly-burly of the market, but crossing present David Street was unavoidable, where they would have encountered sellers and visitors to the city entering via Jaffa Gate. The party proceeded up Christian Quarter Road to the House of Zebedee, the father of the apostles James and John. The story went that Zebedee, a Galilean fisherman, used to sell his fish right here in the city. This House of Zebedee was a mosque in 1601, but it was originally a fifth-century church dedicated to John the Baptist. Today it is famous for being the oldest surviving church in Jerusalem, restored to the Greek Orthodox.

Timberlake and his group probably had fairly quick visits to these churches at this time, as they kept pressing on up Christian Quarter Road, past the Baths of the Patriarch on the right, and came into the courtyard of the Church of the Holy Sepulchre, a familiar place to Timberlake. They went through a doorway and climbed up steps in darkness, following a cord hanging along the wall, until they reached the rooftops of the Church of the Holy Sepulchre, specifically to a place then occupied by the Abyssinians (Ethiopians). They paid two pieces of silver, and were shown the place where Abraham would have sacrificed his son Isaac. This was a rival site to the Haram esh-Sharif, or Mount Moriah.

Returning to the courtyard, they saw the prison of Peter and John, which were cells in the same prison in which Timberlake was incarcerated. In the picture drawn by Antonino d'Angioli that appears in Amico's book (Figure 11), it is identified as no. 61: 'Carcere di Turchi', Turkish prison. It seems to be on the west side of the courtyard here.

The Dutch pilgrim Rauwolf wrote that he came to 'an old heathenish prison' in the court of the Church of the Holy Sepulchre, 'wherein are prisoners kept to this day'.[27] Henry Maundrell noted in 1697 that the prison where St. Peter was apparently incarcerated was close to the Church of the Holy Sepulchre 'and still serves for its primitive use'.[28] Timberlake was incarcerated in the same complex Christians believed was used for St Peter, and he notes: 'we came to the prison where Sainte Peter was... which was the next doore to the prison where I was'.[29]

After this, Timberlake and Burrell were taken to Damascus Gate (Plate 12), where the Captain made further observations. Then, 'havinge well veywed this gate we went directly home, beinge very late and this was my 3 [rd] dayes worke in and about Jheru[salem], beinge very weary with often alightinge to pray, for at every of the said severall places we alighted and said the Lords prayer one our knees.'

Back at the monastery, Timberlake's thoughts must have now turned to his homeward journey. While John Burrell was under no time constraints, Timberlake had travelled to Jerusalem with the clock ticking, with the chance his men might mutiny if he was away too long, and Waldred might give up hope of his return if he was delayed. The journey had taken much longer than he had anticipated, and he had effectively lost a day by being in prison. Al-Fessi could have confirmed a possibility of the fast-track to Egypt: you hired racing camels at Gaza to speed over the sands for four days. In theory, at least, that was what you might do, if you dared. You might not survive.

Al-Fessi seems to have promised to stay with Henry Timberlake until he was safely back at the residence of Benjamin Bishop in Cairo. It would be his return journey also. He would no longer go on to Damascus and Baghdad, because it was his goal now to protect the English Captain. As for Burrell, he was clearly not so sure about returning with Timberlake and his loyal Moroccan companion. Perhaps racing camels were not quite his cup of tea. A return to Cairo was, for him, unnecessary.

15

Bethlehem

Early in the morning of 28 March 1601, Henry Timberlake left Jerusalem, with his group of minders, and took the road southwards to the village of Bethlehem, about six miles from Jerusalem, where an outpost of Franciscans was stationed at the ancient Church of the Nativity. John Burrell seems not to have been present. Timberlake mentions himself and his eight minders only.[1] Burrell is not referred to in the description of his visit at all. He does not indicate any reason for Burrell's absence, or mention it explicitly. It may have been illness, or a kind of malaise that can strike even the hardiest traveller at times. Underlying it, Burrell was surely anxious. He was in Jerusalem with a fellow Englishman who wanted to tear back to Grand Cairo in record speed on a racing camel, and he had no reason to do so himself. Not everyone was as robust and hopeful as Henry Timberlake, and perhaps Burrell himself felt he could not rely on the Captain after the incident in Aceldama.

The way to Bethlehem was a patchwork of grass, trees, flowers and rocks. Vineyards created a striped green rug in the limestone landscape. There were cereal crops, fig and olive orchards, and small turrets where people could stop, climb, and check the road ahead for thieves.[2] As in the case of the pilgrim circuit around and in Jerusalem, so here: pilgrims did not go far without holy places to venerate. The road to Bethlehem was dotted with sites for prayer, to keep minds focused on the sacred stories, both biblical and legendary (see Figure 14). The party left the city via Jaffa Gate, and stopped at the House of Uriah and then the fountain where Bathsheba washed herself when King David saw her and lusted. This was the enormous Sultan's Pool, probably the Serpent's Pool of the first century AD. They then went to the church at the site from which the prophet Habakkuk was, in one extra-biblical legend, conveyed by an angel to Babylon, to meet Daniel in the lion's den. Certain visitors exploded with scepticism at this point. For example, William Biddulph wrote of the place: 'but they might do well first to prove that there *was* such a thing done, before they demonstrate the place *where* it was done'.[3]

They then went to the even less credible place where the Wise Men found the star 'when it was lost', located next to a cistern. This story did rely on a fairly antiquated model of the universe. Legend held that the star fell down and got itself temporarily buried underground. Fynes Moryson, hearing this, in fact, laughed out loud. He writes: 'they shew upon the right hand, a hole in the highest roofe of the Church, by which they say the starre that conducted the Wise-men, fell from above into the bowels of the earth. Can he forbeare laughter who considers the bignes of the starres, yea, even of Comets, as some write that was, specially finding no mention of this falling of the starre to be made in the holy scriptures?'[4]

It was then a short walk further to the spot where the Virgin Mary, again extra-biblically, rested herself near a well, under a terebinth (turpentine tree), and the very tree 'they do still repayre, by setting one other close to the roote of it', writes Timberlake. The place was known as the Kathisma, *Bir al Qadismou* in Arabic, and there had once been a church on the spot dating to the fifth century, now ruined.

The next stop was outside the House of Elias (= Elijah). They were shown the exact place the prophet slept on a rock on the road in front of the main entrance to the monastery. Here, a helpful monk, emerging keenly, usually recited the tale of how Elias fainted with weariness after fleeing from wicked Jezebel., and was sustained by an angel of the Lord who brought him bread and water. Payment for such pious information was always made. More interesting to Timberlake was the fact that 'this house standeth one ahill, soe that from it I did see Bethlem afarre of'.[5] The monastery of St Elias (or *Mar Elias*) first built in the fifth century and rebuilt in the twelfth, is located on a plateau with a view of both Jerusalem and Bethlehem, and sometimes you can glimpse the Dead Sea. Timberlake, the ship's Captain, always appreciated lookouts: places from which he could gaze far into the distance. He would have peered back on the route they had taken, and over towards the little town of Bethlehem, with its great Byzantine church standing proudly in the centre.

From *Mar Elias* they went to the patriarch Jacob's House, where there was the nearby dome of Rachel's Tomb (*Qoubbet-Rahil*), an ancient site kept by Muslims that had been rebuilt by the Crusaders, and again quite recently by Mohammed, Pasha of Jerusalem, in 1560. In general, such Muslim shrines were completely open to Jews and Christians for prayer.

The road then divided into three. The one straight ahead was the road to Hebron. The party took the right-hand road, which led them about two miles on to a town called Bethsula (Beit Jala),[6] whose inhabitants were 'all Christians', a place surrounded by luxuriant vineyards and olive groves. Nearby, the party was shown the field where the Assyrian ruler Sennacherib camped when he besieged Jerusalem. They then backtracked to the fork of roads, and took the left-hand pathway eastwards to the verdant field near Beit Sahour where the shepherds heard good tidings of great joy from the angel (*Siyar al-Ghanam*), where there were the ruins of an ancient church and monastery. Other pilgrims record that here the Bedouin-origin 'Arabs' of Beit Sahour would see Franks coming, ride over to the field, and usually demand some payment.[7]

Finally, after all these mnemonic devices that enabled the party to remember Scripture, the party came to Bethlehem proper, a two-hilled village largely made up of Greek Orthodox Palestinians, with some Armenians and Catholics also. Like Beit Jala, Bethlehem was surrounded by vineyards and olive groves. At the main square loomed the great walls of the Franciscan and Greek Orthodox monasteries and enclosure of the Church of the Nativity. Just over a hundred years earlier the whole town of Bethlehem had been protected by a wall, moat and towers, but the Mamluk sultan had ordered them demolished in 1489, and now it was frighteningly exposed to marauding Bedouin and Ottoman sipahis and janissaries.

Timberlake says that there were about ten friars in the Franciscan monastery attached to the Church of the Nativity, 'which welcomed me very kindlye'. Kind friars, now. Had Timberlake softened? These words are very different in tone to those he employed when writing about the Padre Guardiano in Jerusalem, whom he claimed was personally responsible for his imprisonment, or the 'fatt fryers' who had washed his feet. Somehow, in the two days Timberlake had spent in the monastery of San Salvatore in Jerusalem, he had become open to the possibility of a kindly welcome from friars.

Timberlake says nothing of any other Christian community at the Church but the Latins, the Franciscans, though actually it was divided between the Greek Orthodox and the Catholics. John Rawdon in 1607 wrote that 'at the upper end of it is the praying place of the Graeks, on each side of which is a paer of stayers to go downe into the cratche'[8], which means that the Greeks held the main altar, as they do now. The few Friars Minor of Bethlehem were an outpost of the main centre in San Salvatore, Jerusalem. They concentrated on trying to preserve the sacred grotto, monastery and church, given the terrible abuses of the Ottoman janissaries. The great Byzantine edifice had been first constructed in the fourth century by order of the Emperor Constantine, and remade by the Emperor Justinian in 531. It was a sacrosanct locality to both Christians and Muslims, and the friars were open to all visitors. They also worked hard to educate local Christian boys, by teaching them Italian (which the locals called Frank),[9] in the hope that they could serve visiting pilgrims as guides, and encouraging local crafts, mainly woodwork using inlaid mother-of-pearl. The local craftsmen were at this time just beginning to make the detailed wooden models of the Church of the Holy Sepulchre in Jerusalem that would become famous in years to come. There was also a tattooing tradition: Christian pilgrims could have Crusader crosses, and other symbols, tattooed on their arms.

One of the most remarkable things about the Church of the Nativity in Bethlehem is that Muslims were welcomed. The Franciscans would greet, guide and feed all visitors, regardless of their religion. For example, the great Sufi spiritual master, Sheikh 'Abd al-Ghani al-Nabulsi (so named because his ancestors came from Nablus), and his companions were given great hospitality by the friars when they visited in 1693. They were served dinner and stayed in Bethlehem for one night. Al-Nabulsi mentions how impressed he was by the friars' organ-playing.[10] Al-Nabulsi later wrote in one of his many treatises that non-Muslims might also go to Heaven, not just Muslims alone, for God's capacity for forgiveness was so great. With such an ecumenical assertion, he provided an example of religious openness and tolerance. Perhaps it was the friars of Bethlehem that so impressed him. The friars maintained the Byzantine entrance to the sacred grotto in which Christ's crib once lay (they believed), and used an alternative route through the monastery area, 'out of love for the Moslems',[11] so they would not have to be offended by the imagery of the main church.

It was common for Muslims to go to the Grotto of the Nativity and say prayers. The leading Muslim clerics from Jerusalem led a mass pilgrimage to the site every year.[12] To each Muslim the Christians would provide a plate of food, an oil lamp, firewood, and fodder for his animals.[13] Local Muslims and Christians, Catholics and Greek Orthodox, shared the Church of the Nativity in the sixteenth and seventeenth centuries. It might not have been easy, but it was done. Periodically, harmonious relations were overturned by the few who wanted total control over the church, usually prompted by changes in the established order. Before al-Nabulsi's visit, for example, the Greek Orthodox succeeded in gaining Ottoman permission to make renovations to the roof, and they then wanted to deny Muslims the right to use the main aisles and nave as a kind of *khan* where they could rest and make coffee during their pilgrimages, stating it could only be used for prayers. Muslims reacted to this eviction by claiming the site was a prayer house and retreat for Muslims and should be considered an Islamic sacred site. The Ottoman government, however, did not support the Muslim practice of venerating the place of the Prophet 'Issa's birth, which was also linked with the Prophet Mohammed's night journey. They told Muslims to keep away. In this matter, and in many others, the Ottoman view was different from the views prevailing in their conquered territory.[14] In time, the Ottoman discouragement of Muslim veneration of the Grotto of the Nativity led to most Muslims abandoning traditions of pilgrimage there.

Any move by one community to claim more than is customary, even today, makes other communities in the Church feel intensely hurt and abused. It is a little like the Church has several ardent lovers, each competing with each other, and in fact the only absolutely perfect solution for each one would be exclusivity. Somehow, still, the lovers co-exist, each performing the roles they have been allocated, in the spaces and times they are permitted, looking suspiciously at one another, and sometimes managing to shunt their opponents away.

Certain local Ottoman authorities seemed to have looked to the Church of the Nativity with some ambivalence, and – despite local Muslim veneration – they tended to see it as a resource for exploitation. One story goes that in 1596, an Ottoman official came to Bethlehem and, during dinner, asked for wine. The official knew that Christians regularly drank wine – a white variety – and there were vineyards in the area that had been permitted by a special dispensation, at great cost to the Franciscans. The previous Ottoman governor had, apparently, not only collected 100 gold pieces for the permission, but had requisitioned the entire product, and consumed it with his friends. The new Pasha of Jerusalem, rectifying this error, had specifically decreed that the friars were not allowed to give any wine to Muslims – for whom alcohol is forbidden – without his written order. The friars then duly refused to serve wine to the official.

This official, furious at their behaviour, threw dog excrement into the salad, when the friars had withdrawn from the room, and then called them back in an outrage, stating he had been given fouled salad to eat. He then ordered the imprisonment of five friars, and other local Christians who served the convent, and threatened to have them all hanged for the insult. A messenger was quickly despatched by the friars to alert the Pasha, who responded promptly to his official's over-reaction by sending a janissary to release the prisoners. The friars then had to pay the authorities for the inconvenience.[15]

Such a story illustrates the feelings between the Franciscans and the Ottoman authorities. The friars were upset at the Ottoman officials not only because some of them were coming to Bethlehem ostensibly to 'make inspections' when the actual reason was to get blind drunk, but also because they were of stripping off the lead roofing. This lead roofing had been donated to the church by Edward IV of England when the roof was restored in 1480. Ottoman janissaries wanted the lead to make bullets for their harquebus rifles, and tore off strips, leaving areas of the church very vulnerable to the weather. The friars there were also pressured (by beatings) into giving the janissaries sugar loaves and white candles, and huge amounts of money.[16]

The Ottoman authorities could also make money by playing off the Latins and the Greeks against each other, so much so that both the Franciscans and the Greek Orthodox at different times formally lodged complaints that Ottoman officials were inciting the two parties to move in on each other's possessions with the intention of gaining profits from the resulting conflicts.[17] In addition, any repairs done to churches had to be approved by the Ottoman authorities. A repair of a small breach carved by burglars in the façade of the Church of the Nativity ended up costing a fortune because of the payments for a lengthy process of survey, inspection, and report, before any work was carried out.[18]

In Timberlake's day a thick exterior wall ran through today's Manger Square. Timberlake would have gone through the gateway, tied up his donkey or mule, and then strode forward, past the Armenian monastery on his right, towards the sad little entranceway to the main Church, straight ahead. The actual doorway is tiny.

There were once three massive Byzantine entrances, but they were blocked up by the Crusaders, who designed a smaller arched doorway in the centre, and then this was itself reduced to a tiny one to prevent the janissaries or 'wild Arabs' from carrying off large items, and so that their 'horses may not enter the church' (Plate 13).[19] You bend over, mind your head, and enter a vestibule that makes you think you have accidentally walked into an old barn; the Byzantine narthex was subdivided long ago into different rooms with a low wooden ceiling. You then go through another small wooden door and enter a dark space, where the plain whitewashed walls make you think more of a Puritan assembly hall than a Byzantine basilica.

Once, long before Timberlake, pilgrims coming to the church were awed at the splendour: the gold, the sparkling white marble floors, the mosaics, the precious furnishings, the roof. But visitors coming to the church around 1601 were mostly struck by its poverty: this 'Church is left for the most part desolate, the Altars naked, no Lamps maintained, no Service celebrated,' wrote Sandys.[20] It was a decayed, shabby shadow of its former self, defended by a small group of friars and Greek Orthodox priests who did not have the resources to mend things. Four rows of elegant Corinthian columns over 18ft high, were, and still are, a reminder of what it once was like. The pink limestone columns were decorated with strange medieval encaustic paintings of ascetic saints. The fine cedar roof was impressive, and there were high glass windows, through which birds could find entry through smashed panes. There were twelfth-century mosaics around the walls, above the columns, and between the windows. Some were defaced, others missing, but there were still a number intact, and the friars told a story that a Mamluk sultan of Egypt had once tried to prise the mosaics off to remove them to his palace in Cairo, when a monstrous serpent issued from the wall and broke up anything that was taken.[21] Perhaps that story slightly discouraged future looters from wholesale pillage. The floor, missing most of its marble, was reconstituted by a kind of material made of potsherds mixed with plaster.

The janissaries shot at the figures in the rich mosaics that decorated the interior.[22] It is ironic to think that the beautiful nave mosaics, dating to the twelfth century and sparkling with gold and glass, were shattered by bullets made from the lead of the very roof. In destroying the images, the Ottoman janissaries here could appeal to Muslim law, which forbade the representation of the human form in decorative art. Soldiers also took away precious white marble flagstones that remained, and the alabaster and marble of the wall decoration, in order to further beautify the buildings of the Haram esh-Sharif.

Timberlake mentions no trouble with Ottoman authorities on the day he and his party visited, nor does he mention other pilgrims – Christian or Muslim. He does not describe much of what he saw, but the appearance of the Church of the Nativity and the adjoining monasteries is well recorded by others.

Timberlake was ushered forwards, past the altar, to a doorway with semi-circular steps made of red marble, leading down. At the bottom of the steps were

1. Dovecotes
in Alexandria.

2. Rocky hills.
View from
the Pools of
Solomon.

3. The Old
City of
Jerusalem from
the Mount of
Olives.

Left: 4. The Dome of the Rock, from the middle window of the old Qibla 'Iwwa.

Below: 5. The old courtyard of San Salvatore monastery with Father Athanasius Macora.

Above left: 6. View from the Haram
esh-Sharif to the Mount of Olives.

Above right: 7. The Dome of the Rock.

Right: 8. The Mosque of the Ascension.

Above: 9. The Garden of Gethsemane.

Below: 10. The Kidron Valley.

Right: 11. The Pool of Siloam.

Below: 12. Damascus Gate.

13. The doorway to the Church of the Nativity, Bethlehem.

14. The Church of the Holy Sepulchre entrance.

18. Houses in Titchfield, Hampshire.

19. St Peter's Church, Titchfield.

elegantly-wrought bronze doors, which let light in to the vault below. It is at this point that Timberlake stopped and wondered, but not at anything holy.

He writes: '[the friars] brought me into agreat church, and then into a greate entry, where I sawe the name of Mr. Hugo Stapers twice sett downe one above another'.[23] An Englishman!

He was so excited by seeing the name of another Englishman scratched twice on the stones around this entrance that 'there I sett my name'. Hugo Stapers, additionally, was possibly a son of Richard Staper(s), a principal director of the Levant Company. The friars did not stop his defacement, because writing graffiti was a common pilgrim practice, and it does not seem to have been frowned on. His name scratched on the marble would have shown up white when it was fresh, and as time went by it has blended into a thousand other names on the stone, and cannot now be seen with the naked eye.

This was not the only graffito left by Timberlake in the Church. After he had gone down the stairs into the vault where Christ was said to have been born – to see the manger where he was laid, the site of the gift-giving by wise men, the natural marble which miraculously depicted St Jerome, and also various subterranean tombs – he was led upwards, not only to the main church but high, to the roof. In fact, Amico writes that pilgrims were taken to the roof by a stairway marked '30' on his plan of the Christian buildings of Bethlehem where 'under the arch formed by [the roof] there is a balcony with seats and a square of stone where often the Fathers with the pilgrims on their return from visiting the surrounding places used to take their meals.[24] Timberlake writes: 'Going up to the top of the Church, I saw upon the leads the name of M. Hugo Stapers againe ingraven, which made mee looke the earnestlier for some other Englishmens names: but finding none, I carved downe my name and came away'. Timberlake was far more excited to find the name of an Englishman than he was to see the nativity grotto.[25]

Timberlake 'came away and dined with the Friers', probably then in the dining hall next to the kitchens, located on the upper storey of the monastery. The dinner proceeded according to the tripartite division that was normal in Jerusalem: with the reading of the Golden Legend, followed by silent eating, followed by talking.[26] Perhaps Timberlake was allowed to walk in the Franciscan monastery gardens, one of which was planted with orange trees and surrounded by vines, and another was full of different trees, especially pomegranates.[27]

After dinner Timberlake was led down a rocky path to the Milk Grotto, so called because this was where, allegedly, the Virgin Mary hid herself when the angel warned the holy family to go to Egypt, to save them from Herod's massacre of the innocents. The story goes that while she was nursing the infant Jesus in the cave, a few drops of milk spilt on the ground, turning formerly red limestone to white, and ever afterwards the stones have a miraculous power. Both Christians and Muslims believed that if you took stones from the cave, washed and pulverised them, added the powder to water and gave this mixture to nursing mothers (or animals) to drink, it would greatly increase the supply of milk.[28]

Just out of Bethlehem they were given another chance to say the Lord's Prayer, this time the well of David (cf. 2 Sam. 23:15–17). The party returned to Jerusalem at 4 o'clock in the afternoon. Timberlake liked to record times.

As Timberlake made his pilgrimages, where was al-Fessi? I have already mentioned that I think Burrell was not present on this day. Was al-Fessi there? He is not explicitly mentioned either. But if Bethlehem was remembered as the birthplace of the Prophet 'Issa, and visited by Muslims at the time, he could have been, following his own devotions. More importantly, if he felt it was his job to protect Henry Timberlake, and not leave him alone in a strange land, as he had vowed to do, then surely he would have accompanied him wherever he could. Should we see Timberlake's journeys around the holy places taking place with al-Fessi somehow observing, on guard, perhaps with a small group he had assembled, perhaps solitary, trailing behind the party of friars (who must have wondered what on earth was going on)? Since Timberlake did not trust the friars in general, al-Fessi's presence would have made for extra security. Maybe.

But there was one place that al-Fessi would not have gone.

When Timberlake returned to San Salvatore, word came that he and Burrell would be permitted entry to the 'Temple of the Sepulchre', the Church of the Holy Sepulchre, upon payment of nine pieces of gold to the Ottoman authorities. It was here they would spend the night. No Muslim would enter this place.

16

The Temple of the Sepulchre

The Church of the Holy Sepulchre in Jerusalem includes within it the traditional location of Jesus' crucifixion at Golgotha and his entombment in a garden. It was here that the Roman Emperor Constantine constructed a magnificent basilica in the fourth century AD, to commemorate the place where his mother, the Empress Helena, claimed to have found the 'True Cross' – the very wood of the cross Christ was crucified upon – and the location of Golgotha. The adjacent tomb – which was more important to the Jerusalem church – was soon afterwards enshrined in a huge circular building known as the Anastasis. Both these glorious Christian edifices were torn down by the Fatimid Caliph Hakim in 1009. Under the Byzantine Emperor Constantine Monomachus a rotunda was built around the tomb in 1048, utilising what could be retrieved from the ancient structures. Then the Crusaders, when they took Jerusalem in 1099, built a brand new edifice to adjoin it, designed by the architect Maître Jourdain, so that it formed one ecclesiastical building. This church was consecrated on 15 July 1149. What existed in 1601, as today, was basically the same church, with modifications, and was popularly known as the Temple of Christ's Sepulchre.

The most common reaction of people now coming into this building is slight confusion. You might expect Chartres, but instead you find yourself facing a wall (around the choir) hung with religious paintings, with a rectangular stone in front of it on which are many pendulous lamps. This is the 'Stone of Unction', where Christ was traditionally anointed after his death. From there you wander to your right in a circle around a series of small chapels, on different levels, all in a mishmash of different decorative styles, so that it is very hard to get a sense of the whole.

Late in the afternoon Timberlake and Burrell walked in to the grey, austere church, with its wide Crusader pillars and draftiness. A huge circular aperture in the centre of the high rotunda let in air, which in winter and on spring nights is cold.

The Ottoman authorities did not allow anyone to open the door to the Church of the Holy Sepulchre unless visitors paid them the money required for entry, so that there were always local Christians inside who had been shut up for days, sometimes weeks, pilgrim traffic being more of a dribble than a torrent. Word always soon spread that the door was to be opened, and pilgrims stood with a throng of local Christians ready to enter the church, especially clergy who were to relieve those who had officiated inside without a break. The careful control of Christian access to the Church of the Holy Sepulchre dated back to Salah edh-Din, who had entrusted a Muslim family of Jerusalem with the keys to the building. Muslims, as noted above, respected almost all the places associated with Jesus – Prophet 'Issa – except this one, and Christian veneration of this (in their view, bogus) holy place was an allowance. That they permitted Christians to continue worshipping here, even though it offended their religious sensibilities, was out of a certain mix of accommodation and avarice. Christians had to pay. The price was 4.5 gold pieces for the Greek Orthodox, and nine gold coins for Franks. Nine gold coins was an exorbitant fee. The rate of exchange for such coins (the Turkish sultani = the Venetian zecchino = the Spanish ducat, more or less) was between 6s 8d and 9s,[1] let us say 8 shillings, which meant that the entry was £3 12s. A servant in Elizabethan England could earn £4 a year.[2]

Already as they paid their money at the doorway, and left their usual party of minders, Timberlake had asked the Muslim gatekeepers – who usually arranged themselves extravagantly on a stand by the entrance covered with carpets and cushions[3] – why there was a kind of 'great hole, whereat a little child may easily creepe in' through the door, and was told that 'the hole served to give victuals at, for them which lie within the Church'. He states that the number of people living inside the Church was 300, men and women, who could not get out or in except when a pilgrim enters 'which happeneth not sometimes in 14. daies'. Because people actually lived in the Church they 'have there their whole housholds, and boorded lodgings there builded for them'. There were around 100 strings hanging down at the entrance doorway, connected to bells in the lodgings of people encamped in the Church, and when servants or family members came with food, they would ring the right bell, and the lodger would come to collect the food passed through the hole.[4] There were latrines for men and women. It was a cross between a church and a khan.[5]

Inside this place Western visitors found themselves locked into a strange world, where they had to come face to face with all the varieties of Christianity that existed in the world. For Western pilgrims, accustomed to the simple animosity between Catholics and Protestants, they were suddenly hit by the recognition of ancient, seemingly weird forms of the Christian religion that tended to relativise their battle. It is common for European visitors then to take note of all the different sects, and Timberlake does so briefly himself. He lists them in order of their numbers within as (1) 'Romaines', the Catholics; (2) Greeks; (3) Armenians, who he says have their services in Arabic; (4) Nestorians, likewise Arabic-speaking and 'slaves to the Turke'; (5) Abyssinians, 'people of the land of Prester John', namely

Ethiopians; (6) 'Jacobines' – Syrian Jacobites – 'who are circumcised Christians, but slaves likewise & servants to the Turke'. There were also Georgians, Syrian Maronites, Copts, and at Easter time – presumably Orthodox Easter – up to 1,000 people would be lodged in the locked Church.[6]

The men were easily distinguished from one another by the particular garments of the clergy, and by the turbans of the laity. In Turkish lands, with religion indicated by the colour of a man's turban, it was easy to see who was who: the Nestorians had peach turbans; Armenians wore blue; the Greek Orthodox, Maronites and Syrians had white with blue bits. They all had their own spaces, 'and by-roomes for ease... continually there lying, & praying after their manner', writes Timberlake.

Each had their own place for services, and their routes for processions, which proceeded, in one place or another, for hours. Arabic, Syriac, Coptic, Greek, Latin, Armenian, Georgian, Ethiopic... all the different languages of diverse liturgies wafted around this structure as in the tower of Babel, each chanted loudly to emphasise their presence to the others. Western Christians, observing the passing of strangely clad dark-skinned Christians of faraway places, sometimes found it hard to even think of some of these sects as Christian at all. Rauwolf, after noting how the Syrians spoke Arabic and dressed in rough goat-hair coats and tunics, with high shoes, derided them for becoming too Turkish and, with all his prejudice blazing, noted: 'If a Christian hath to deal with them, and desireth to buy something of them, either Opium, Scammony, or any other the like drug, which they commonly falsify, he must look to himself as if he had to deal with Jews.'[7] The drug-trafficker complains about the dealers. Fynes Moryson considered them 'poore rascall people, mingled with the scumme of divers Nations, partly Arabians, partly Moores, partly the basest inhabitants of the neighbour countries'.[8] The feelings were mutual. As the Englishman Bodington would say: 'These Religious People bear little respect one to another, speaking very basely of each other.'[9]

The record of firmans shows how the Ottoman authorities constantly shifted in favour of one religious community to the next, but generally they favoured the Greek Orthodox, since most Christians in their domains belonged to this denomination and the Greek Orthodox were the oldest Christian denomination in the region. The Latins (Catholics) and Ethiopians were small Christian groups in Jerusalem whose main bases were outside the Empire. The Copts were allowed to build a chapel behind the Tomb of Christ in 1537. An upper gallery was taken from the Latins and given to the Armenians, who were also Christians of the Ottoman empire. The Franciscans were naturally aggrieved at the loss, while the other communities vied to impress the Sultan for further favours, often with generous gifts. Ottoman policy tended to be the maintenance of a certain detachment about the Christian holy places, but this policy was interrupted at times by decisions to bend to local Muslim pressure or the lobbying of one Christian group.[10]

The Sultan Suleiman the Magnificent, as we have seen, drove the friars out of Mount Sion in 1551. Another thirty-two years after Timberlake's visit, the Franciscans were dispossessed of the Grotto of the Nativity in Bethlehem, which was given to the Greeks. They also lost the Rock of Calvary, and the Stone of Unction. The sites were returned to them two years later, to be lost again two years after that, returned to them in 1690, lost partly in 1757, and so on. As the Grand Vizier of the Sublime Porte would coolly announce in 1759: 'These places belong to the Sultan... and he gives them to whomever he wishes. They might have been always in the hands of the Franks, but today his highness wants them to belong to the Greeks.'[11]

Timberlake and Burrell were given a guided tour of the sacred buildings by the Franciscans, who would have used the opportunity themselves to relieve those on duty and bring in supplies. The tour was designed so that visiting Catholic pilgrims could collect all the indulgences attached to each place in order. It was itself a procession: a ceremonial walk. The friars dressed in surplices, and the visitors were issued with books of Latin hymns to sing. This was the friars' chance to have Latin – the language of Western Christianity – ring loudly around this shrine, resounding in the ears of the Greeks, Copts, Ethiopians and others. The leading friar held a great silver cross in front, with two men at each side swinging incense pots. The processors followed behind with pilgrims holding candles and friars flaming torches.[12]

At each altar there was the need to say the Lord's Prayer and Ave Maria. Catholic pilgrims would have the opportunity to touch rosary beads and other artefacts to the actual sites, and a formulaic explanation of each site would be given. For this reason, as in the case of all the holy places, pilgrims invariably repeat the same information in their accounts. The locations may be seen on Amico's plan (as printed here in Figure 16 from the book in Essex University library, with interesting scribbled additions by an Italian who knew the work of Francisco Quaresmio from 1639), which is the most accurate for this period. From Timberlake's listing of places, it seems that he and Burrell were taken around on the standard route of prayer stops. They began in Our Lady's Chapel, belonging to the Franks, where there was (from Amico) A. the Column of the Flagellation. They went then to B. (Christ's Prison); C. where soldiers divided Christ's garment; D. where the True Cross was found by Helena; E. the Chapel of St Helena; F. a piece of column where Christ was crowned by thorns ('which I could not see,' says Timberlake, 'til I was glad to give the Abashenes that kept it two pieces of silver'); G. the place where Christ was fixed to the cross; H. the site where the cross was raised, and where the rock was rent at his crucifixion; I. the Stone of Unction, where the three Marys anointed Christ after he was dead; K. the Chapel of the Angel, where he appeared to Mary Magdalene; and L. the holy sepulchre itself, Christ's tomb 'which is the last place where they use any prayers'. The guides may also have noted in passing that the Turks had stolen items from this site, just as they had from the church in Bethlehem.[13] It was covered over with alabaster panelling, and apparently belonged to the Franks.[14]

After this tour, Timberlake and Burrell were free to wander around or sit still, following their own interests, watching other processions and rituals at various different altars.

As always, Timberlake was remarkably unimpressed in terms of personal piety, and was moved with wonder at things other pilgrims tended to pass over. For example, given that the cleft in the Rock of Calvary is pointed out to him, he makes a point of examining the feature with great interest, and comments:

> The Rocke that rent at his crucifying... is a thing well worth the beholding for it is slitte, like as it had bin cleft with wedges and beetles, even from the top to the two third partes downward, as it were through the brow and breast of the Rocke: nor is the rent small, but so great in some places, that a man might easily hide himselfe in it, and so groweth downeward lesse and lesse.[15]

There is something rather poignant about this observation, for the indications from archaeological excavations in the church undertaken from the 1960s onwards is that this part of ancient Jerusalem was in fact originally a quarry, one in which people would have indeed used wedges and beetles (= heavy hammers). But the cleft in the rock at the side of the rocky protrusion identified as 'Calvary' was the reason it was left jutting upwards from the excavated stone all around: it was useless because of this imperfection.

Timberlake loved measuring things. He was one of the most intrepid measurers ever to visit Jerusalem. While other pilgrims spent their hours in prayer and contemplation, Timberlake was busily beavering around counting his steps and making compass-readings. From the point he had finished praying at the sepulchre of Jesus he went first to see the tombs of the Crusaders, King Baldwin and Godfrey de Boullion, located alongside the chapel of Calvary (12 on Amico's map, though now no longer, because the tombs were destroyed as an anti-Catholic act by the Greek Orthodox in the nineteenth century). Then, 'returning thence backe to the Sepulcher, I measured the distance between place and place, spending thus the time from five of the clocke before night when I went in, untill the next day at eleven of the clocke at my coming foorth, writing downe all things which I thought note-worthie'.[16]

Timberlake notes that the area of Calvary – the area of the Church of the Holy Sepulchre – was once outside the city, but now inside, which is confirmed by modern studies. Looking at the Rock of Calvary, he states that it is 'not so high as to be called a mount, but rather a pyked or aspyring Rocke: for I noated the scituation of it, both when I was at the toppe of it, and when I came to the Sepulcher'. He is absolutely right. It is more like a finger of rock jutting out from the surrounding levels. He paced out the distance between the Rock of Calvary and the Edicule, with compass in hand, and came to the conclusion that the tomb was 173 feet westward. Indeed, that is not a bad guess, though a little exaggerated. The distance from the top of the Rock of Calvary to the bench where Jesus' body lay in the Tomb is about 144.5 feet.

Timberlake busied himself also in the actual sepulchre itself, stating that the bench was 2.5ft from the ground, 8ft in length, and 3ft 9 ins broad, 'being covered with a faire stone of white colour'. He measured the vestibule of the Tomb, known as the Chapel of the Angel, and noted its dimensions, and went on to measure everywhere else as well, concluding that it was '422. fadomes about', and 'the one side of it likewise I found to be 130. fadomes'. A fathom is six feet.

Now there was something to take the attention of clerics away from processions and chanting: an English measurer. What must they have thought, to see this fair-faced foreigner pacing out distances – one, two, three, four – and scribbling in his note-book details of heights, lengths, directions, widths? What must Burrell have thought?

Timberlake was also glowing with national pride as he went about his tasks. He considered the Church a result of an English initiative. Rather than ascribe it to the Byzantines and the Crusaders, he states that it was 'builded by the fore-remembred Queene Helena, mother to Constantine the Great, shee being (as I have read in some Authors) an English woman, and daughter to king Coell, that builded Colchester'. An Englishwoman! To think that Christianity's most sacred shrine was the work of England.

The English town of Colchester is to this very day proud of its link with Helena, Constantine's mother and finder of the True Cross. King Cole – allegedly – gave the town its name 'Cole-chester', and is indeed the man of the nursery rhyme. Old King Cole was a legendary 'merry old soul,' who liked to be entertained by fiddlers. The imposing Colchester town hall has a statue of St Helena built into it. This association came about as the result of a medieval English story, but everything else we know about Helena points to her being far from royal in origin and far from England. The real Helena was no princess. Bishop Ambrose of Milan noted once that Christ had raised Helena 'from dung to power'; she was in fact a *stabularia*, a girl working in an inn or stable, and the she more likely came from Bithynia, in what is now northern Turkey.[17] For Timberlake, issues of the reliability and antiquity of historical evidence were not of great concern; he trusted English tradition. He had proudly noted elsewhere when friars had mentioned St Helena. But, to his dismay, here, when he suggested Helena's English provenance to the friars, Timberlake had no luck: 'being urged to them, they denied it'. You can feel Timberlake's indignation. He urged. They denied.

Timberlake continued all night long with measurements and notes, as he would have written up navigational notes on the stars in his ship as he went into unknown waters. His was a scientific mind.

Perhaps during his investigations in the Church Timberlake, like Fynes Moryson before him, was shown a spot in the Greek chancel identified as 'the centre of the world', the *omphalos*. Moryson, also having a scientific mind, just had to state his case:

> I... objected, that the earth is round, and that in a Globe the center is in the middest, all centers in the outside being but imaginarie, and to be placed wheresoever the measurer will. Also that in measuring (after their manner) the outside of the earth, Palestina was farre distant from the Equinocticall line, which divideth the World into equall parts. And if Palestina were just under that line, yet that all the countries having the same Meridian, should be the middest of the World, as well as Palestina.[18]

There was Moryson, bursting with science, reciting this logic to the baffled faces of the Greek Orthodox priests, with the help of a struggling interpreter. He might as well not have bothered. The Renaissance had not yet reached Jerusalem. The priests replied that David had said in a Psalm (74:12), 'in the midst of the world I will work their salvation', to which Moryson replied, logically, that the verse didn't mean the 'middle', as in 'centre', but meant 'in the sight of the World, so as none should be able to denie it'. At this point, according to Moryson, the Greek Orthodox 'grew angry, and said, that the Scripture must be believed, in spite of all Cosmographers and Philosophers'. That was the end of the discussion. It was probably best to leave it, given the underlying animosities between Greeks and Latins. An argument on whether there was actually a 'centre of the world' could easily have ended in a brawl.

17

The Englishmen
of Aleppo

Timberlake and Burrell left the Church of the Holy Sepulchre at about
11 o' clock on the morning of 29 March 1601 and returned to the mon-
astery of San Salvatore for dinner (lunch). They might have felt some concern.
There would be new arrivals to meet, or perhaps they would have to sit with
Jesuits. But then news came that would turn things around. The news was that five
Englishmen had arrived at the gate: merchants coming from the city of Aleppo.

Fathers Angelo and Aurelio of the Franciscan order were sent out to meet the
visitors, who had done the right thing in requesting the sponsorship of the Padre
Guardiano. The two friars greeted them warmly by kissing their hands, and told
them of Timberlake and Burrell's presence in the monastery.

Fellow Englishmen! That was extraordinary. The English, in 1601, were far from
being a world power. Despite their pride, England was only one area of a small
island and the English had colonised only Wales and Cornwall, with occasional
forays into France. While they were intrepid sea-voyagers and merchants, as well
as pirates and raiders, they were still quite contained, and very few people outside
their borders spoke their language.

The chances were that at least some of this party had heard of Captain Henry
Timberlake already. His ship was sailed for the Levant Company. Captains were
well known anyway. How surprised they must have been, however, to find him
here rather than at a port, or in Cairo.

The party from Aleppo were searched at Jaffa Gate, as expected, and gave
up their weapons to the janissaries of the Citadel. They were then searched
again outside the monastery, very thoroughly. The guards looked in every bag
to check for gunpowder, which goes to show how worried they were about
incoming Christians. Finally, they were allowed to enter San Salvatore, where not
only Francesco Manerba welcomed them, but also Timberlake and Burrell, just
returned from the Holy Sepulchre.

Timberlake and Burrell would have been told of the Englishmen's arrival by the
messenger who came from the gate to summon a Franciscan welcome. They must

have been absolutely dumbfounded. The chances of Englishmen from Aleppo – a Levant Company agency – arriving at the same time as them in Jerusalem were slight, and here they were!

The Englishmen from Aleppo received a welcome from the Padre Guardiano very different from that offered to Henry Timberlake. They were led to a room where they were given supper, with the friars serving them cordially. The Englishmen could talk together in their language. There was no mention of a ceremony in which candles would be held and feet washed and kissed. There was no reticence on the part of these Englishmen to stay in the monastery, and there was no hostility on the part of the friars. It is all very strange, a sudden shifting of attitude, just a few days after Timberlake and Burrell arrived.

And how do we know all this? Because one of the Englishmen – William Biddulph – wrote about it.

Biddulph wrote a letter to his friend (and relation?) Bezaliell Biddulph after staying for some time in Jerusalem and experiencing the Catholic Easter celebrations in the city, for which a number of new European pilgrims arrived. Given that these visitors would be returning to Europe, he gave them the letter, and it eventually made its way to the intended recipient in England. This letter and others found their way into Purchas' compendium in 1625. Before then Biddulph's correspondence had another fate.

Like Timberlake's letter, Biddulph's letter from Jerusalem ended up in print, though it was very heavily edited. As Nathaniel Crouch – Timberlake's later publisher – hid behind the pseudonym of 'Robert/Richard Burton', so the publisher William Aspley may have hidden behind a pseudonym: 'Theophilus Lavender'. Biddulph's letter would appear in one of his books, entitled 'The Travels of certaine Englishmen into Africa, Asia, Troy, Bythinia, Thracia and to the Blacke Sea and into Syria, Cilicia, Pisidia, Mesopotamia, Damascus, Canaan, Galile, Samaria, Judea, Palestina, Jerusalem, Jericho and to the Red Sea and sundry other places, begunne in the yeere of Jubile 1600 and by some of them finished this yeere 1608, the others not yet returned'. The title (not exactly snappy, but designed to prick the interest of those intrigued by certain areas of the East) advertised the book as being, 'Very profitable for the helpe of Travellers and no lesse delightfull to all persons who take pleasure to heare of the Manners, Governement, Religion and customes of Forraine and Heathen Countries'.

The plural 'some of them' and 'others' in the title, in reference to the letters 'Lavender' has drawn on, corroborates his own admission that 'Lavender' blended in anything useful into his chopped-and-changed Biddulph source material. William Biddulph is not even indicated as the author of the work on the title page.

Lavender notes in his introduction:

The fourth and last letter [in this collection] was written from Jerusalem, wherein he maketh relation of his travell by Land, together with foure other Englishmen, from the

City of Aleppo in Syria comagena, to Jerusalem, by the Sea of Galile or Tyberias, and Lake of Genezareth, and so throw the whole Land of Canaan, which way was never travelled by any Englishman before, neither possibly can be travelled againe at this day, in regard of the turbulent and troublesome estate of those Countries, which is like every day to grow worse rather than better. And this may serve partly for a Confirmation of M. Henry Tymberley his voyage from Grand Cairo in Egypt... to Jerusalem, performed the selfe same yeere, and at the selfe same time, for all of them met together at Jerusalem.'[1]

At any rate, this was all in the future. The two as yet unpublished English authors, Timberlake and Biddulph, met in Jerusalem in the spring of 1601 without any prescience of their future publishing splashes. Biddulph, Preacher to the Company of English Merchants resident in Aleppo, was accompanied by four of the staff: Master Jeffrey Kirbie, Merchant; Master Edward Abbot; Merchant; Master John Elkin, gentleman, and Jasper Tyon, Jeweller.[2] Timberlake may have known Tyon by reputation as being a bit of a thug who had assaulted the ill-liked John Sanderson in Constantinople a few years earlier.[3] Tyon's attitude may well also have been one who had seen it all before, for he had already been to Jerusalem, when Fynes and Henry Moryson visited in 1596.[4]

The names of the Aleppo party given by Biddulph are exactly those given by Henry Timberlake, though he sometimes spells them differently, and gives more details, for example, Edward Abbot, we learn from him, was 'servaunt to the right Worshipfull Sir John Spencer'; Kirbie was 'servaunt to the worshipfull M. Paule Banning' and they were both 'liegers for them in Alepo'. 'Servant' here means agent or assistant. He mentions that the last named were 'two other young men', which implies that the group was made up mostly of young men.[5]

Rather interestingly, Timberlake writes that the Englishmen came to the 'house' of San Salvatore 'hearing of my being there'. Maybe they told him that. Perhaps he thought that the fact that he was staying would reassure them that they could themselves live at the monastery without fear, though they were carrying letters from illustrious merchants at Aleppo and clearly intended to stay at San Salvatore all along. Timberlake is pleased that they can validate his presence in Jerusalem, in case anyone doubts he ever went there:

> These (though they sawe not mine imprisonment, nor were with me at the sight of those things in and about Jerusalem) can witnesse that they were acquainted there-with at the gates [with my name], and testifie the other truthes beside.

William Biddulph had taught at Oxford before ending up as the preacher at Aleppo, and was a rather strange-looking personage with a very long beard, a 'spare leane man' with the 'weake body', wrote Lavender in his introduction.[6] He and his party had not decided to come to Jerusalem out of a great desire to see the holy places, but because they were in a fix.

Aleppo was struck by the plague, and corresponding famine, and was no place for foreigners to stay, if they could help it. They were told it would not lift until the sun entered the constellation Leo in July. Therefore, arrangements were made for their departure. They obtained letters of recommendation from Clarissimo Imo, the Venetian consul, and others from leading Italian merchants, asking for 'our kinde usage there, with liberty of conscience'. They clearly had good relations with the Catholic merchants of the city, hence the letters of introduction, which seem to have made all the difference to the Franciscans.

Over food and drink in San Salvatore monastery the Aleppo party, who were good-humoured and full of jokes, told Timberlake and Burrell of their journey. Coincidentally, on the very day Timberlake and Burrell left Cairo, 9 March 1600, Biddulph and his company had left Aleppo on horseback, well supplied and accompanied by janissaries, as well as other English, Italian and French merchants who rode with them for some miles' distance. Their party included not only themselves and hired janissaries but servants and a cook, apparently all on horseback.

This group of Levant Company factors had many tales to tell of their own journey (Figure 17), for example of a Syrian village named Lacmine, deserted and derelict, because the inhabitants – fearing the Ottoman janissaries of Damascus – had fled to the hills. The Turks 'used to take from them, not onely victuals for themselves, and provender for their horses without money, but whatsoever things els they found in their houses.' The Englishmen found a 'church' (mosque) in which they were allowed to shelter, upon payment of a little money, and eat. They walked about, and saw the poor villagers gathering 'Mallows and three-leafed grass', which they boiled for food. The travellers gave them bread, which they were very happy about, saying 'they had not seene any bread the space of many moneths'. This relates to what the Palestinians south of Jerusalem said to al-Fessi, that they did not have bread. There was some problem.

Despite the human hardship the jokey Englishmen made a pun on the name of the town – Lacmine – saying it was not just 'Lack-men' but 'Lack-money' too.

Then there was their story of Tyaba, where no one would give them a place to lodge, so that their chief janissary Byram Bashaw stormed into a house, and offered to pull out man, woman and child so that they could stay there. Biddulph writes: 'When we saw the pittifull lamentation they made, we intreated our Janizarie either to perswade them for money, or to let them alone.'

Or there was the story of a shared house of worship: in an old Christian town called Charrah there was an ancient church of St Nicholas, where both the Christians and the Muslims prayed, the Christians on one side and the 'Turkes' on the other.

The Englishmen told the story of a funny incident at Quneitra where they went for a stroll up and down the market streets, as Englishmen are wont to do, until a local asked them why they kept walking around and not sitting still.

Where were they wanting to go? They replied they were walking around 'for our pleasure'. To which their questioner replied it was a greater pleasure to sit still that walk up and down when you didn't need to. Crazy foreigners!

They too had had their brush with highwaymen. As they were coming down the pass from the Golan Heights, they were stalled by men Biddulph calls 'Turkes and Arabs', who faced them 'with Maces of Iron and other weapons' and demanded 'tole money' before they were allowed to pass. They gave them what they asked, but the caravan of Christians behind them fared worse.

The party also did something surprising: they visited the village of Safad where there was, as Biddulph would write, 'a Universitie of the Jewes, where they speake Hebrew, and have their Synagogue there' on a high hill with three tops, one part being inhabited by Jews, and the other two by 'Turks' (Muslims). They met there Jews they knew from Aleppo as merchants, who had come to Safed to spend their old age. He writes: 'The Jewes have here more libertie then in any part of the Holy Land. They dare not come to Jerusalem, for feare lest the Christians there dwelling, stone them.' He also notes how Muslim men departed from the town for Mecca while they were visiting, and they saw 'many women playing with Timbrels, as they went along the street' who 'made a yelling or shriking noise as though they cryed'. They asked them (through an interpreter?) what they were doing, and were told that 'they mourned for the departure of their Husbands, who were gone that morning on Pilgrimage to Mecha, and they feared that they should never see them againe, because it was a long way and dangerous, and many died there every yeere.' So must al-Fessi's wife or wives have mourned his departure.

Then there was their humorous tale of Mount Tabor. They had come to a place called 'I-nel Tyger' (Ayyun at-Tujjar), translated as the 'Merchant's Eye', just beside Mount Tabor, the highest hill in Galilee. The party took Ali, one of their janissaries, and a group of the villagers, he calls 'Arabs', to go up the mountain with them. They ascended partly on horseback, and then on foot. The party proved themselves to be not particularly fit for this undertaking, much to the amusement of the locals, who tried to spur them on. One of the Englishmen cried, melodramatically, 'For the love of God let us returne, for I can goe no further; Oh, I shall die, I shall die!' This unfit specimen is kindly not identified by Biddulph in his account, but since Tabor is only 1,960ft high the inability to climb up it seems slightly feeble. At any rate, one of the more sprightly members of the party shouted back, 'Come cheerefully, I am on the top'.

So much laughter. The Englishmen together were more than merry. Perhaps they could laugh even at their tale of what happened next.

On 25 March, which the Englishmen counted to be the first day of 1601, they journeyed through pleasant fields, where fat cattle grazed in the Jezreel Valley, to Jenin, 'a very pleasant place, having fine Gardens, and Orchards, and waters about it'. They arrived in Jenin on the day that Henry Timberlake and his party arrived

in Jerusalem, and while Timberlake went through total misery, the Englishmen
from Aleppo enjoyed a pleasant recuperation in this lovely village. On 26 March
they remained in Jenin, for this was the day that Ramadan had ended: the beginning of the Idh al-Fitr.

On 27 March they continued southwards, and were halted by men who
claimed tribute to let them pass. They paid a certain amount and rode off, but
these men pursued them with bows and arrows and other weapons. One of the
janissaries, Fatolla, had a musket, and was ready to fire it, except that another
janissary saw that the men with bows and arrows had also got messengers ready
to ride off 'to raise up the whole rabblement thereabout upon us'. They then paid
all the money the men demanded, asking that they no longer pursued them, to
which their leader replied: 'God forbid, God forbid, we should do you any harme,
if you pay us what we demand.'

Perhaps someone could have defended the justice of the 'theeves'. They considered certain lands to be theirs, and that if people wanted to walk through their
lands they should pay a toll. This was very common in cities, and the Ottomans
charged a toll themselves on the road from Egypt. To walk through an area without paying a toll was, for the travellers, a good thing, but these men who stopped
travellers thought otherwise. They would have seen it as their income. It was
their territory, and therefore they were due payment if anyone entered it. They
were 'theeves' to the travellers because the travellers did not recognise they had
any right to the payment, while the Turks were considered the legitimate owners of the land and could charge customs duties or whatever by right. In terms
of the justice system at play here, if anyone did not pay the toll they would be
beaten until they did. If they flatly refused they might be killed. Harsh. But it
was not simple robbery, for the so-called 'theeves' in this area did not abscond
with whatever they could lay their hands on in terms of booty, or strike to make
a raid.

The Ottoman authorities had in fact appeased powerful local nomadic tribes
by giving them administrative and fiscal responsibilities as tax collectors. The
Ottomans had sought to limit the power of the Druze, an independent eth-
nic and religious group who live to this day in what is now northern Galilee
and southern Lebanon, led at the end of the sixteenth century by a chieftain
named Fakhr al-Din. The Ottomans had supported a Bedouin leader named
Mansur, who was given authority over a large area in return for subduing the
Druze, but they had executed him in 1594, and backed Fakhr al-Din's son in the
region of Sidon, Beirut and the Beqa` valley. The region where Biddulph and
his party were chased by toll-chargers was in fact officially under the authority
of Bedouin: Lajjun was governed by Tarabay ibn Ali, until his death sometime
in 1601. So no wonder they wanted the duty. The villages of the region had to
pay protection fees to the Bedouin, and the Ottomans had on-again off-again
relations with the sheikhs, at one point recognising and co-opting them (as

sanjakbeys of certain regions and guardians of roads), and at other times out-lawing them.[7] So that partly explains the complexities recorded by European travellers.

Timberlake had to make up his own mind about their story. He was told also that when Biddulph's party entered a wood further on there seem to have been different kinds of people, more the classic highwaymen who killed people reck-lessly. They 'tooke away both a man and Horse from the Caravan which followed after; and a woman also riding on an Asse with their carriage'. The party charged their pistols, and they fired warning shots, a strategy that seems to have worked, for they were not attacked. At night time they came to the city of Nablus, next to Mount Gerizim, and drank from Jacob's Well. They slept in a khan, but discovered in the morning that they had had some things stolen.

The next day, 29 March, they took to the road again, and met now Ottoman soldiers 'who knowing our Janizarie, and other Turkes in our Companie, let us passe by them quietly'. They themselves may have charged money to let them pass. Biddulph's journey seems to be a kind of slalom ski course in which they had to swerve past every possible kind of thieving hazard in the entire region: Arabs, Ottomans, Bedouin, miscellaneous highwaymen, you name it.

At this point Timberlake and Burrell must have told their own story of attack in the desert. Perhaps they did not over-do the terror. Drama and near escape always looks so much less hazardous in hindsight. But then there was the trauma of Timberlake's incarceration. That could not have been told with amusement.

Yet somehow I think this group must have followed it with wit and black humour that would take everyone's minds away from reality. They were a group who liked to have a laugh, especially at the expense of Jesuits. When they them-selves later encountered the stern Jesuit Father Benedictus at San Salvatore they did not argue with him, but rather they joked about him behind his back in dit-ties, and noted that, even though he was called 'Benedictus', a name that might be translated 'Well-speak', he could 'neither *benedicere* nor *benefacere*, 'neither say well, nor doe well, by any that were not of their sect and sort', and that he should not be called 'Benedictus' but 'Maledictus'. They quipped:

Audi, tace, lege, benedic, benefac, Benedice
Aut hac perverte, maledic, malefac, Maledicte

Literally:

Listen, be silent, read, well-speak, well-do, Benedictus,
Or here pervert (them), bad-speak, bad-do, Maledictus

'Maledictio' is 'abuse, revile'. Biddulph made up a rhyming English version:

'O Benedict, heare, hold thy peace,
Doe well, say well (O Scorner)
Else let thy name be Maledict,
Perverting all the former.'

Then there was the Jesuit they laughed about in the pilgrim party behind them who would not pay a robber. He was 'shrewdley beaten with iron maces'. The Jesuit 'counted it meritorious, in that he suffered such misery in so holy a voyage'. This man, battered and bruised, would also, in due course, turn up at San Salvatore in Jerusalem, where one from his order (Benedictus?) would commend him and say 'that he merited much to sustaine such travell and labour, and be at so great cost and charges, and suffer so many stripes for Christs sake'. Biddulph, sarcastic, would comment: 'but I know, had it not beene more for love of his purse then for love of Christ, he might have escaped without stripes'. So we get an image of the wise-cracking Englishmen, quick to pull to shreds any Jesuits that they encountered. They seem less prone to be defensive and offended than many other Protestants, given their good relations with Catholic merchants in Aleppo, but they did make the Jesuits figures of fun. Cruel humour.

As for Biddulph, he was not quite the paragon of virtue as an English preacher that one might initially expect. Biddulph would be caught with his trousers down, literally, in a compromising situation with a lady on the island of Zante. Biddulph was a man who liked wine and women, the classic irreverent reverend, and something of a gossip-monger. He could stir up trouble, and did, later on, in terms of the Levant Company consul who replaced Henry Lello in Constantinople, Thomas Glover.[8] A post in Aleppo, or anywhere else far away from Protestant eyes, could be a licence to do anything you would not dare do at home, and it was likely that much of the tittle-tattle about debauchery was quite true.

Though perhaps Timberlake could size up his compatriots very quickly. Their mode was not quite his mode. Their frivolity was not his humour exactly. He could take them for what they were: a familiar type of expatriates, clearly a better sort than Bishop in Cairo.

Timberlake would also have noted the reaction of Burrell to the newcomers, which was positive. With their arrival, another option had now presented itself to his travelling companion. Burrell, whose courage was not the courage of Timberlake. He could choose to stay with the larger, richer party of Englishmen of Aleppo, with their janissaries, cook and servants, and journey with them back to Syria, or elsewhere in Palestine. He clearly did not have a pressing timetable, and could choose where to go, and when. They opened up a different world, one in which he did not have to rely on a Captain prone to take notes of a somewhat incriminating nature – if anyone could translate them – and a mysterious Moor who seemed oddly attached to him. Burrell was in no hurry to return to Cairo, after all, he could press forwards into new areas. This footloose and open-minded attitude fits with an identity of Burrell as a kind of scholarly backpacker, ready to look for new experiences and new fields of knowledge.

As he looked at Burrell during the stories that were told, perhaps Timberlake realised that there would be no chance of Burrell returning with him to Egypt now. Their paths would split. The Englishmen from Aleppo were just exactly Burrell's perfect travelling companions: generally young, intelligent, witty and moneyed. Timberlake may have wished that they might all decide to go on to see Cairo, and travel back with him, but that was not mooted. Their destination was Jerusalem, and that would be enough. Timberlake alone would strike out across the desert again, with only his Moor for company. As he smiled and lifted his glass to toast their safe arrival, he surely felt a pang of loss.

But he would still have relished the moment. It was a relief simply to speak his native language. The Englishmen, in their excitement, could speak loudly, laugh strong. Confident of being understood by no one else, they could ridicule the Ottoman janissaries and parody the Jesuits. They were working for the same firm as Timberlake, and had the same interests in trade and the world. The room was a capsule of London. They could relax.

Now let us return to the welcome given by Francesco Manerba to the Aleppo Englishmen. In that greeting in the courtyard, with Timberlake and Burrell smiling by his side, Manerba had been cordial and open. He welcomed them and let them alone to be Englishmen together, taking them to a chamber where they were served food by the friars alone. It was as if the Padre Guardiano was bending over backwards to be accommodating. There was no ceremony of candles and feet-washing, no kissing of feet and singing, no sermon to them kneeling before an altar. Just as Timberlake appears to have softened when it came to the friars of Bethlehem, the Custos appears to have softened when it came to the new Englishmen. He did not make them jump through the hoop he had made Timberlake and Burrell jump through. They were completely exempt.

Was it the letters from the powerful Catholic merchants in Aleppo that had swayed him, or their accompanying gifts? Or was it some change of heart in the Custos, as he had observed Timberlake and Burrell? He could stand back, detached, and look at the dynamics between the visiting Jesuits and the Protestants, and think. And, in the background, he knew that the Sanjakbey was alert to any disruption brewing among the Christian visitors who came to the city, ready to pounce on them if they transgressed. They had no idea how dangerous his position was, how vulnerable they were, how delicate this was.

However, Biddulph did not think particularly generously of the Padre Guardiano's welcome. He put it down entirely to the fact that Francesco Manerba would not cross his benefactors in Aleppo, and warned that any Protestant traveller should not think of coming to Jerusalem without letters of recommendation and a lot of money, or else they would have to 'partake with [Papists] in their idolatrous services'. Perhaps he got this impression from what Jasper Tyon had warned, given the pretence to Catholicism of the Moryson brothers he had accompanied earlier. Tyon himself must have pretended to be a Catholic before. But he may also have suspected that Timberlake and Burrell had participated in practices and rituals that they should not have done, even despite their protestations. Biddulph noted that the Greek Orthodox were too poor to have non-Greek Orthodox guests. Furthermore, despite the granting of liberty of conscience and the fact that the friars were 'very kind and curteous to strangers in all things' Biddulph suspected cynically that this was just a cunning ploy 'to seduce them from their Faith, and to winne them to the Church of Rome'. Therefore, 'this kindnesse and libertie of conscience, which wee found amongst them, wee imputed not so much to the men, as to our owne money'. Biddulph was snide and ungrateful, while conceding Manerba's kindness and his acceptance of their liberty of conscience – this at a time when Catholics and Protestants in general could not accept such liberty at all, anywhere in Europe. Biddulph comes across as a meanspirited and cold.

The monastery of San Salvatore preserves to this day a register book from the period Timberlake and Burrell visited. The pages are quite white – well-preserved – and only the constellations of bookworm holes really indicate the antiquity of the volume (Figure 15). On the date of Timberlake's emergence from the Holy Sepulchre, 8 April 1601, Gregorian calendar, their names are recorded:

Henricus Timberlare de Anglia, Ereticus
Joannes Boreel de Anglia Socius dicti Henrici[9]

Henry Timblerlare of England, heretic;
John Boreel of England, friend of the said Henry.

Heretic. Apart from the diplomatic Padre Guardiano, the friars were not quite comfortable about Henry Timberlake. The friar responsible for writing in the names of pilgrims in the record book kept by the monastery of San Salvatore in Jerusalem ensured that Timberlake was preserved in the book with a damning label reserved for Protestants. You can imagine the friar sitting there, with quill in hand, hearing the loud laughter of the Englishmen in the background and their incomprensible tongue, writing in the two names with some consternation.

It is nevertheless another example of independent testimony to Timberlake's presence in Jerusalem at this time, and it tells us also something of the Franciscans' attitude. When it came to recording the names of the other Englishmen: 'Godifredus Kerbiius, Joannes Elchinus, Gulielmus Bidellius, Gaspar Cianus, Eduardus Abbati', they were noted simply as 'an Englishman', 'Anglus', or 'from England', 'de Anglia'. Timberlake is the one who was given the label 'heretic'.

But then, he was also the one who had made the most trouble, and he had not finished making it.

18

A Missing Journey

Henry Timberlake may have been one of those people who really do not need much sleep. This would have been very helpful to a sea captain: a man who should always be alert. It is useful as a traveller.

It seems that on the night of 29 March 1601, by English reckoning, he did not sleep much at all. It is easy to imagine him staying up talking to Biddulph and the others, with his note-book in hand, asking them details of what they saw on their trip for his own information. Later in his account it is clear that he used their information for what he writes of distances in Galilee: 'These places last specy-fyed beinge att Samaria I was not in but the other fyve Englishmen that were in Jherus. comminge through Gallile came through them and of them I have these descriptions, and like wise they receyved of me the description of my jornye threw Palestina'.[1] But there was something else he was up to that night, some-thing he had arranged perhaps with al-Fessi. He does not write directly about it in his account, but it is clearly there.

Towards the end of Henry Timberlake's letter to his friends in England, some-thing goes wrong. From the moment that the Englishmen of Aleppo arrive the orderly description of what took place, in chronological sequence, is interrupted, and then an entire day is skipped over. It is as if the narrative expresses an inter-ruption and disorder in Timberlake's mind, and then he hides something.

He hides what he did on Monday 30 March. Timberlake did not leave Jerusalem just immediately after the Englishmen from Aleppo arrived. Their arrival was on Sunday 29 March. He left on Tuesday 31 March. He had a missing day, left unrecorded.

It would be perfectly understandable if, during this day, he took it easy, pre-pared himself, bought in provisions, spent some time with William Biddulph, and so on. However, his account contains an anomaly that can only be satisfacto-rily explained by giving him an extremely energetic Monday, consisting of an extraordinary excursion.

The evidence as to what he did is found in an aside, not as part of the chrono-logical narrative. Before he left, he writes, he received two patent letters, one sealed with the Padre Guardiano's own seal, stating that he had visited the holy places, and a second patent: 'that did showe that I did wash in the Ryver Jordan'.[2]

Nowhere in Timberlake's narrative account does he explicitly describe his journey to the Jordan River to wash in the water.

But he did go to the Jordan River, and to the Dead Sea. When Timberlake lists places he had gone to and their distances in relation to English towns, he also mentions Quarranto, where Jesus spent forty days and forty nights, the River Jordan, Jericho, and the Lake of Sodom and Gomorrah (the Dead Sea): Quarranta 'is from Jheru. as Chelmesford is from London'; the 'Ryver Jordan is from Jheru. the nearest parte of it as Eppinge is from London'; 'Jhericho, the plaine of it, is where it is nerest from Jheru. as Lowton halle Robert Wroths house is from London' and the 'Lake of Sodom and Gomora, is from Jheru. as Gravesend is from London'.[3] He even writes of the bitumen found on the Dead Sea 'wherof I brought some part from thence'. He has brought bitumen from the Dead Sea.

In other words, on 30 March 1601 Timberlake raced down to the Dead Sea, the River Jordan, Quarantia, and back to Jerusalem in time to depart from there on March 31.

The scenario needs to be reconstructed out of these fragments. The gates of the city of Jerusalem were locked and bolted at sunset and reopened at dawn; in early April in Jerusalem the sun rises around 5.30 in the morning. Timberlake would have been ready, as would horses. He simply could not have done the trip on mules or on donkey in the time parameters. It is about twenty-eight miles from Jerusalem to the site of Jesus' baptism in the River Jordan. It was an extremely dangerous route. The Ottomans officially held the region of Palestine as part of their territory, but the land of the southern Jordan Valley was in reality held by the Bedouin, who guarded access.

The Custos was not in favour of any pilgrim under his care going independently to the Jordan River. From all other accounts the Padre Guardiano of the Franciscans sternly warned travellers against the journey. As Fynes Moryson writes:

> The Friers our guides seriously protested, that if any living thing were cast into this Lake of Sodom, it could not be made to sinke... We had a great desire to see these places, but were discouraged from that attempt, by the feare of the Arabians and the Moores: for they inhabite all these Territories. And I said before, that the Arabians, howsoever subject to the Turk, yet exercise continuall robberies with all libertie and impunitie, the Turkes being not able to restraine them.[4]

Did Timberlake do it on the sly? Was that why he was loath to describe his actions? If so, how could he have engineered it?

Perhap by plotting, with al-Fessi. The Maghrebi had to organise things. A discussion has been taking place over some days, secretly. They have been whispering outside the monastery gates: a regular meeting under cover of darkness. Horses. Bribe money for the guards. A quick exit at midnight. A meeting by the shrine of Moses. Burrell is not involved. How else could it have happened?

It is hard to see how Timberlake could have arranged this without al-Fessi's help. Suddenly he comes into view again in the story. While Timberlake was busying himself being guided around the holy sites by Franciscans, al-Fessi would also have had his own holy shrines to visit, some of which were the mosques frequented also by Christians, and also perhaps tombs of Sufi masters. He would have kept up a meeting with Timberlake to arrange their homeward journey. Along with these arrangements, the opportunity had presented itself of something quite different, something of which the Padre Guardiano did not approve. Perhaps, for Timberlake, that was part of the attraction.

In other later accounts by travellers to Palestine, no one seems to have done a visit to the River Jordan in a rush. The visitors wanted to see things, take matters slowly and carefully, make observations. Had a novelist been making up this story of Henry Timberlake's visit to Palestine he or she would not – on the basis of the parallels – have invented a day's outing of this nature. We seem to be stuck with it regardless.

There was a route from al-'Aizariyya past the Nebi Musa (Prophet Moses) shrine along the Wadi Daber and then to the Dead Sea. To Nabi Musa the way wound around, through desertic hills and rough valleys. The shrine was very much visited by people devoted to the Sufis of Jerusalem, who hung flags there on special occasions. Worshippers gathered there with thirty-three prayer beads strung in a necklace, reciting the ninety-nine names of God.

Nabi Musa was in Bedouin territory. Indeed, the Bedouin would have had to be the guides and protectors for the trip to the Dead Sea. The view ahead is stunning: purple mountains of ancient Moab, across the Jordan, and the crisp blue of the lake, with a shock of vivid green around the oasis of Jericho. From Nabi Musa the road drops three hundred feet to the lowest point on earth. There lies the plain where the Wadi Nabir debouches its occasional water towards the lake and here horses could go faster, speeding towards the shoreline.

The Dead Sea was visited to see a pillar of salt identified as Lot's Wife. Both Christians and Muslims would break off bits of it to take home. And here was an Elizabethan Englishman of 1601 – roughly dressed, and wearing a wide-brimmed hat – collecting bitumen from the shore of the Dead Sea, and looking towards the outlet of the River Jordan into this strange lake. Timberlake writes:

> The Jordan runneth into this Lake, and theire dyeth, which is one of the greatest
> secrets in the world, that a fresh ryver should runne contynewally into a salt Lake, and
> theire dye. And the Lake is contynewally soe salt that noe weight of any resonable

substance will sinke but allwayes flote above the water, as a dead man, or dead beast, or any other dead thinge will never goe downe. And whatsoever is brought into it by the Ryver Jordan it keepeth contynewally uppon the superficies of the Lake, and soe beinge tossed thereon by the force of weather maketh a congeled substance or froth, which froth being dryven uppon the bankes, it becometh a kinde of blacke like pitche, which they call theire Bitumum, whereof I brought some from thence.[5]

Accounts of English-speaking travellers who visited Jericho, the River Jordan and the Dead Sea in the sixteenth and seventeenth centuries are not that common. As noted above, Fynes Moryson, in 1596, was discouraged by the friars from going because of the dangers. This was normal. The friars did not want anyone to go. According to William Lithgow, visiting in 1612, there was a single annual journey to the Jordan, Jericho and Quarantia undertaken by the Padre Guardiano between Palm Sunday and Good Friday, which he joined. He writes: 'These places cannot be viewed, save only at that time.'[6] No friars would accompany pilgrims without being in a huge, armed party. Lithgow reports that his party was composed of 100 soldiers (sixty horsemen and forty footmen), and cost each participant seven French crowns. They departed on a Tuesday, and once down in an inhospitable part of the valley, in darkness, they were attacked by the Arabs who shot arrows at them. They went along the Dead Sea, and then up to the River Jordan, where the pilgrims went naked into the river. Lithgow, still naked from swimming, then climbed up a 'turpentine tree' (terebinth) and cut down a rod (which he later presented to King James). Unfortunately, while he was doing this, the rest of the throng went on, unaware he was not in the party. They were then assailed by the Bedouin. Lithgow heard the shot of a harquebus rifle in the distance and, looking around, realised his company had gone on. He was in something of a quandary, given he was naked: whether to stay up the tree, or go down. He decided in the end he had better jump out of the tree and rush after his group, which he did, nude.

He then describes how he met up with one of the soldiers on horseback guarding the procession, who was so furious with Lithgow for staying behind that he jabbed at him with his lance. When he got to the main party, the Padre Guardiano, horrified presumably, took off his own friar's habit to cover him up. Presumably someone else then covered up the Padre Guardiano.

The Bedouin are described as naked too. There is another mention of Bedouin clad only in loin cloths in the writings of the Spanish Franciscan Juan Perrara: the 'wild Arabs... go about naked except for the private parts'.[7] That is not 'traditional' Bedouin dress now. Nakedness and semi-nakedness are usually frowned upon in Islam, but then there are references to holy men, who would go around semi-naked or naked, who would be looked after by the Muslim community, like Indian sadhus.[8] So maybe at this time the same sensibilities as today did not apply.

How do you know when a whole story is true, and when it is false? People can perceive things as real, when they are not real. Or people can behave in very unexpected ways. Did Lithgow believe he was telling the truth, or did he actively take poetic licence, or was his editor glossing his work?

When Bodington and his party wanted to go to the Dead Sea in 1669, they had to seek permission from the Ottoman Pasha, and pay for an armed guard of about fifteen men, janissaries, including – surprisingly – the Pasha himself, 'mounted on a Mare valued at a thousand Livres'.[9] They went to Quarantia and Elisha's fountain, and then Jericho. They swam in the River Jordan, and then went to the Dead Sea, where they also bathed. They spent two days in this enterprise.

Why would the Pasha have gone there, even with a guard of fifteen? To put himself in such a completely vulnerable position would have been reckless. Perhaps the Pasha went there to send a message to the Bedouin: here I am, and I am in control.

Henry Maundrell in 1697 set off to the River Jordan in a large party headed by the governor of Jerusalem, and accompanied by 'several bands of souldiers'.[10] So here the governor, the Pasha, is clearly present, but with a much bigger guard. Maundrell expressed the opinion that 'without this guard, there is no going thither, by reason of the multitude and insolence of the Arabs in these parts'. Each Frank paid twelve gold coins for the privilege, but locals and ecclesiastics paid less. The operation was devised as a great method of making money out of the Christians. The number of pilgrims to the Jordan (both local and visiting) was about 2,000.

The party went down past Quarantia, and encamped at Jericho overnight. Next day they went to Jordan, where 'troops of Arabs' appeared on the other side, firing three shots, and then departing. They also went down to the Dead Sea, returning to the camp in Jericho after the excursion. After two days in the camp, the entire party returned to Jerusalem.

But, muddying the waters, Sandys indicates that the relationship between the Pasha of Jerusalem and the Bedouin of the Jordan Valley and Dead Sea was much more complex than it might appear at first sight. When Sandys visited in 1610 he was told by the Custos that he could not go to the Jordan because the annual visit there had already taken place, the pilgrims returning on the same day he entered the city. He describes this journey (headed by the Padre Guardiano) like this: 'A journy undertaken but once a yeare in regard of the charge, the passengers being then guarded by a Sheck of the Arabians, to resist the wilde Arabs; who almost famished on those barren mountaines (which they dare not husband for feare of surprisall) rob all that passe, if inferiour in strength. Yet paid we towards that conduct two dollers apeece to the Sanziack.'[11] So here payment was made to the Sanjakbey, but there would be Arab (Bedouin) protection en route, which would guard the large throng against other Bedouin and highwaymen. Perhaps the reason information is inconsistent is because the situation was immensely volatile: one year there would be better relations between the Pasha and the sheikhs of the Bedouin than another. One year there would be war between the clans, and another year not. Volatility in Middle Eastern affairs is not a recent phenomenon.

The volatility of relations between rulers and Bedouin seems sure. Ibn Battuta indicates a situation in which Bedouin acted as guards en route between es-Salihiya and Gaza,[12] and we find that indicated also in European sources.[13] If the Bedouin had actually guarded travellers on that route under the previous empire of the Mamluks, and the Ottomans did not accept their guardianship, then the Ottomans were depriving the Bedouin of their revenue derived from *caphar*, payments, for the job. Perhaps then it is no wonder that the Bedouin made it their business to attack travellers on that route. Fynes Moryson, visiting in 1596, simply sees the Bedouin as 'disobedient' to the Turks: 'the Arabians are... subject to the great Turke, yet being poore and farre distant from his imperiall seat [in Constantinople] they cannot be brought to due obedience, much lesse to abstaine from robberies'.[14] The Bedouin did not accept Ottoman hegemony, and wanted deals whereby they were the guardians of travellers on 'their' roads. If they did not get the deal, then they would get their dues by ambush.

Therefore, some kind of deal was made by Henry Timberlake with the most powerful Bedouin of the Jordan Valley. If you had a deal of friendship and protection with them then things would be different. Moryson himself recognised that this kind of deal could take place. He writes:

> Yet these Barbarians doe strictly observe their faith to those that are under their protection. And all the Merchants chuse one or other of the Arabian Captaines, and for a small pension procure themselve to be received into their protection, which done, these Captaines proclaime thier names through all their Cities and Tents (in which for the most part they live) and ever after will severely revenge any wrong done to them, so as they passe most safely with their goods.[15]

Timberlake, somehow, made a contract with the Bedouin. He and al-Fessi rode not fearing the Bedouin, for they were their protectors against real highwaymen, against rival Bedouin, against the Ottoman sipahis. We can then imagine Henry Timberlake, al-Fessi, a party of Bedouin, on horseback, galloping around the Jordan Valley, this quite uninhabited place where there was only the little village of Jericho, where rival tribes of Bedouin watched each other carefully. The sun beat down, and dust rose behind the horses' hooves. At dawn they had departed, covertly, through St Stephen's gate, and skirted the Mount of Olives towards the east, to the Sufi holy place of Nabi Musa, and down to the Dead Sea. Timberlake collected bitumen from the shore, and tested the water for buoyancy. Then they went to the Jordan River. Dismounting here after the journey through a landscape of desolation, Timberlake would have dropped to his knees and said the Lord's Prayer, as he had become accustomed to doing. Here there was verdant growth. Timberlake busied himself picking branches of trees: tamarisk, willows, oleanders. He gathered a few spring flowers. It was quiet and peaceful, with the sound of the rushing waters and this narrow river. This was the water in which Christ had been baptised. He walked away from his companions, found seclusion, took off his clothes and plunged into the surprisingly warm, muddy water. He submerged himself. He rose. He saw the sunlight peeking through the vegetation, and birds flutter off from top branches, or so we can imagine.

Whatever the case, truly Timberlake had gone where no Englishman had gone before, at least, not for a very long time.

Gathering plants? That is supposition, but there were certain plants that only grew next to the Jordan. With such evidence, and the bitumen from the Dead Sea, he could prove to the Padre Guardiano that he had definitely gone to the Jordan River, and receive a certificate stating that he had bathed there. Henry Timberlake must have wanted this very much, to have a kind of medal showing he had gone one step further than Englishmen like Hugo Stapers, or the jokey merchants from Aleppo.

But how would the Padre Guardiano have reacted to the return of the Englishman who had been accused of being a spy, and released with great difficulty? What had Timberlake done to the Custos? When had he managed to return? The gates would have shut at sundown, around 6 o'clock. It is easy to imagine the consternation in the monastery.

And here there is the reason, perhaps, Timberlake did not provide a detailed account of his most extraordinary enterprise. The Custos discouraged anyone from going to the Jordan River because of the dangers, but also it was his responsibility to make sure that Christian pilgrims did not do anything alarming to the authorities. For the Custos, Timberlake must have transgressed.

The Custos must have been waiting for the Englishman's return. All day he would have done his best to keep everything low-key, not showing his own alarm. His job was to 'protect' pilgrims, which meant keeping a close eye on them.

There was perhaps a moment when Timberlake pulled out the leaves and branches he gathered at the Jordan River, a now squashed bouquet, along with the bitumen, and gave them to Manerba. Such was the proof.

The Padre Guardiano resolved to give Timberlake a certificate that he had bathed in the Jordan River. So be it. But – in order to account for Timberlake's silence in the letter – there seems to have been a request by Manerba. He should keep quiet about it.

How could Manerba communicate to the Englishman the precarious position the Franciscans were in? How could he make Timberlake understand that the Ottoman authorities could sweep away the privileges of the Latin enclave in Jerusalem instantly, if they could demonstrate that trust had been broken? For Timberlake to go to the Jordan Valley without the blessing of the Sanjakbey (who could not have been pleased with the man accused of spying hurtling off with Bedouin to Jericho) or the Padre Guardiano was an offence to them. The Ottoman authorities could arrest the Franciscans for acts of rebellion against the Sultan. The Sanjakbey could kill them all and close the monastery.

So here is a proposal: not only did Timberlake visit the Dead Sea and River Jordan, but on his return he promised secrecy to the Padre Guardiano. He agreed, on his honour, that he would divulge nothing of this sojourn, or encourage other Englishmen to make the journey, for the sake of the friars in Jerusalem. If the Franciscans were working hard to discourage pilgrims from going to the River Jordan and Dead Sea, for their own safety, it would be a public relations disaster if Timberlake broadcast his successful trip to all and sundry.

A man like Timberlake would have been bursting to announce his success, surely, if it were not for some restraining request. He wanted the proof of his washing in the Jordan River in the form of that certificate. Therefore, in his letter to his friends in London, his journey to the Jordan is not explicitly indicated except by implication. He did state that he had this proof of bathing in the River, and carefully described what he saw of the places. As for that: Timberlake, the adventurer, just could not help himself. But he kept to some promise that he would not make a relation of his journey there and back. It is left to his readers to imagine it.

19

Dromedaries from Gaza

Early the next day, on 31 March 1601, Henry Timberlake took his leave of the monastery of San Salvatore in Jerusalem, and said goodbye to John Burrell, who had decided to stay behind and travel onwards with the Englishmen from Aleppo. Now, with their presence, Burrell was no longer one of the only two Protestants in the land, and he could journey with them, to Damascus, Aleppo, and wherever else he wanted to go. He was free, and in no hurry; he clearly wanted to explore. It made sense that he would choose the Aleppo party over Timberlake, but it meant that Timberlake was without an English companion. His only companion now would be al-Fessi, the Moor.

The long-bearded William Biddulph, the other Englishmen, the friars and the inscrutable Padre Guardiano also gave their farewells. The departure of a pilgrim required a ceremony at which certain certificates were conferred, in which the sites visited by the pilgrim were listed.[1] The seal on the certificates depicted Christ with the twelve apostles below. As noted, Timberlake's certificate was accompanied by another separate certificate to record that he had washed in the water of the River Jordan.

> And soe havynge my pattent sealed with the greate seale of the Pater Guardian and
> also pattente that did showe that I did wash in the Ryver Jordan... I departed from
> Jheru[salem] in company of the Moore that holp me out of prison.[2]

A letter in Latin listing all the holy places a pilgrim had gone to was given as proof of the indulgences earnt by visitors, and there is a version of one of these letters in John Locke's account of his travels to and from Jerusalem in Hakluyt.[3] When Fynes Moryson left Jerusalem the Padre Guardiano also gave him an Agnus Dei ('Lamb of God') and some earth and stones from the holy places. An Agnus Dei was a wax disk stamped with an image of the Lamb of God holding a cross or flag, which could act as a Christian talisman. This was blessed by the Pope, and was worn on a string or chain around the neck. Timberlake would not have accepted this, if it were offered. Fynes Moryson did so because he was pretending to be a Catholic. There was also an opportunity to have your arm tattooed with a Jerusalem cross, or the names of Jesus, Mary, Jerusalem, and so on,[4] but Protestants generally did not go in for this.

What did Padre Guardiano, Francesco Manerba, think as he watched Captain Timberlake turn to go? The meeting of two, very different, strong-willed people is always interesting to observe. Had they both been changed by the encounter? And what did everyone make of Timberlake and al-Fessi, preparing mules together in the street, just the two of them setting off with the muleteer on a perilous journey? Did anyone expect, in their hearts, that they would get to Cairo successfully, alive?

In terms of Timberlake's date of departure from Jerusalem, the manuscript here is corrupt. This passage contains one of its errors of transcription. The copyist had Timberlake and the Moor leaving on 30 March, because it would be natural to think of the day of Timberlake's departure as occurring after his exit from the Church of the Holy Sepulchre, and would mean that one did not have the problem of a missing, undescribed, day. The copyist could sometimes make errors like this, putting 'Arabians' for 'Armenians', for example. Both the early and later complete editions, and also the independent short edition of Purchas (made from another manuscript copy), have the date as 31 March, thereby ensuring that the missing day is clear.

Both the manuscript and the first printed edition have it that Timberlake and the al-Fessi reached 'Ramoth Gilead' on 31 March 'at night'. No other stopping place is mentioned, and it would be natural if they left Jerusalem early in the morning and arrived at this first locality at night on the same day.

As for the mention of 'Ramoth Gilead' it is very unlikely that the travellers returned to Ramat al-Khalil and then went over to Ascalon. In Purchas' short version there is the word 'Ram', not Ramoth Gilead, and this may well have been what was in Timberlake's letter. If the original had 'Ram', it would explain why both the British Library manuscript and the edition of 1603 understood the reference to indicate Ramoth Gilead, when in fact it did not. In the later edition there is the name 'Rama' instead of 'Ramoth Gilead' which is an appropriate correction. 'Ram', in fact, would make absolutely perfect sense. Timberlake and al-Fessi would have gone west to Ramle, usually called 'Rama' by visiting Europeans. Ramle was a major town en route to Jaffa. To go to Ramle meant travelling slightly north-west, but then down the coastal road.

Ramle was founded around AD 715 as the capital of the Umayyad province of Filastin (Palestine) and was famous for its beautiful White Mosque and palace, but an earthquake had destroyed the city in the eleventh century. The Crusaders rebuilt it, with a Church of St John at the centre, a church that was then turned into a mosque. From the end of the fourteenth century the Franciscans had a pilgrim hospice in the town, and it became a common stopping-place for European travellers.

Timberlake and al-Fessi went here, not south to Ramat al-Khalil. It could be reached in a day from Jerusalem on a mule. It was about twenty-eight miles distant from Jerusalem. Allowing for stops, it would make sense if Timberlake and al-Fessi arrived at night.

They must have looked an odd and rather vulnerable sight: a Frank and a Maghrebi, travelling together. Just these two men and a muleteer leading the way.

From Ramle they could head down the coast towards Gaza. From Ramle to Ascalon was about the same distance from Jerusalem to Ramle, about twenty-six miles, so it worked in terms of another day's journey. Ascalon was a small town famed for its fantastic shallots. And then it was only about twelve and a half miles further on to Gaza, which they reached on 2 April.

At this point let us pause to reflect again on the different versions of Timberlake's account: the manuscript which is used here as the foundation for this reconstruction, the 1603 edition, the 1609 edition, and the condensed version found in Purchas' compendium. While Archer's later revised edition of 1609 seems right that the first stop was 'Rama' and contains some useful additional information at various points, new information is provided that cannot be right. It has, regarding Gaza and Ascalon:

> at one of those two places I hoped to have some passage by water, either to Alexandria, or to Damietta, but fayling thereof, I was in a maze and knew not what to do; whether I were best to go backe againe to Jerusalem, or to put myselfe desperately into the hands of the wilde Arabians, to be by them conducted to Grand Cayro. One of those two courses I must of force take. So there was no hope of passage, and yet I had another hope, but to no end, which was that I should finde passage at Joppa, and for that cause I stayed at Gaza, and sent my Moore to Joppa to seeke for passage, but there was none to bee had. At last considering with my selfe that my hast into Egypt was great, for I had left my man Waldred in Cayro with my stocke of one thousand two hundred pounds, and my ship lay in the roade of Alexandria, with sixtie men in her, and whether they would depart without me, or no, I knew not – for that, when I went from them to go up to the River of Nylus to Cayro, I had no intent to go for Jerusalem – my business standing at that point, I was forced to this extremity, to make away all the money I had about mee, and to put myselfe into they hands of two wilde Arabians, that undertooke to carry me and my Moore (without whom I durst not go) to the Citie of Cayro in foure dayes.[5]

In the first place, this entire passage sounds apologetic, as if a critic had said: 'Why didn't stupid Captain Timberlake go back to Alexandria by sea rather than going over the desert with wild Arabs and a Moor?' This would have been an ignorant question, and one that a sea captain could have answered directly. That Timberlake might have hoped to get to Alexandria or Damietta from Gaza or Ascalon would be like someone hoping to get on an international flight at a domestic airport. The ports of Palestine had long ago been destroyed by the Ayyubids and Mamluks to avoid another Crusader stronghold. Gaza had a small wharf, but the others only had natural anchorages without docks or wave-breakers, so few Mediterranean ships berthed in them.[6] These ports were normally used for local sailing and fishing vessels.

Additionally, for Timberlake in the 1609 edition to send the Moor off to 'Joppa' (Jaffa), from Gaza, to check whether there was a ship leaving from there is absurd. If they had wanted to check what was in port at Jaffa they would have both gone there from Ramle. Since it is over forty miles from Gaza to Jaffa, we would have to imagine al-Fessi going for a very long and tiresome errand that might take him three days, which does not fit with the chronology. The 1609 edition makes it sound like Jaffa was just a little way up the road, to be reached in a couple of hours, and this section must then have been written by someone with only a faint knowledge of Palestinian geography.

The publisher, Thomas Archer, has therefore inserted a section in which Timberlake anguishes about what to do, and is forced to the situation of crossing the desert on camel back, with a Moor and two Arabs, against his will. He has woven in some interesting information about Timberlake's ship and stock to ensure it looks credible, but it is not. In the manuscript and Archer's early printed edition (reflected also in Purchas), Timberlake has this plan all along, and shows no serious concern about it.

In Gaza, according to the manuscript chronology, the Englishman and the Moor spent only one night resting in the town. There, Timberlake and al-Fessi made an agreement with two Bedouin with racing camels, who would convey them to Cairo within four days for a large fee that would be paid only upon delivery. The next night they prepared themselves, and left civilisation for the dark ocean of sand.

Timberlake writes: '...with those 2 Arab. and my Moore I dep[ar]ted and that night, being the third of Aprill, we rann soe hard uppon those Dromedaries and the day that I began to wax weary'. Of course, 'and the day' seems a little out of place, but it is the kind of language that reflects someone speaking, or writing quickly. All the night and all the day the Englishman and the Moor, with the two Bedouin, were 'running' on camels. You could see why a publisher would want to tidy up a sentence like that, but it was tidied wrongly in print: 'With these two Arabes and my Moore I departed from Gaza, having no other companie, and that day (being the 3. of Aprill) wee ran these Dromedaries so hard as at night I began to waxe very wearie.'[7] No. Timberlake left at night, and it was in the late afternoon of the day that he started to feel exhausted, as is apparent from what follows.

'Dromedaries', Timberlake called the animals they rode. He distinguished dromedaries from ordinary camels. Actually, what he meant to do is to distinguish

camels bred for racing, or speed, from regular camels. Most of the world's camels are dromedaries: *Camelus dromedarius*, the Arabian one-humped camel. Those
bred for racing can go about twelve miles per hour.

Timberlake was quite interested in the details of a racing camel, and described
these at some length:

> Dromedaries ar a kinde of beaste much like to a camell, only his heade is lesser and
> his leege is some what longer, and [he hath] avery smale necke. Theire is this dif-
> ference betweene a camell and him even as theire is between a Mastie dogg and a
> grayhound.

Timberlake liked technicalities, measurements. He considered a dromedary to
be built for speed, though 'I thinke a good horse will runne faster', but no horse
could manage to get through the desert with the endurance of this animal, for
on his journey 'I never sawe them eate nor drinke' and 'it is saide that they will
fast from water 10 days and never drinke but not soe long from meate'.

However, despite his positive interest in the camels, the camels let him down

It was still daylight, but late in the afternoon. Exhausted, Timberlake asked the
Bedouin for a short break. This area was apparently slightly hilly, with some
scrub and thin vegetation. They managed to find somewhere where they could
tie up the camels.

The party dismounted, sat down, ate some raisins and drank water.

Then something terrible happened.

One of the camels took fright, broke free from its tethers and bolted off.
Perhaps when it did so, Timberlake gazed after it partly with fear and partly
with a curiosity about the speed the animal was travelling.

Quickly, one Bedouin jumped on the remaining camel and tore off after the
first one, while the other ran to a crossroads on the other side of a hill to look
where the camel went. Timberlake tells the story in his own words:

> ...soe we all alighte[d], for you rode two uppon a beast ...and soe went to supp. In
> the meane tyme one of them [the dromedaries] brake lose and rann away backe
> againe. Then one of those Arab. tooke the other beast and rode after him that
> brooke loose. And the other went to a cross way over a sandy hill to turne him soe
> that both men and beasts were out of sight.

The Englishman and the Moor were left alone in the wilderness, in the middle
of the desert, with no camels, no camel-drivers, no bags – which were surely
tied up to the camels – and only a small amount of food and water.

One of the few pieces of written-down Frank that survives is a translation of the Lord's Prayer. It illustrates how one Frank speaker tried to use the language. It runs:

Padri di noi, ki star in syelo
noi volir ki nomi di ti star saluti
Noi volir ki il paisi di ti star kon noi
I ki ti lasar ki tuto il populo fazer volo
di ti na tera, syemi syemi ki nel syelo.
Dar noi sempri pani di noi di kada jorno
skuzar per noi il kulpa di noi
syemi syemi ki noi skuzar
kwesto populo ki fazer kulpa a noi
Non lasar noi tenir katibo pensyeri
ma tradir per noi di malu
perke ti tenir sempri il paisi
e il fortsa e il gloria. Amen.[8]

Our Father, who is in Heaven
We want your name to be saluted.
We want your Land to be with us.
And that you let all people do your will
on Earth in the same way as in Heaven.
Give us always our bread every day
and excuse us for our sins
in the same way that we excuse
those people that do sins to us.
but lead us from bad [things]
Do not let us have bad thoughts
because You have always the land
and the strength and the glory. Amen.

In times of crisis, religious people often pray. Perhaps Timberlake said the Lord's Prayer in Frank as well as English at this point, so that al-Fessi could participate: this prayer of the Prophet 'Issa.

They waited for a long time. There was no sign of the Bedouin returning.

Silence. And as they waited the sun started to go down.

At sundown al-Fessi would also have prayed, as all Muslim men are supposed to pray. Al-Fessi would have purified himself with sand, his face, his hands and arms to the elbows, his head, his feet, and waited, standing ready.

He would have checked the place of the sunset, and roughly calculated the direction of Mecca. Facing it, a Muslim at prayer places his hands on either side of

his head, with his thumbs touching his ears, and the palms forward. 'God is Great',
he says in Arabic.

He moves his hands down to his sides, and then to rest by his stomach and
says: 'In the name of God, most compassionate, most merciful. Praise be to God,
Lord of the Universe, most compassionate, most merciful, Master of the Day of
Judgement. You alone we worship. You alone we ask for help. Guide us in the
right path: the path of those whom you have blessed, not of those who deserve
wrath, nor of the strayers.'

As he bows forward from the waist, he says, 'God is great.' And while he remains
bowing he adds, 'Glory be to God, the great.' He raises himself up. 'God responds
to those who praise him.' He pauses, standing. Then he drops down to his knees,
saying, 'God is great.'

He kneels, with his head touching the floor. 'Glory be to God, the Most High.'
He sits up again, and says, 'God is Great.' He touches his head again to the earth
saying, 'God is great. Glory to God, the Most High.' He stands again, and repeats
the sequence twice, and at the end of the last prostration he sits up.

He says: 'I bear witness that there is no other God besides God. He alone is
God. There is no other.' He looks to the right, and says, 'Peace to you.' He looks to
the left. 'Peace to you.' He sends deep peace out to the universe.

Two prayers in the wilderness: Christian and Muslim. But no sign of the camels.

Henry Timberlake decided to run up a nearby hill and – like a navigator searching the seas and skies – look to the distance for some sign of the Bedouin.

> ...And it began to be darke and I beinge alone with my Moore went my selfe alone
> to the top of the sandy hill to see yf I could espey comminge towards me eyther of
> the theives.

In the last sentence Timberlake uses the adjective 'alone' twice. And 'theives'
he writes. The Bedouin – since their attack on the caravan in the desert outside es-Salihiya – he saw as thieves: thieves like those who attacked the man and
left him for dead in Jesus' story of the Good Samaritan. After all, that story was
located on the way to Jericho, and Timberlake knew that area to be in control of
the Bedouin. It was a simple equation.

But instead of seeing the Bedouin they had made the contract with in Gaza,
Timberlake saw the worst alternative.

> When soe deuly I espied comminge towards me fower other theives.

Four other Bedouin with whom no agreement had been made! He was like a
mouse seeing four cats.

And what was worse, the Bedouin saw him.

Timberlake turned around and raced back as fast as he could run. His impulse was to get back to al-Fessi, waiting. Two were better than one in this kind of situation. They could stand back to back and fight to the death.

Furiously, he ran down the hill and on to al-Fessi, now pursued by the Bedouin, who ran their camels quickly round the edge after this speeding Frank, sure of their prey.

As Timberlake reached al-Fessi the Bedouin were almost at his heels, but the turbaned Moor stood in front of the Christian, pointing whatever weapon he had – I presume a gun – straight at the leader of the party, allowing them no further.

Al-Fessi clearly took his commitment to Timberlake very seriously. He had decided he would protect the stranger in a strange land, and he would not renege on his decision. This was life or death. If death came, so be it.

The Bedouin looked at the Maghrebi – who must have been holding his pistol firmly, ready to shoot – and stopped. They could proceed no further, and there was a tense stand-off. The leader of their party tried to make a deal with al-Fessi. From what Timberlake writes, the conversation proceeded something like this:

'Give us that Frank,' said the Bedou to al-Fessi. 'And we will let you go free.'

'I will not. I will not let you take the Frank. He is no good to you anyway. He has nothing. All his money is in Cairo, and all he has with him is on the back of a camel that has run away. We have made a contract with two of your tribe, who were in Gaza, Mustafa and Ali, to take us to Cairo in 4 or 5 days, for 24 sultani, and they have led us to this place with two camels. One of them took flight, and they have gone after it. For this reason we are alone in the desert, trusting to your hospitality.'

Timberlake, in his description of what took place, is oddly passive. He does not ready his own weapon, perhaps because he does not have a pistol on him, or perhaps it is simply not prepared and loading took time. Al-Fessi would have had time to load a pistol, when he saw from afar what was happening, or perhaps it was already done. Timberlake might have had a knife, but that was no good in this situation. He appears to be completely at the mercy of others, and entirely dependent on al-Fessi to protect him. At this stage, he would have listened to the Arabic negotiations, unknowing.

'Give us the Frank.'

'I will not give you the Frank. He has nothing on him but his clothes, which are of no value.'

But the Bedouin knew that a slave like Henry Timberlake would fetch a good price. He was strong. They would have seen how he could run.

Al Fessi probably suspected that the Bedouin thought he was lying, to cover the fact that Timberlake had plenty of money in his rough coat. Al Fessi might not have trusted them to keep him alive once he longer posed a threat. They could not sell him, a Maghrebi, because he was a Muslim, so it was easier for them if he were dead. All the same, the other Bedouin might not return. Their escape after the camel might have been a ploy, to leave the foreigners here abandoned. They may have alerted these others. How could he know?

At some stage, as the Bedouin talked amongst themselves, to make a decision, Al Fessi must have explained the conversation he had had to Timberlake.

'Then if it is true what you say,' said the Bedou, in due course, 'Mustafa and Ali will return with the camels, and we will let you go free. But if they do not return, you will both be ours.'

Al-Fessi kept the Bedouin at bay, protecting Captain Timberlake in the desert.

20

The *Hajj*

Timberlake writes:

> And by that tyme I hade recovered the place where I lefte my Moore, one of them
> was att my heels and bad the Moore delyver me to him. The Moore told him that
> I hade nothinge, but was to be caryed to Cayro in 4 or [5] dayes by two of theire
> companions, namminge them to him. He said yf that were trew they would doe me
> noe harme but yf they came not with the beasts they would then make us both theire
> slaves. My Moore said I had nothinge to lose but the clothes about my backe, which
> were worth nothinge for I had promised to pay those two men 24 peices of gold
> when they had brought me to Cayro, soe that yf they did not kill me I cared not.[1]

What did Timberlake think of 'his Moor' then? This man had saved his life in
Jerusalem, and now refused to hand him over to the Bedouin in the desert. He
risked forfeiting his own life in the process. What reward would justify this kind
of action? What was his motivation? Would a Christian have done the same thing
for a Muslim?

The desert gets cold very quickly.

And the moon shone sweetly, over a scene like in a Christmas card of the
three magi visiting Jesus in the manger: camels, the great bejewelled desert sky,
the bright star of Venus. But this was no happy birth of a prophet. Under this sky
there was no little town of Bethlehem, and a stable. The camels were poised, and
their owners were not thinking of giving any precious things to anyone, but how
much money they might make by enslaving these unfortunate travellers who had
dared to stray into their domains.

There are two men resisting being their victims: a Muslim and a Christian
together, far away, alone, captured, united in fear.

But then there was a noise. Some time later, the two men that had run after the
camel returned. The stand-off was over. The Bedouin offered Timberlake and al-
Fessi raisins and water. No hard feelings. It was just one of those things.

Timberlake writes:

Soe after ii howeres those Arabians came againe and soe the other 4 and those ii were all fellowes. Soe they gave me a fewe raysons and a litle water and they departed. But yf this Moore hade not bine with me in this place I hade bine caryed quite away.

How must that have felt to a Christian like Henry Timberlake, to owe your life for the second time in a few days to a Muslim who you had come to know only recently, who had no reason to put himself in danger for your sake?

But for al-Fessi this would have been yet another reason to think that God had indeed required him to be of assistance to the Captain, for without him this man would be dead. The attack was confirmation that his aid was required.

Il ham du lila, praise be to God, he would have said.

After all had been settled, the journey continued through the night. They kept on going, riding all that night, with several stops for water, and the next day. The next evening they came to a Bedouin camp.

It was a village of black tents, sheep and goats, camels, women painted with henna and trimmed with silver bracelets, wild-haired children. Timberlake and al-Fessi would have dropped off the camels, and had to pay their respects to the Sheikh, shakily. The Sheikh brought them all into his tent, where they were given camel's milk to drink. Desert hospitality.

The 'thieves' that would have enslaved Timberlake now looked after him.

The 4 day at night we came to a place where the theyves had tente and theire they gave me milke of cammells.

Leaving the now-friendly Bedouin after some hours, they journeyed on, with the two men they had originally contracted. The following night they reached es-Salihiya, the border of the desert where the caravan had encamped. By this time, Timberlake had had enough of camels and desperately wanted horses. His body was sore and aching. The manuscript has it that he was 'soe over taken in my bodye' that he felt 'wounded with roles'. Because of this bodily pain he was 'constrayned to give [the camels] over and hyer 2 horses.'

So Timberlake insisted on hiring horses for himself and his Moroccan companion, while the Bedouin would have continued with the camels, one on each.

He writes:

So I rode 3 dayes and 3 nights for hast to come before my shipp should be gone and the 4th I toke those horses and soe the next daye by 6 at night I came to the cyttye of Grannd Cayro agayne & payd my Theives and my ii horses and sent them away.[2]

Once again, however, at this point it is necessary to contend with the alternative version of the 1609 edition. Here it was agreed that the Bedouin would take Timberlake and the Maghrebi to Matariya, not Cairo itself, and it was there that they received the twenty-four gold coins, but in the manuscript and the 1603 version, as well as in Purchas, no one got paid until Timberlake reached Cairo. This amended version reads:

> But the reason why the Arabians did grant to get me horses, was not because they pityed me for my wearinesse, but for that they durst not go any neerer to the inhabited Countrey with their Dromidaries, and there one of them stayed [at Salhia], and the other went with me to Materia, from whence I sent my Moore to Cayro, to fetch mee their hyer, and there I payd them that let me the horses, six pieces of Gold, and therewith they delivered me in safety into the custody of my Moore, within three miles of the Citie Cayro, where I was welcomed by the Consull and others there resident.[3]

Maybe there are some bits of truth in all of this, and the original letter Timberlake wrote simplified a more complex situation, but perhaps this passage was also apologetic, designed to answer a query about the arrival of the Bedouin in Cairo. Since Timberlake had characterised the Bedouin as 'thieves', perhaps English readers – thinking of English parallels – thought it unlikely that such thieves (highwaymen, robbers) would have shown their faces in the city, imagining them to be outlaws. Perhaps that was something that made people doubt whether Timberlake was telling the truth. Therefore, the publisher, Thomas Archer, may have added this complex arrangement to ensure that it seemed more credible to the English audience. This version has the Moor dashing off to Cairo, just as it had him dashing off to Jaffa, and renders him more subservient.

In the manuscript Timberlake and the Moroccan left Gaza with two Bedouin in the night, or rather early morning, of 3 April. That evening, still the 3rd, they had been accosted by other Bedouin. The following evening, on 4 April they had stopped at the Bedouin camp in the Sinai. Next evening, the 5th, they had reached Salihiya, and by six o'clock in the evening on 6 April, they arrived back in Cairo. It was a record for speed travel in the year 1601, a journey that spanned a total of four days, from 3 April to 6 April, as Timberlake had asked. Timberlake writes:

> Upon this beast [the dromedary] you may see by this discourse that I came soe farr in 4 dayes as I was goeinge outward from Cayro in 12 dayes.[4]

It must have felt glorious, to have achieved this speed, to have covered a distance of 224 miles in this time. That would have meant averaging fifty-six miles per day. It must have felt fantastic to saunter into Bishop's residence in Cairo, having been all the way to Jerusalem and back, within one month. Here he was, alive and well.

Bishop would have been surprised. Had he expected the Captain to return at all?

Waldred himself had been pessimistic. He had already sold the stock and departed for Alexandria, returning to the ship. He had not waited for the Captain's return. Given this, it is clear from what Timberlake writes that he was now very anxious that the *Trojan* might sail without him, and that made it imperative that Timberlake return to his ship now as fast as possible, for the men would be even more restless. Why wait for a captain who had gone off on a journey to Jerusalem and might never return? Everyone would have been ready to sail now, to get going to another port and then home.

So Timberlake had to say goodbye to the Maghrebi, the Moroccan Moor, al-Fessi, who had rescued him from danger, and helped him on his journey to the Holy Land and back. Timberlake writes nothing emotional about their goodbye. But he calls him 'good':

> [I] gave my good Moore 6 peices of gold and some other thinges and sent him to Mecha with the carravan.[5]

'Good'. The word clangs out over time.

When the publisher, Thomas Archer, came to print Timberlake's letter in 1603 he deleted that problematic word. No one would like the sound of a 'good' infidel. He changed it to 'honest'.

Six gold coins might not seem such a huge amount given the sacrifice al-Fessi had made to interrupt his own journey to help the Captain, or the extreme risks he had taken to defend him from danger. It is hard to know how the business of payment worked out. Perhaps al-Fessi refused to accept any more. Perhaps this was what he himself had paid to gain Timberlake's release in Jerusalem.

Timberlake paid twenty-four pieces of gold to the Bedouin. This glaring discrepancy gives the impression that al-Fessi refused payment, and that six gold coins was all that Timberlake could foist upon him, because it constituted expenses. Six gold coins, if they were equivalent to a Venetian ducat, would have amounted to about forty-eight shillings.

He also gave him 'some other things' though. Perhaps this masks what Timberlake did manage to give al-Fessi, the true value of his gift. What could such things have been? His compass? His chronometrical device? His quill and ink? Clothing? A ring?

The 'sent him to Meccha' line means that Timberlake furnished him with all the supplies he needed for his pilgrimage, and in the later 1609 printed edition this is made explicit: '[I] bought divers provisions for him to furnish him in his journey to Mecha'. That he facilitated the *hajj* journey of his friend here is clear. A Christian pays for a Muslim to make the *hajj* to Mecca. It was sheer gratitude and respect.

To give al-Fessi gifts and expenses rather than a payment would, in Muslim society, have preserved al-Fessi's honour. If he had been a hired help, a payment would have been appropriate, and there would have been an imbalance of status between the Englishman and the Moor. In giving gifts and expenses only, they remained equal in dignity, friends.

So there were the two men the day after they arrived back in Cairo, namely 7 April 1601, buying food and other items, for the *hajj*. There was this freshly clothed Frank and the turbaned Maghrebi, shaking hands, speaking to each other with some intensity, then turning and walking away.

We cannot know what was said between the two men. How could Henry Timberlake thank al-Fessi enough?

'*Bselama*, Signor Capitan. *Treq salama*,' al-Fessi would have said, and he was gone. The *hajj* would soon depart from Cairo in great style, and he would be part of it. He had done his duty to God and to the Sultan of Morocco.

The good Moor.

21

The *Trojan*

Henry Timberlake's return trip to Alexandria was a continuation of the speed-racing of the previous days. The manuscript reads:

> The 7th daye [of April] I stayd in Cayro all daye and at night I came to Bollake and tooke a boate, and soe the 10th of Aprill at nyne of the clocke in the mornninge I came to Rosetta, and theire taking horse with a Janizarie I came that night to the walles of Allexandria where I lay all night because the gattes were shutt before I came. Soe one the morrowe, beinge the 11th of April I came abord my Shipp the Trojane in good health and good saftye. I praysed be the Almightie, having bine out in my pilgrimage from Allexandria just fiftye dayes.[1]

Timberlake continued his dash back to Alexandria, on his own, paying for passage on a boat, and paying for a janissary and horses at Rosetta. With his assistant, Waldred, back at the ship, and apparently fearing the worst, Timberlake was anxious that the ship might sail without him. He galloped the horses, with his janissary guard, as fast as he could, but still he reached the city after nightfall, and the gates were closed. He had to wait all night outside the gates, which they would not open for him. At daybreak, at last, to his relief, Timberlake was permitted entry, and found 'my shipp not ready to departe'. Thank God.

The later 1609 printed edition of Timberlake's account alters this final dash back to Alexandria to make it even more exciting:

> I fell into greater danger than any I had during my journey, for that betweene that Towne [Rosetta] and Alexandria, there were diverse great Janisaries that came from Constantinople, that were newly landed at Alexandria, who having tyred their horses, would have taken our two Mules from us, which my Janisarie refused them, and therewith drew out his sword, and they to be revenged came running to take me, and having laid hands upon mee, foure of them beate mee cruelly and drave me to the passage that was hard by, and there would have killed me, which my Janisary perceiving, and seeing that nothing could appease them but our two Mules, after he had

been sore wounded, he delivered them unto the other Janisaries, or else I had there beene slaine, after my long and weary journey, being within five miles of my ship, that lay in the Roade at Alexandria, and so he being sore wounded, and I well beaten, at last we got to the gates of Alexandria...[2]

Here Timberlake and his hired janissary start off on horseback, and suddenly we find they have mules, not horses. They get attacked by janissaries from Constantinople, who would not have attacked a fellow janissary hired to take a traveller to Alexandria. There is some improbable 'passage' nearby when the whole route is sandy desert. This silly, spurious tale has been inserted here to give the story action and excitement right up to the last sentences. Like a good Hollywood director, Thomas Archer, the publisher, makes sure there is tension to the end.

So where did this story come from? What if some encounter with janissaries lately come from Constantinople actually occurred while Timberlake and the Moor were riding mules from Jerusalem to Gaza – it could have been some-where in the mountainous region outside Jerusalem, where a 'passage' between hills would not have been inappropriate. But if they had had some altercation there, why had Timberlake not written about it in his letter? It could have come from any traveller's tale.

Following the manuscript, Timberlake's journey down the Nile to Rosetta, and then quickly on horseback to Alexandria, was fast and peaceful. His only problem was not getting to the city of Alexandria before nightfall. But at dawn he was on board his ship once more. Waldred was probably very surprised.

This is how his letter ends, successfully, in Alexandria: the grand finale. Everyone wants a story to finish with the idea that our hero lived happily ever after. He made it. It was in his ship that Timberlake sat down to write his account of his travels to Jerusalem and back, and the letter was sent off with other merchants going more directly back to England.

There was the Captain in his quarters on board ship, surrounded by his familiar navigational equipment and maps, writing his account to his friends. He was back in his right context again, dressed in fine clothes, no longer the pilgrim 'weeds' he had put on in Cairo. A fitting ending.

But real life is not so easily divided into stories with happy endings, for strands unravel from each segment of our lives into other, new sequences, as we travel on from victories to failures, and back again, and into the unexpected future.

Timberlake would not set his sails for home.

Timberlake's ship, the *Trojan*, had remained in Alexandria the entire time he was in the Holy Land, and, upon the Captain's return, would set sail again for another foreign port.

Where then did he go?

History is full of holes, and you can have a wealth of information about some-one for a short time, only to find little else about the person in any surviving records. However, we do have some more information about Henry Timberlake. Sir William Forster's book containing the writings of the eminent, self-righteous and slightly unappealing Levant Company merchant, John Sanderson, tells us what happened.

John Sanderson was an important man, a former Levant Company consul and treasurer at Constantinople. He visited Palestine from Aleppo, via Damascus. He arrived in Jerusalem, where he, like Timberlake, got into a crisis.

Sanderson sailed from Constantinople for Jaffa in the *Mermaid* on 14 May 1601, and arrived in Sidon, where the Captain delayed because of bad weather. Sanderson grew impatient, and chose not to wait behind with a party of three other Christian pilgrim travellers on the *Mermaid*, but to set off alone. He linked himself with a party of Jewish merchants, whom he came to respect and like, travelling to Jerusalem via Damascus. This shows a good side to Sanderson, given the appalling anti-Semitism of the times, though it is also indicative of Sanderson's complete lack of regard for anyone else's opinion.

When he got to Jerusalem, on 30 June, he was met by two Franciscan friars, who welcomed him, perhaps Fathers Aurelio and Angelo who had met Biddulph's party, but Sanderson was determined to resist all offers of protection by the Franciscans. In a letter he carried, he was recommended to the Greek Patriarch of Jerusalem by the Greek Patriarch of Constantinople and therefore rejected the Franciscan offer of hospitality.

Sanderson, full of self-importance, then tried to enter the city carrying his sword, and took umbrage at having to surrender it, when the Jews in his company were allowed to retain theirs. He could do nothing to prevent its loss. This challenge was reported to the Ketkhuda, the Pasha's military commander or Agha in charge of the janissary guards, before which Sanderson had to appear, presumably in the Citadel. Luckily, he also had a very useful letter from Sultan Mehmet III that he was to be treated with respect throughout all Ottoman dominions, which you might think would mean that he was treated with kid gloves. Unluckily, the letter impressed the Ketkhuda only sufficiently to allow Sanderson's presumption to enter the city with his sword go unpunished, but he still demanded a gift of velvet cloth for the Pasha and silk cloth for himself, which Sanderson stubbornly refused to provide. He was ordered to be sent to prison by the insulted official.

At this point, the Jews with whom he had travelled, and who had accompanied him to his audience, fell down at the Ketkhuda's feet and entreated him, kissing his hand and garment, begging that he pardon the (stupid?) Frank's bold behaviour and offensive words. They negotiated a settlement that Sanderson should give twelve chequins (gold pieces) to be allowed his freedom.[3]

Sanderson, like Timberlake, considered all of this commotion a Papist rather than a Turkish plot. Like Timberlake, he was reliant on the immense generosity of people of a different religion who had befriended him (despite, in his case, his obstreperous disposition). Sanderson, like Timberlake, was, however, bigoted in regard to Catholics. He refused to call on the Padre Guardiano, Francesco Manerba, despite the many entreaties of the Greek Orthodox Patriarch for him to do this, and such a snub to the man who was officially the guardian of all western Christian pilgrims, was not received happily in the monastery of San Salvatore.

Manerba seems not so much offended but worried about whether Sanderson was posing as a Protestant Christian when he was in fact a Jew. Given Sanderson's very close association with Jews, and his preference for their company, since he went around the city with a Greek Orthodox priest and a Jewish interpreter, that was not such an unreasonable supposition. The Church of the Holy Sepulchre was as out of bounds for Jews and Muslims as the Haram esh-Sharif was to Christians and Jews. Perhaps responding to the paranoia, Francesco Manerba was in a difficult position. If the Padre Guardiano failed to protect an act of desecration by a Jew in the Church of the Holy Sepulchre, he would have failed miserably in his job. The Padre Guardiano therefore, it seems, resolved that Sanderson – whose true religion could not be ascertained – would not set foot inside the Church.

When Sanderson tried to do so, all hell broke loose. He writes:

> I had paied these nine chequins and had by the Turkes the church doore opened for me, was within and entring the sepulcher, [when] the Roman friers and other fell in an uproare, saying I was a Jew.

The 'Turks' apparently told him to enter the church anyway, but the resulting fracas was such that both Sanderson and the friars had to come before the Qadi. Sanderson describes the fiasco before the bemused Qadi in this way:

> The Padre Guardiano sent his drudgeman (= dragoman, interpreter) and accused me to be a Jew, because I came in the company of Jewes. Divers Turkes followed to heare the matter. One old Turke came and earnestly exhorted me to become a Musselman in the presence of the Cady. I gave him the hearing, and told him that I was a Christian, and no Jew. Then he said, in the hearing of all the Jewes, Turkes, and Christians: 'Let him be searcht (= examined) [to see whether he was circumcised].' But the Cadie before whom we were, being a very discreet man, did reprove that Turke and also the drugman and friers, my accusers, and so did dismisse me. But (as I was afterwards told) it cost my adversaries above 200 chequins. I spent not past some twentie in that businesse.[4]

Eventually, thoroughly offended, Sanderson left Jerusalem, departing on 8 July. Sanderson then went from Damascus to Tripoli on the coast of Syria, and witnessed to the *Trojan* being there.

Timberlake's ship, the *Trojan* sailed into Tripoli harbour, which is shaped like a half-moon. There were many small boats and some larger merchant vessels. This harbour was fortified by towers, in one of which there is an artillery, and one being the Tower of Love, because it was built by a Venetian merchant, to escape death, after he was caught in bed with his 'Turkish' (Muslim) lover. Along the harbour were store-houses and shops, though this was not as thriving a mercantile hub as Damascus or Aleppo. The city of Tripoli itself was inland from the harbour, along a sandy road with lush cultivations on either side. Beyond was huge Mount Lebanon, where, on the lower slopes, Maronite Christians and Druzes lived.

Tripoli and its port survived despite the constant threat of being swallowed. They were 'annoyed with sande',[5] for a huge sand bank threatened the surrounding agriculture.[6] Fynes Moryson was shown a pillar: 'fastened upon a hill of sand, by which they say the sand is inchanted, lest it should grow to ouerwhelme the City. Likewise they shew other pillars, under which they say great multitudes of Scorpions were in like sort inchanted, which of old wasted all that Territory; and they thinke that if these pillars were taken away, the City would be destroied by the sand and Scorpions'. With this enchantment keeping scorpions and sand at bay, the land around Tripoli, and the city itself, was well-watered and fruitful, with olive groves, fig orchards, vineyards that produce a rich wine, and gardens full of silkworms, for the people sold raw, very white silk to the Italians. The sheep are so huge, said Moryson, that the 'very tailes of them, hanging in many wreathes to the ground, doe weigh twenty five pounds, and many times thirty three pounds'.[7]

Even though there was all this verdant productivity of the countryside, and the river running through the town, Moryson described the narrow streets of Tripoli itself as having air and water that is 'unhealthfull'. He stayed with a Christian, who used to entertain the French, and found a bed made for him and his brother with clean sheets, so that 'I could scarce containe my selfe from going to bed before supper, because I had never lien in naked bed since I came from Venice to this day, having alwaies slept by sea and land in my doublet, with linnen breeches and stockings, upon a mattresse, and in betweene coverlets or quilts, with my breeches under my head.' This is a lovely description of how all our travellers would have slept. Despite his eagerness to go to bed without his supper, however, Moryson was disappointed: 'But after supper all this joy vanished by an event least-expected: For in this part of Asia great store of cotten growes (as it were) on stalkes like Cabbage... and these sheetes being made thereof, did so increase the perpetuall heat of this Countrey, now most unsupportable in summer time, as I was forced to leape out of my bed, and sleepe as I had formerly done.'[8]

Timberlake's own experience of cotton sheets, whether positive or negative, was brief. Sanderson writes:

Our people of the *Trojan* passed some troble in that bad governed place. Our men of the ship *Trojan* were most of them imprisoned in Tripoly jayle (the castle), and five were in great hazard to have beene executed; for the Emiers people accused them to have robbed a caramisall of the Emers of sope and other merchandise.[9]

Soap was an expensive product from the region, and one of the main exports from Tripoli. But, as we all know, foreign trade can involve terrible misunderstandings. The merchants in the boat selling soap felt aggrieved and accused the men of the *Trojan* of theft from the Emir. It was Timberlake's responsibility as Captain to control his crew. Was Timberlake himself imprisoned with his men in Tripoli castle? I think not, in fact, because if he were then Sanderson would have mentioned it. Sanderson's words – 'our men of the ship Trojan' – implies the crew. But Timberlake may yet have been under some kind of house arrest. He would not have been allowed to leave Tripoli.

The castle dominated the city, built on the side of a hill, to facilitate taking advantage of a brook that provided the water supply. The castle was built high, looming over the streets, towards the south-west corner, inside the city walls. It was built by the Crusader Raymond de Saint-Gilles in the eleventh century, and was now held by the Ottomans with a garrison of 200 soldiers, and a large artillery, under the governor of the city. The crew of the *Trojan* would languish in a medieval dungeon.

Since the *Trojan* was a Levant Company ship, its fate was Sanderson's concern. There seems little reason why else Sanderson would have gone to Tripoli apart from having to act for the release of the *Trojan*'s crew. The usual port used by the Levant Company was Scanderoon (Alexandretta), further up the Syrian coast. Tripoli only became important in 1609, when the Ottomans temporarily closed Scanderoon. In 1601 there were no English, French or Venetian consuls there. Why Timberlake decided it was the right place to put down anchors is anyone's guess.

Sanderson himself, who was a rather sour and humourless man, not shy of his own achievements, took pride in his successful negotiations. He writes:

> But (as God would have it) the Cadie of Tripoly, being a greenhead (that is, one, a holy man, of the parentage of Mahomet their prophet), who came passenger with me to Sidon in the *Mermaid* from Constantinople, he and his having beene well entreated in that voyage, together with my very often and earnest solicitation, did to his utmost power favour our people, so effectually that every one of them were freed, without further harme, from those false accusing Moores.[10]

Sanderson therefore is the hero of this drama, as he describes it, frequently pleading with the Qadi of Tripoli to speak to the Emir on behalf of the *Trojan*'s crew. Timberlake would have been extremely grateful to both him and the Qadi. However, Sanderson was one of those men no one would have really wanted to be grateful to. Sanderson comes across in his surviving papers as prone to alienate people very easily, with a tendency to think badly of others and to have outbursts of violent temper.[11]

In their respective positive appreciation of non-Christians, Timberlake's Moor and Sanderson's Jews, both Timberlake and Sanderson are idiosyncratic individuals who can value humanity before religion in a time of harsh religious prejudice, yet both of them draw the line of their openness at the feet of the 'Papists'. Sanderson was even more virulently anti-Catholic than Timberlake, and had caused more anxiety among the Franciscans in Jerusalem. The altercation left Sanderson out-raged, and when he came to Tripoli he was extremely suspicious of an old friar who came to Sanderson's abode to bid him welcome.[12] He claimed the friar (unseen) shot at him on two occasions, when he was lured out on a particular pathway by, in this case, a conspiring Jew.[13] Given his intercessions on behalf of the crew of the *Trojan*, the gunshots may have been fired just as easily by one of the caravan's aggrieved members, but Sanderson placed the guilt on the old friar, with only the flimsiest circumstantial evidence to support him.

Perhaps Timberlake distanced himself from Sanderson, despite the circum-stances. In a note in the edition of Sanderson's travels published in *Purchas His Pilgrimes*, there is a reference to the place that 'Henry Timberly (alias Captaine Timberly)' was imprisoned in Jerusalem, 'which he himselfe recordeth in a printed booke; but thus much I had copied from his owne hand'.[14] However, this is probably Purchas' note, not Sanderson's. Purchas himself had a handwritten copy of Timberlake's letter, which he then partly printed, independently.

However, there is a letter written by William Biddulph of Aleppo on 22 October 1601 that must have been sent to Sanderson when he was in Tripoli, which is also published in *Purchas*. Biddulph does not here mention the fate of the *Trojan*, but he writes at the end: 'I pray commend me to Master Timberley, John Brochurst, William Pate, &c.' He then also knew of Timberlake being there.[15] Timberlake was not completely alone. Other Englishmen were there with him

.

With the release of his men, and the situation resolved, Timberlake would have been immensely busy organising his ship's rapid departure. The ship could finally be loaded up and prepared for her homeward journey, after many months. Sanderson intended to board for the journey back to England. But Sanderson never took his passage in the *Trojan*. Neither did anyone else.

Sanderson writes:

> The 10th day [of February 1602] the shipp *Trogian* was caste awaye upon the rocks in the road of Tripolie by boysterous billowes that broke her anchors and shov'd her on the shore.

In his autobiography, Sanderson recounts: 'The *Trogian* broke upon Tripoli Rocks. Ther I had a losse of some things I was provid[ed] of.'[16] That he lost goods means that the ship had been loaded up. Elsewhere, Sanderson also lists the *Trojan* as one of the vessels he intended to sail in, but did not, stating: 'The Trogian broke one the rocks at Tripolie Road. In hir I purposed to goe for Christendom, but after went in the *Edward Bonadventure*.'[17]

Sanderson himself shows no emotion at the sinking of the *Trojan*. He went off in the second ship six days later, on 16 February 1602, presumably leaving Timberlake to sort things out alone, with the other Englishmen who had stayed behind.

The situation of Tripoli harbour meant that this kind of destruction was a constant risk. The Tripoli port itself – *al-Mina* – was not a harbour proper, but was a 'road', that is a stretch of water near the shore where ships can ride at anchor. Ships were partly defended from the force of the waves by two islands – the Bird and Coney Island.[18] There are a number of other tiny islands here, and very sharp rocks to the west and north of the road where ships had to anchor. Ships could be very vulnerable in a storm. As William Lithgow wrote: 'There is no haven by many miles neere unto it, but a dangerous rode, where often, when Northerly windes blow, ships are cast away.'[19]

Was Timberlake aboard his ship at the time? It was normal for the crew at least to sleep on board when at harbour. Did he dive into the sea from the decks as his precious ship and cargo were lashed by waves and wind towards the jagged stones? Did he watch the ghastly accident from the shore? Many scenarios are possible, but clearly the utter devastation for Henry Timberlake, to see cargo, ship, some crew, everything, drown in turbulent waters at a foreign – and hostile – port is almost unimaginable.

22

Disaster

Timberlake was alone, a shipless Captain. Upon the *Trojan's* annihilation, after so much misery with the Tripoli authorities, Timberlake could not have turned to Sanderson for any comfort. Sanderson was not a very sympathetic figure, and was clearly peeved at losing his own possessions. Sanderson left, sailing to the island of Zante in the *Edward Bonaventure*, a ship co-owned by Timberlake, and then to Venice in the *Cherubin*, travelling overland back to England through France, which would have been quicker than the sea voyage.

Timberlake did not return.

After all he had gone through, he was faced with this. Henry Timberlake believed in divine providence: God's protection and care of the world. It is not so hard to believe in it when things are going well for you, or if you are basically of an optimistic disposition. But when disaster strikes, what then happens to belief in the beneficent care of God?

In Timberlake's day they believed also in the power of evil forces, like Shakespeare's weird sisters: the witches that Macbeth meets, to his doom, on a heath.

This was not an age of widespread maritime insurance. There were rudimentary insurances for cargo, but generally a wrecked ship was a total loss. You can see this being played out in Shakespeare's *Merchant of Venice*. Antonio, the merchant, has put all his money into ships and freight, and raises a loan from Shylock of 3,000 ducats for his friend Bassanio on the condition that he is bound to repay it in three months. He is relying on the success of at least one of his ventures. From his ships he expects return of 'thrice three times the value of this bond': 27,000 ducats. He is so confident and dealing with such huge sums that he agrees to give the Jewish money-lender (whom he hates and who likewise hates him) a 'pound of flesh' from near his heart if he does not repay the loan. Antonio, however, strikes complete disaster with his ventures: all his ships are wrecked. As Bassanio exclaims, horrified, questioning:

Hath all his ventures fail'd? What, not one hit?
From Tripolis, from Mexico, and England,

from Lisbon, Barbary, and India,
And not one vessel scape the dreadful touch
Of merchant-marring rocks?

Antonio clearly does not have insurance to compensate for his losses. He is penniless, and therefore Shylock is determined to have his 'pound of flesh'. Antonio had believed that he could not lose everything since:

My ventures are not in one bottom (= hull) trusted,
Nor to one place

He had felt secure. For there was an assumption that if one ship should be wrecked Antonio could still completely compensate for its loss by the huge profit he would make on another. The sums involved show what astronomical profits and losses could be made in overseas trade.

If possible, merchants would go on rescue missions to try to salvage lost goods. There's a story of the wrecking of a ship off the coast of Scotland in November 1556; the goods were subsequently pillaged by the local inhabitants. A deputation was sent from London to recover these, and they managed to take back £500 of the material.[1] That was all.

The agony of Henry Timberlake, trying to recover what was left of the wreckage and the stock he had on board the *Trojan* – let alone dealing with dead and injured sailors – must have been great. Given that the purpose of his voyage had been to earn money not only for himself but for a raft of Levant Company merchants, including Richard Staper himself, the tragedy of the loss was desperate. In today's terms, he had lost millions not only belonging to himself in the form of his ship and property, but also belonging to others. There was simply no way to recoup the loss. The only thing to do was to stand up, work out the most practical course, gather up what could be recovered, and go on.

Timberlake and his remaining crew would have spent weeks scouring the shore and town to salvage all that they could.

He still did not return to England. After the recovery of anything salvageable from the wreck, he could have gone back to London with his tail between his legs, and sorted out his finances and a better venture as carefully as possible. But Henry Timberlake's nature was to fight for success, not to succumb to defeat. He simply would not return as a failure.

Then there is something else Timberlake did. He returned to Alexandria. He knew the place now. He could work out his future.

This return to Alexandria is conjecture on my part, but it is reasonable to suppose he went back to Egypt, because he made a point of finding out what happened to al-Fessi. At Alexandria, the Moroccan pilgrims would have gathered to return on ships bound for the Maghreb. There was a Moroccan presence in the town. People knew people. Who left and who returned was remembered. He could find al-Fessi, or people that knew him.

But here Timberlake found out something else.

The *hajj* was dangerous. The 'wild Arabs' could attack the caravan, but more deadly still was simple disease. The plague at Aleppo could easily have spread to Damascus, and then to Mecca itself through the pilgrims. The plague that the Englishmen of Aleppo had fled from was not likely to have stayed in one city. Plague was a terrible scourge everywhere, and it was one of the most dangerous things for pilgrims.

For all his commitment to protecting Henry Timberlake, al-Fessi himself succumbed to forces that would rob him of life.

Timberlake's original letter did not of course contain the information about the death of the Moor. It was only the 1609 printed edition that included it, along with all the apologetics, for only some time after he sent his letter from Alexandria did Timberlake learn of his friend's fate and news of this could not have reached Archer until after Timberlake's return to London. In the relevant insert of the 1609 edition of the account, tacked on to the description of the Moor's departure for Mecca, there is nothing about how Timberlake came by news that would have been impossible to procure without a return to Egypt:

> I... bought divers provisions for him to furnish him in his journey to Mecha, in which journey, as hee returned againe, hee dyed.

When misfortune strikes in the Muslim world people say '*Allah aqbar*', God is great. That is the call you hear from the minarets when it is time to pray. You cannot understand the workings of God; you can only submit. You praise God when life is good; you call him great when life is hard. The Maghrebis who told Henry Timberlake of al-Fessi's death would have said those words: *Allah aqbar*.

How would Timberlake have reacted, given the cataclysmic loss of his ship, and now the news of the death of the man who had saved his life when he journeyed in a strange land? He was alive, and al-Fessi was dead. He was alive, and his ship had been destroyed. This was a bizarre dance of fortune. How could it be explained?

Some Muslims might have said that God acted with favour to al-Fessi, in taking him when he did. It was said that there were *hajjis* who blinded themselves after they made the pilgrimage, so that they would see nothing profane ever again. It was said that every man's destiny was written on his forehead. Surely God himself had taken al-Fessi to Paradise, having completed his sacred journey. He would see no more sin. All his sins were forgiven. We all must die, and he died at the perfect time. He was rewarded. *Il ham du lila.*

The Christian notion of divine providence was something else. To a Protestant like Henry Timberlake untimely death could not have been a blessing from God. A blessing from God was an easy death after a long life of health and prosperity. It was a blessing for a traveller to return to his loved ones waiting at home, to feel the wind and the waves, to seize every day with full sails. That was God's blessing, to trust that Heaven awaits after living a good, long and prosperous life. It fuelled the Protestant work ethic. That was what Timberlake hoped for.

To one who deserved God's providence, God had – for Timberlake – withheld it.

And was al-Fessi in Paradise, after the *hajj*? Timberlake, like many Christians of today, believed there could be no salvation for anyone unless they believed in Christ as their Saviour, and were baptised and confirmed, trusting in the death and resurrection of the Son of God. Muslims like al-Fessi did not even believe that Christ was crucified, let alone risen. To Christians, he should be classified as a damned infidel.

Did the Good Samaritan go to Hell? Timberlake had called al-Fessi 'my good Moor', reflecting the epithet 'the good Samaritan'. He had made the association himself.

When you are a traveller, worlds open up that are not only physical, but also philosophical. The death of 'my good Moor', cannot have been taken easily by Timberlake.

By the spring of 1602 Timberlake had buried two of his infant children, suffered imprisonment and seen his ship and stock claimed by the terrible sea. He had been away from home for a year. Some of his sailors may also have been drowned. The man who had saved his life in Palestine had died. Timberlake stood bereft of much money, in a foreign land, with few around him to give him any support, and hardly anyone who spoke his language. How very fierce the world must have seemed. In not returning to London, perhaps he went off searching for some solution to the way life had turned out for him. Henry Timberlake would not return to England for another year, by which time his friends in London had already offered his Alexandrian letter for publication to Thomas Archer.

But Timberlake did return, and went on to be a wealthy and successful man.

23

Publication

Henry Timberlake was an incredible survivor. The kind of misfortune that would have crushed lesser men did not crush him. If he went back to Alexandria, it was perhaps to take command of another ship. Whatever he did in the following year was a success. Somehow, Timberlake salvaged some stock. Somehow, he bought and sold astutely. Somehow, he called on one port and another and traded well. He did not return to London destitute. He did not return until he could come back victorious.

By the time of his arrival home to his wife and family, the first printed edition (with amendments) of his letter had been published. The Elizabethan public was pleased to hear of the exploits of this maverick Captain, who voyaged so daringly to the strange city of Jerusalem. The news of the loss of his ship, the *Trojan*, and his subsequent recovery from disaster would also have been talked about.

At All Hallows Barking, in the records of baptisms, marriages and funerals in the register, there is the record of the birth of Timberlake's youngest son: Richard 'Timberley' was born on 20 January 1604 – that is, 1605. This proves he was back in London by May 1604 at the very latest, but how long before that is impossible to say. In mid-1603 a plague struck London, and if he had returned at that point it is likely that he and his family would have evacuated the city. Again – for how long? It is anyone's guess.

The publisher Thomas Archer published Timberlake's account in that plague year, the year of Queen Elizabeth's death and King James' accession. 1603 was a time of anxiety and momentous change. The mood in the palace was shifting. Two years later there was the Gunpowder Plot. Relations between Catholics and Protestants hit an all-time low. Muslim-Christian relations likewise plummeted. James reversed the open-minded policy adopted by Elizabeth in regard to Morocco and Barbary as a whole. He was a much more fundamentalist Protestant in his religion, and fiercely suspicious of Muslims as well.

Thomas Archer, the publisher, marketed Timberlake's work at 'Pope's Head Pallace, neere to the Royall Exchange': a narrow thoroughfare with Archer's bookshop on the corner. On those streets Timberlake would have walked to see his letter sold as a booklet at this little shop, upon his return to London.

Given the zeitgeist in 1603 and the decades following, some people did not like Timberlake's work at all. In the preface to the publication of William Aspley's version of Biddulph's travels, published in 1609, the pseudonymous 'Theophilus Lavender' (probably Aspley himself) was critical of Timberlake (whom he calls, like Biddulph, 'Master Tymberley') because he thinks that he made so many mistakes that people say 'it is a shame it should come in print'.[1] Who were these people anyway? It is always wise to distrust anyone who begins a sentence with, 'People say...'.

Lavender was writing after the later edition of Timberlake's work has appeared in 1609, for the page numbers he cites are to this, not the first edition, but he is utilising six years of discontented mutterings in his critique.

Timberlake, he says, writes that Mount Hermon and Mount Tabor 'stand very neere together, Tabor being the greater'.[2] Lavender scoffs at this and corrects Timberlake by using Scripture. He claims that Tabor lies 'towards the West of Canaan, and Hermon towards the East'.[3] Lavender is wrong. Hermon is a large mountain north-east of the source of the Jordan at Dan and Tabor is in Galilee, not really east, but more in the centre. Lavender then goes on to announce that 'Tabor is twenty miles beyond the Sea of Galile, and Hermon is a little hill by Jordan'.[4] Actually, Hermon is a mountain 6,506ft high about twenty-two miles north of the Sea of Galilee, which Biddulph would have seen from the Golan, and Tabor is a hill 1,929ft high in Galilee, but not by the Jordan. With such gaffs, Lavender testifies not only to never having been in Palestine, but not even reading Biddulph properly, whom he quarries for his publication. In fact, Timberlake's information that the mountains Hermon and Tabor lie very close together must reflect what Biddulph would have told him that evening in Jerusalem: he learnt that in Galilee there was a hill called 'little Hermon' (now called Givat Hamoreh, 1,690ft high) that lies close to Tabor.[5] It is Lavender who proves himself ignorant of the topography of Palestine as he huffs and puffs over Timberlake's inaccuracies.

Lavender claims that Nazareth is twenty miles from Mount Tabor, and that Timberlake is wrong to say it is five miles away, when Timberlake is completely right, accurately here reflecting what Biddulph must have said to him, though Biddulph never wrote it in his letter. There certainly was a small village of Nazareth (Nasira), even though Lavender wishes to assert that 'neither is there any such City standing at this day, but the place where it stood was neer unto the Sea of Galile'[6] perhaps on the basis of Biddulph's omission of Nazareth in his letter, blended with a hasty reading of the Gospels. Nazareth is twenty miles from the Sea of Galilee.

Lavender claims that Timberlake never visited the Jordan, Jericho or Sodom, when Timberlake states that he received a patent letter that he washed in the waters of the Jordan River and that he took bitumen from the Dead Sea. Lavender seems to have misread Timberlake as easily as he misread Biddulph. He misses the allusion. The Padre Guardiano would have been pleased.

It is always very irritating when critical reviewers quote you incorrectly, or misinterpret your words, and then refute the misinterpretation as if you have said something you have not said, or if they 'correct' you by writing complete rubbish. Timberlake would have felt this. Lavender uses a classic supercilious put-down of the 'I-could-say-so-much-more-but-I-won't' variety: 'Besides these particulars (and many other which I could name, but modesty forbeare) that Pamphlet setteth down all things for truth which were told unto the Author, whereas many of them are most false and ridiculous.[7] Timberlake is gullible, then, and Lavender is being modest in not listing how many errors there are in the printed text – how nice of him!

So Timberlake gets a bad review, and a tendentious one, because Lavender is doing this to promote his own publication of Biddulph's renovated letters, printed by Thomas Haveland, for William Aspley, sold at his shop in Paul's Church Yard, at the sign of the Parrot. Actually, if 'Lavender' is in fact a pseudonym for William Aspley himself, one may suspect he is being truly peevish and self-promotional. He admits (so big of him) that 'all men speake well of Master Tymberley: and my Author [Biddulph] reporteth him to be a very honest and judicious man'. Biddulph also said to him that 'they have wronged him in publishing his travels before his comming into England, and inserting thereinto such untruths against the Author's will'.[8] Really? Which untruths exactly? So Lavender and Biddulph discussed Timberlake, and Biddulph thought any errors were actually inserted by Thomas Archer, the publisher, and were not Timberlake's own.

They thought it was wrong to publish Timberlake's account before his return. Lavender writes: 'The voyage of Master Tymberley was imprinted (as I understand) without his consent, and before his coming to England, by a Copy which hee sent to his friend.'[9] Lavender excuses Timberlake for not correcting errors, because he never got to see any proofs. Evidence of this lack of input is even in the title, he says, because it mentions 'English pilgrims' when, as we all know, 'Pilgrims goe with a superstitious devotion to worship Reliques at Jerusalem; but master Tymberley and his companions went thither onely as travellers to see the Holy Land.'[10] The taint of Catholicism was a dangerous thing, and Archer had certainly erred by putting the word 'pilgrims' in the title. Interestingly, Archer had avoided mentioning that Timberlake and Burrell dressed in pilgrim attire, but had botched the title.

Lavender has this devious way of condemning Timberlake while ostensibly defending him from his critics, those 'many men of learning and judgement'. He could not possibly have agreed to call himself a pilgrim or even have permitted the book to be published at all, he writes, because, 'if it were his owne doing, he being both wise and Religious (as he is accounted) would never bee so simple to publish his owne disgrace in Printe, in going to Masse, and observing many other ceremonies as are mentioned in that booke which goeth foorth under his name.'[11] Timberlake never went to Mass exactly. He went to services, but he never partook of the Catholic Eucharist.

Timberlake, as far as is known, did not bother to engage in a refutation. At any rate, time itself is the greatest disprover of bad reviews. Perhaps he did not want to lower himself to engage in discussion with a hypocrite.

Despite his comments about Biddulph, the 'sweet smelling lover of God', Theophilus Lavender, alias William Aspley, appears to have published Biddulph's letters without his permission, just as he did Shakespeare's plays, with inserts from all kinds of sources, and mashed the originals together out of order. Aspley had already made a name for himself in publishing unauthorised copies of popular London plays, including (in quarto form) Shakespeare's *Henry IV Pt II* (1600), *Much Ado About Nothing* (1600), and an anti-Catholic treatise called 'The supplication of certaine Masse-priests falsely called Catholikes' (1604). In the case of the plays, booksellers such as Aspley would get a shorthand writer to copy a play as it was spoken in the theatre. In publishing Biddulph's work without permission, as well as Shakespeare's, who is he to criticise anybody else?

Lavender/Aspley's efforts with the Biddulph material in fact reaped the wrath of John Sanderson, which was significant wrath to reap. In January 1609 [1610], just after Aspley's edition of Biddulph's material was published, Sanderson wrote a letter to his friend John Kitely saying that he should keep any letters or papers of his safe in case someone 'most malitious' got hold of them and published them 'with malitiouse additions and faulse flatteries'. He feared a 'Lavender' might get his hands on his own material, after his decease. Sanderson notes that 'some affirme that they weare in print without his [Biddulph's] knowledge and consent, and so may be verely thought'. The edition of Biddulph 'stinkes of lies and foolerye'. He tore out pages to prove the point and sent these with the letter to Kitely. Sanderson, it has to be said, was no friend to Biddulph: when Sanderson once saw Biddulph in London his 'hart rosse at his gotes beard' and he could not bear to say hello.[12]

Kitely replied with an attack on Biddulph as the source of the publication through and through. He insinuates that Biddulph was a bit of a tippler in Aleppo, and, writing with weighty puns, adds, 'I would take some paines with my penne to perfume Theophilus Lavender, but you know the nature of the stuff is rancke and not to be stird in. What maie be done besid in other places wilbe knowne... In the meanwhile I smell his kinsman Theologus Spickenard... and ever hath shewed more beard than witt or religion in all his 10 yeares travils.' Spikenard is a kind of lavender bush, and 'Theologus' must refer to a theologian, or minister of the church: Biddulph himself.[13] Kitely makes that plain by adding the reference to Biddulph's well-known long beard and ten years of travel. By Kitely's understanding, Biddulph would perhaps have invented Theophilus Lavender to hide behind, so he himself could chop and change his own letters and write such a nasty preface against Timberlake, with other snide things inserted as well. Such a conspiracy theory might seem a little extreme, especially given the appalling errors in Palestinian geography Lavender makes, but it shows how much animosity was lurking in the Levant Company, and how careful you had to be about what went into print of a religious nature.

Archer did not have a monopoly on Timberlake's work. Rival publishers could take it into their own hands to make their own editions, to cash in on the popularity of a bestseller. Copyright laws were only in their infancy, and came in the form of a decree from the Crown. For example, at the beginning of Fynes Moryson's account of his travels, published in 1617, there is an announcement that no one else is allowed to print the book for the next twenty-one years 'upon paine of his Majesties high displeasure', with the penalty of £3 per book. That would certainly have kept rival publishers off Moryson, at least for a time, but others were not so protected. Bootleg editions were rife.

Timberlake's *True and Strange Discourse* was usually in the hands of Archer or legitimate associates of Archer, but in an unauthorised edition printed in 1611 by John Norton for another bookseller, Hugh Perry, there is something shocking. An artist has created a visualisation of a scene in which Timberlake and the Moor cross the desert on a camel together (Figure 18), and it is supposed to be funny.

This artist had a very dim idea about what a camel looked like, and perhaps drew a 'cameleopard'. He had a dim idea about what a Moroccan looked like too, and depicted the Moor like a puppet, or a court jester, only with a very black face. He is sub-Saharan African, not a North African from Fes. The English, with ultra-pale skin, perhaps lumped together anyone with darker skin into one amorphous 'black' category.

As for Henry Timberlake, despite his fervent Protestantism, he is outfitted like a Catholic pilgrim to Santiago di Compostella. A little scallop shell, associated with that site, is positioned on his cloak. Another symbol, perhaps a ship, is on his hat. The artist had obviously been in touch with Timberlake's critics, as evidenced by Theophilus Lavender, who tightly considered the journey far too Catholic-sounding to be read by wholesome Protestants, despite the fact that Timberlake comes across today as one of the most flagrantly anti-Catholic people you could have met at the time. In total, the whole ensemble in the picture looks like a couple of clowns riding a (two-men-in-a-costume) circus horse. Then there is another feature that makes the entire portrayal even more obnoxious: the camel has a huge erection.

Despite the offensiveness of this image, it is a very useful piece of evidence to have, because it serves to show the preconceptions of Timberlake's audience, and also gives us a sense that his story was read by some as somewhat ridiculous. And perhaps what was most ridiculous to them was what is most interesting to us: the relationship between an Englishman and a Moor. The erection of the camel is a terrible insinuation, and is reflected also in the upright baton carried by the Moor. Timberlake gets branded a Catholic and the Moor a fool and their relationship as one of lascivious homosexuality. Why would a Muslim be friendly to an Englishman unless he wanted to have sex with him? The Moor's friendship with Timberlake could then be dismissed as base, in terms of the standards of the day, rather than honourable.

How could anyone understand the motivations of a Muslim to protect a Christian? How could Timberlake ever have expected them to understand what he had gone through? How could his account be anything but an entertaining curiosity?

Timberlake did not, apparently, interfere with Archer's enterprise, even with additions of new information and emendations that crept in. He had not written his letter to be published. It was not a work of literary craft. Perhaps Timberlake really did not care enough, or perhaps he had no rights. Whatever the case, it was a reasonably popular work, given the numerous reprintings it enjoyed.[14] His name would have been known by many. And yet Timberlake's interests were not in literature; they were with the sea and the world out there.

Importantly, however, the name of his ship, *Trojan*, was removed in the later edition. Perhaps the memory of her loss was too terrible, and he would rather ask for it to be deleted from the text than have himself reminded again of her destruction. Despite all his critics, he would have had those who relished the glimpse of the world he had opened up.

Meanwhile, Timberlake concentrated on new travels. Henry Timberlake's name appears as a member of the Company of Merchant Adventurers of London, formed in 1612 to discover a north-west passage between the Atlantic and Pacific Oceans, an easier route to the lucrative East.[15] He is not mentioned regarding the ships that sailed off to Canada in search of this elusive, indeed non-existent, passage, but his involvement would have been as a fundraiser and financial supporter. He had the wealth to provide. He was rich enough to hold first joint stock in the East India Company until 1617.[16] There is no indication that he ever received royalties for his book. Rights to its publication were later in the hands of the East India Company.

More importantly perhaps, he looked to America. He sailed there in 1618. The Virginia Colonial Records mention a meeting for 'Smythes Hundred'[17] attended by Henry Timberlake on 5 August of that year.[18] Virginia, an English colony, spelt for the few entrepreneurs who ventured there a golden future, and he owned land. His dealings with the Virginia Company would apparently lead him to the sister Bermuda Company, and a purchase of land in Bermuda, the Somers Islands. Timberlake's land is now part of the Port Royal golf course.[19]

From Jerusalem in the east to Virginia in the West, from the Russian port of St Nicholas in the north, to Africa in the south, Henry Timberlake voyaged thousands of miles in the various ships he captained, in search of adventure and business. He would be recorded in death as 'the great Traviller'.[20]

Henry Timberlake was one of the extraordinary men who built the modern world, and while he has been eclipsed by more flamboyant travellers and explorers, his tale of adventure in the Holy Land, and his witness to the compassion of a Moor, still resonates to the present day. It is not a story of conquering and discovery; it is a story of endurance and, if you like, knowledge. When we travel we lay ourselves open to be challenged in ways we do not expect. Likewise, real stories of history challenge us at times to think differently about the world. The past does not always behave as we expect.

Epilogue:
The Great Traveller of
Titchfield

Henry Timberlake's will exists in the records of the Commissary Court of London,[1] in the Guildhall Library, just down the road from where his book was once sold, by Thomas Archer (Plate 17). The will of Henry Timberlake was recorded by the Commissary Court of All Hallows Barking by the Tower of London, since this was his home parish, and was written on 10 July 1625, in the first year of the reign of King Charles I.[2] It indicates that before he died he moved away from London to live in Chilling in the Parish of Titchfield, close to Southampton and Portsmouth.

He records that he is 'at this present [time] sickly in body and lame in my limmes'. Lameness would have been a terrible restriction on a man like Timberlake, a great adventurer who had sailed off widely, who had conquered his fears and taken huge risks, both with his life and his finances. Lameness means you cannot travel anywhere, for even to leave the room is a torment. At such a time, he could only travel in his memory.

The will lists his land and houses as well as his existing family. His eldest son Thomas Timberlake receives 'such lande and Tenements, and shared or partes of Land as I now am, or at any time hereafter during my life shalbe, seized of in the Somer Ilands or Virginia in the Partes beyond the Seas, or in either of them with all profittes and commodities ernninge and increasinge in and upon the same.' In addition he and his heirs receive: 'one parcell of land with a tenement thereon erected, called or knowne by the name of Hobbes or Madame Land, situate, lyeinge and beinge in Barking in the Countie of Essex.'

Then there is a younger son, called Henry, to whom he bequeaths 'one Cottage and one Parcell of Land called or knowne by the name of the Mount Marshe, or by what other name soever the same is called or knowne withall the Salt Marshes thereoute belonginge or therewith enjoyned. All which are situate and lyinge and beinge in Prittlewell in the said County of Essex.' He also gives to his son Henry 'two cottages in Lambeth Marsh neire the Cittie of London'.

According to the records of All Hallows Barking he had buried his son Henry as a baby. Given the loss of his namesake son, the son born on 20 January 1604 (1605) – though baptised as 'Richard' – perhaps took his father's name. Alternatively, Richard died and this is another younger son, baptised somewhere other than in All Hallows Barking.

These lands and buildings are bequeathed with strings. There is a complex arrangement to make good his debts, for he is 'now indebted unto diverse persons in diverse great somes of money'. The payment of these debts has been guaranteed by his good friend Arthur Bromfield Esq. Meanwhile, Sir William Cope of Hanwell, Oxfordshire is indebted to Timberlake the sum of £3,947 'or thereaboutes'. That Timberlake dealt in large amounts is not surprising given what was required for adventuring overseas. The sum has been conveyed to Timberlake as security from some mortgaged lands called Withcombe in Oxfordshire and Wakering in Essex, and he had obtained a decree in the Chancery for receiving the debt out of the rents due to Sir William Cope out of Custom House Quay. So all creditors would be justly answered. The National Archives contain records of Timberlake's decree from the Chancery: C 3/385/28 and C 3/385/ 29 labelled 'Timberlake v. Cope: Oxford and Essex, dated 1621–1625.

Timberlake then turns to his daughters. His daughter Sara is identified as being 'now the wife of Timothie Blyer of Tichfield' who is a 'Clarke', actually the vicar of the church. She is bequeathed a legacy of £200, but not until 1630, as long as she is still alive. He gives £5 to 'Timothie Blyer the younger'[3] who is 'my apprentice [in] the Company of Browne Bakers, within the Cittie of London, whereof I have been a member'.

As for his daughter Hester, she is 'now the wife of Thomas Williams', but she had children from a previous marriage to a man named Mitchell. Of these children, two still live with her: Thomas and Judith. Two others, John and William, appear to be boarding elsewhere. Hester is to be given £30 yearly out of the rents and profits of Timberlake's leasehold tenements in London'. The National Archives have a document from 18 May 1609 (E 214/928), with the parties given as 'James I' on the one hand and 'Henry Tymberlake and Robert Bradbury of London, gentlemen' on the other, concerning 'the lease of tenements, a wharf, gardens etc. in [the parish of] St. Peter edVincula within the Tower of London, and All Hallews Barking, for 80 years from the death of Sir Henry Lee, Master of the Arsbury'.

Timberlake gives inheritances also to Hester's children Thomas, William, Judith and John. Timberlake is clearly much concerned that his grandsons be properly maintained until they can be 'placed out, apprenticed or otherwise disposed and settled in some course to enable them to live'. Hester is also bequeathed, additionally, £20 to be paid one year after his death. There is no mention of his other daughter, Marie, who must at the stage have been already dead.

He gives then legacies to his sister Katharine Burrowes and her husband Jeremy. Then there comes something for his friends: 'I give and bequeath to my loving friends Arthur Bromfield and Mary his wife, and to Elizabeth his daughter, to William Beeston, gent[leman] and to my kinsman Jasper Dartnell and to his wife, to everie one of them fortie shillinges to make each of them a Ring to be worne in remembrance of mee.'

Timberlake was generous in his will. His first wish was to give the poor of Titchfield £3. All sorts of people, from godchildren to servants and associates, get a cut, and also Dorothy Pescod, 'a poore innocent that I keepe' who receives £5, and his executors are instructed that they should 'provide some fit place for her, that she may not wander nor begge.' His old servant, Joane Rieves, is given 'one cowe and a calf' and six 'yewe sheep', and then twenty six shillings and eight pence in money for her to buy hay 'to winter her Cowes with'. All his household servants 'such are not before named and such shall dwell with [me] at the time of my death forty shillinges a piece'. As for what remains, 'of all my goods, cattell and [chattells], anuities, plate, Jewells, household stuffe, implements of the household and husbandrie, and adventures beyond the seas, my debts and legacies aforesaid being paid, and my funeral expenses being defrayed, I give and bequeath unto Margarett my Lovinge wife'.

The 3rd Earl of Southampton, Henry Wriothesley, was very active in the fortunes of Titchfield. After the dissolution of the monasteries, in 1537 Henry VIII had given the twelfth-century abbey belonging to Premonstratensian monks to his grandfather Thomas Wriothesley, who became the Earl of Southampton in 1547. The redesigned abbey became his principal country residence: Place House. The 3rd Earl was distinguished locally for reviving the woollen industry, closing the River Meon at Hill Head in 1610 to reclaim the floodplain, building a canal to the sea (designed to carry goods from a mill, tannery and the village and to irrigate the water-meadows), and building a Market Hall on the square, and he was distinguished nationally for being involved in the rebellion of the Earl of Essex in 1601, for his incarceration in the Tower of London, and for being a friend of William Shakespeare. Local legend holds that one of Shakespeare's plays was premiered at Place House and that Shakespeare was in Titchfield, writing plays and sonnets, under Wriothesley's patronage.

Arthur Bromfield, Timberlake's friend, was an agent of the 3rd Earl, and worked to administer the Fontley Iron Mill.[4] The water-powered iron forge on the River Meon was built in 1603–5 and by 1623 the first tin-plate mill had been established, to make kitchen utensils.[5] The Earl tried to boost Titchfield industries, and Bromfield was the man in charge.

But more than that, Timberlake was associated with the 3rd Earl. A book recording the history of the Earl of Southampton Trust, a charity dedicated to helping the poor of Titchfield, has Henry Timberlake's name on the cover: the cover art work is simply a facsimile of the founding deed, made on 18 May 1620, and copied 11 August 1739, which was drawn up by Henry Wriothesley. Timberlake is the second named in the list of eighteen men, after that of Arthur Bromfield. The third name is Timberlake's son-in-law, Timothy Blyer (written Bloew).[6] So by 1620 Timberlake was the landholder of Chilling Manor and a reasonably wealthy man active in helping the poor of the parish. The deed gives the reason for establishing the charity as being because Titchfield, though an ancient market town, is of late 'much decayed and impoverished for want of trade and commerce'. The men who signed the deed thought of improving its fortunes because, since it is situated near the sea coast, it is a 'very fitt place for the making of wollen cloth or for some other good and profitable trade'. The charity was designed not simply to dole out necessities, but so that 'trade might be renewed and continued... for the good of the inhabitants thereof and the poore people of the said Towne sett to worke whereby they may be better enabled to sustayne themselves and their families'.[7] It was a kind of job creation scheme, and fits with the 3rd Earl's interests in improving the industries and enterprises of the town. He gave part of his land to the charity so that some sort of profitable trades could be set up in these areas.

In the National Archives a letter of attorney from the 3rd Earl, appointing 'Arthur Bromfield of Titchfield, Hants., esq., Philip Gifford of London esq. and Henry Timberlake of London, marchant' power of attorney on 1 January 1624 (E 44/335). So, even with residence in Titchfield, Timberlake was still identified as a London merchant.

Despite local charities, it is Henry Wriothesley's association with the Virginia Company that is most intriguing. He was a founding member and Treasurer (from 1620) of the company, which lasted from to 1609 to 1624, and a member of the Somers Islands or Bermuda Company.[8] He too was a backer of Henry Hudson's quest to find the north-west passage.[9]

The early 1620s were a critical time for both Henry Wriothesley (who spent a couple of months under a kind of house arrest after falling foul of King James in 1621), and Virginia. Between August 1620 and February 1621 six ships of settlers had gone out to America, and the following year another twenty-one ships, with 1,300 people. But in March 1622 the colonists in Jamestown were massacred by native Americans who had been dealt with badly by the colony's leaders, and this was then followed by a famine during the winter.[10] Timberlake and Wriothesley would have had much to discuss.

Henry Timberlake's burial is recorded in the Titchfield Parish Register, in September 1625:

> Henry Tymberlake gent[leman], the great Traviller, in the Chancell of Titchfield, the xith day.[11]

Timberlake was buried in the chancel, where only the tithe-holders, the most important landholders, were interred.

On a summer evening my husband Paul and I, with our two children, drove towards Titchfield to find the vestiges of Henry Timberlake. The area between Southampton and Portsmouth is quite populous. The Earl of Southampton's seat at Place House is cut off from Titchfield now by the A27. It was sunset when we arrived, and very quiet in the little town of cobbled streets and jettied houses (Plate 18).

We ate dinner in a local pub, the Coach and Horses, which seemed to be crowded with Henry Timberlakes. I even drank a glass of an excellent local beer called 'Henry's Ale'.

The next day, which was sunny, warm and mellow, we drove out a short distance (about two miles) from Titchfield to Chilling. Chilling Manor Farm is now a livery, Chillingbarn Riding Centre, and we found the owner, Mr Hewlett, in his garden, outside a 1980s house. Mr Hewlett was friendly, and showed us a great old barn.

Apparently, the old manor had been destroyed as recently as 1951 (despite it being subject to a protection order as a historic place) by the American Sun Oil Company, who had purchased the land and were seeking planning permission to build an oil refinery here. One of the obstacles to the planning permission had been the presence of the manor house, even though it was seriously delapidated, and so there had been an 'accident' with a tractor. Whether that story is entirely true or not in all the details, the destruction of the manor house was recent. The oil refinery was, in any case, never built.

Mr Hewlett continued to explain that when he purchased the property in the 1980s there was nothing that remained of the manor, except a cellar, which they found in the course of building his new home. They had concreted it in. But there was also a spooky story. When the builders came to construct the house, they discovered that the architect had unwittingly drawn up the plans to match the dimensions of the old manor 'to the inch'. The entrance-way was in the same place, even the front door. Mr Hewlett pointed out how carriages would have swept around the driveway to deposit their passengers.

Timberlake, with his careful taking of exact measurements, would have been pleased to have the new house match the dimensions of the old manor that had been so ignominiously destroyed.

Thanking Mr Hewlett, we walked to the sea. From the upper storey of the Chilling Manor, you would have been able to get a good view of the Solent, where shipping from Southampton passed by. Perhaps this is one reason why Timberlake chose this location. He could see the ships and the sea, and feel the breezes.

It took us about eight minutes to walk via a wheatfield to the cliffs and the rocky shore, where over to the east there was the Solent Breezes Holiday Camp, and across the water in the distance the grotesque black lines of Fawley Oil Refinery. So Timberlake had gone to the Middle East, and now the Middle East came to England, in the form of that very dangerous substance.

Along the beach there were men enjoying flying in the air with birdlike hang-gliders and yachts sailing on blue, glimmering water. We went further, through Chilling Copse, where people were walking their dogs.

Later, I visited St Peter's Church (Plate 19) with an odd recollection of entering the Church of the Holy Sepulchre in Jerusalem. Here I was, looking for the grave of Henry Timberlake, as I and countless others had entered that sacred shrine looking for the tomb of Christ. I was traipsing around Titchfield seeking objects of association in the same way that Christians looked around Jerusalem. I walked down the aisle to the chancel, where there was a brightly coloured stained glass window, hoping that Henry Timberlake's ledger stone would still be there, and readable. But again I was disappointed. The floor area was completely covered over with Victorian tiles and a blue carpet. Henry Timberlake was not mentioned in the surviving stone memorials on the walls. I looked at all the other ledger stones on the floor, thinking it might have been moved elsewhere, but no luck.

Nevertheless, Henry Timberlake lay beneath the chancel area, even if the exact location of his mortal remains were unknown. Of this illustrious former resident of the parish, this author and adventurer, wealthy London merchant and 'great Traviller', today's Titchfield itself knew nothing apart from what was in the Parish Register. Of Shakespeare, whose visit to Titchfield was pure speculation, there are many legends, and none that has any solid evidence to commend it. It is strange, in history, who is remembered, and who is forgotten.

Back in London, I returned to the Guildhall Library, and Timberlake's will. I wanted to double check there had really been no mention of his book, and indeed there was nothing. On 26 September 1626, the rights, held by the East India Company, to Timberlake's *True and Strange Discourse*, valued at £1,000 – quite a sum – apparently passed to one Abraham Jacob.[12] The rights may have been transferred to the East India Company sometime before Timberlake's will was made. Timberlake's account would not be printed until Nathaniel Crouch took the opportunity to republish it, eighty years after its first appearance, in a form based on the 1609 edition.

I looked also for other records. Soon after their loss, Henry Timberlake's widowed wife and children suffered another blow. The Parish Records of Titchfield contain the notice of the burial of his son, Henry, on 13 December 1627. If this was the boy christened Richard then he would have been only twenty-three, but it may have been yet another younger son. Henry the younger's will indicates that he had no children.[13] But there was another Henry from Titchfield, a grandson who would leave Titchfield to immigrate to Newport, Rhode Island,[14] where he would have six children with his wife Mary, including a Henry, and a long line of Timberlakes would be established in America.

This emigrant may have been a son of Thomas, Timberlake's elder son. I soon held the original copy of his will in my hands, with its browned edges and archaic handwriting. It was written on 10 July 1642, in Surrat, India. Thomas Timberlake followed in his father's wandering footsteps, and ended up as a factor for the East India Company at their Surrat establishment. But the will is a sad inventory. It is as if Thomas is lying in bed, looking around his room, and noting down everything he sees to give to his fellow factors: his shirts, coats, quilts, books, pictures, silks. Then there are some things that appear to have come from his father: one beaver hat, one hanging compass and box, books of navigation and a ring with Persian characters on it.

He gives money to his sisters, and surviving nieces and nephews. What remains of money, land and tenements he bequeaths to his son, named Thomas, if his son was still alive. Perhaps Thomas senior did not know he had a second child, the mysterious Henry who would be an emigrant, when he was installed in faraway India, or perhaps the Henry Timberlake who sailed to Rhode Island was an illegitimate son. The will records on the outside '17 August 1643', the date of probate, and the name of Thomas' sister Sara Balier (Blyer). No clues.

I returned Thomas' will to the librarian at the desk and thought of Captain Timberlake's navigational books and equipment, lying in a room full of remarkable Indian furnishings. This dying man was the same as that little baby Henry Timberlake had left behind in London in 1601 to travel all the way to Algiers, Alexandria, Cairo, and beyond. This was Henry Timberlake's son's fate, to die far away from England at the age of forty-one, not even knowing whether his children lived.

But genealogical searches were not my concern. I walked out into the Guildhall Yard to a clear day in London now, where old and new blend together. The buildings of the Yard are an architectural reminder that the past is built into the present. People like Henry Timberlake are never entirely gone. They leave legacies of their remarkable lives. We can open a book, or a document, and find them again. We carry them with us.

Notes

Prologue: An Old Book

1   Mayer (1993–4). The volume also included another story of fourteen Englishmen visiting Palestine in 1669, and various essays on Palestine, the Bible and the history of the Jewish people by Crouch himself, as 'R. B.' Richard/Robert Burton.

2   In 1608, 1609, 1611, 1612, 1616, and 1620 and 1631. It also appeared in Dutch in 1678. See also the *Harleian Miscellany* I in 1808.

3   *DNB* 56:401; *ODNB* 54:809.

4   See Maclean (2004); Dimmock (2005), contra Matar (1999), 14. The term 'Turks' was used of Muslims of Ottoman lands.

5   Sloane 2496. Timberlake's letter appears on fol. 62r–70v. This volume was put together in February and March 1693, by 'R. B.', Richard/Robert Burton alias Nathaniel Crouch. This volume ended up in the library of the antiquarian Peter LeNeve (1661–1729), and was sold at auction to be bought by Sir Hans Sloane (1660–1753), whose library formed the basis of the British Library.

6   Timberlake (1625/1903-5).

1: Henry Timberlake

1   Willan (1956), 264–5, cf. 5.

2   Willan (1956), 264–5.

3   Wheeler (1601), 87–93.

4   Morton (1979), 205–6.

5   Wood (1935), 17.

6   Hakluyt (1589/1903–5).

7   See for surveys Imber (2003); Finkel (2005).

8   Both quotes from the introduction by David Howell to Maundrell (1810/1963), xxvii-xxviii; Wood, (1935), 230.

9   A crown was 5 shillings.

10 As listed in the *Calendar of State Papers*, vol. 4 ed. Green (1869).

11 [Biddulph] (1609), B.

12 AH/RR/A1/1.

13 See Billings (1994), Chapter 5.

14 Wood (1935), 35–7.

15 Forster (1931), 214.

16 Wood (1935), 209–12.

17 See Harris (1956) for this and what follows.

18 Wood (1935), 36–7, and E210/10336 in the National Archives, Kew.

2: The Ship and the Sea

1   Wood (1935), 17.

2   Wood (1935), 23.

3   Webbe (1590).

4   For such stories see Maclean (2001).

5   [Rawdon] (unpubl.), 27–8.

6   Bent (1893).

7   [Biddulph] (1609), 1–2.

3: The Moor

1   Matar (2005), 5-6.

2   Wood (1956), 42.

3   Wood (1956), 60.

4   Wood (1956), 13, 25–6.

5   Wood (1956), 61.

6   Timberlake (unpubl.), 64v–65r.

7   Timberlake (unpubl.), 64v.

8   Holm (1989), 606–8; Hancock (1984).

9   Locke (1589/1903-5), 90, cf. Forster (1931), 50, n.4.

10 [Biddulph] (1609), 2–3.

11 Bent (1893), 16.

12 Hakluyt (1589/1903-5), 4: 426–34

13 See Barbour (1965), 97–114.
14 Matar (1999), 33; Harris (1956); Yahya (1981), 185–7.
15 Harris (1956), 9.
16 Matar (1999), 100.
17 Wood (1956), 229 notes that ideally a journey between England and the Levant would take forty-two days, but of course it could also take much longer.
18 Blount (1636), 35.

4: Alexandria

1   Webbe (1590), B4r to Cr.
2   Timberlake (1603), 1.
3   Timberlake (unpubl.) 70v. Similar words appear following the initial greeting in the 1603 edition.
4   From the itinerary of Father Simon Fitzsimons (1322–24), in Hoade (1952), 11–12.
5   Davis (1955), 63; Sandys (1673), 115.
6   Hakluyt (1589/1903–5), 5: 153–67; Purchas (1625/1903–5), 6: 149.
7   Lithgow (1614), S3.
8   [Rawdon] (upubl.), 3r.
9   Lithgow (1614), [S4] - T.
10 Blount (1636), 32.
11 [Rawdon] (unpubl.), 3r.
12 Sandys (1673), 114.
13 Sandys (1673), 113; for Alexandria as a whole 111–15.
14 Sandys (1673), 115.
15 Sandys (1673), 110.
16 Sandys (1673), 116.
17 Blount (1636), 36.
18 Sandys (1673), 116.
19 Sandys (1673), 108.
20 Forster (1931), 52.
21 Simon Fitzsimons, in Hoade (1952), 22.

5: Grand Cairo

1   Said (1978/1995).
2   Irwin (2006), 109.
3   Blount (1636), 38.
4   Lithgow (1614), S3v.
5   Blount (1636), 38–44.
6   [Perrara] (1927), 60.
7   Webbe (1590), C.
8   Blount (1636) 42.
9   [Rawdon] (unpubl.), 4v.
10 Blount (1636), 44.
11 Webbe (1590), C.
12 Sandys (1673), 126.

13 Lithgow (1614), S3r.
14 See Raymond (2000).
15 Forster (1931), 211; Wood (1935), 34–5.
16 Wood (1956), 217.
17 Wood (1956), 240.
18 Hakluyt (1589/1903–5), 6: 413–18
19 Timberlake (1609), 29.
20 [Rawdon] (unpubl.), 1v–2r.
21 Alcarotti (1596) 4v and see Morris (2005), 363–83 esp. p.367.
22 Moryson (1617), i, 447.
23 See Aldersley (1589/1903–5) and the instances cited in Chew (1974), 58–9.
24 Wood (1956), 240–1, 244–5.
25 Lithgow (1614), S2r.
26 Raymond (2000), 209.
27 Gonzales (1977), 110.
28 Lithgow (1640), 122.
29 Forster (1931), 78; [Biddulph] (1609), F2r.
30 Ray (1693/1738), 280–1.
31 Dannenfeldt (1968), 69.
32 Forster (1931), 294–5.
33 Timberlake (1609), 22.
34 Sandys (1673), 122.
35 Lithgow (1614), Sr.
36 Sandys (1673), 127.
37 Lithgow (1614), S2v.

6: The Caravan and the Chickens

1   Wood (1935), 32–3.
2   Ray (1693/1738), 285.
3   Ellis (1851).
4   Loftie (1884).
5   Locke (1589/1903–5).
6   Aldersley (1589/1903–5).
7   Mandeville (1582), cf. Milton (1996).
8   Webbe (1590).
9   The assertion by Dimmock (2005), 1, that Timberlake's journey was 'by no means exceptional for an educated and wealthy Englishman at the dawn of the seventeenth century' is not correct, see Morris (2005), 363–83: 'The registers of the Holy Land Custody of the Franciscans indicate that only a few dozen pilgrims a year were visiting Jerusalem at this time' (p. 367). The situation changed somewhat as the seventeenth century progressed.
10 Moryson (1617/1907–8).
11 Adrichomius (1595).
12 For a complete list see Gómez-Géraud (1999), and see her comments on p.240. For a wider collection of travel literature see

Yerasimos (1991).

13   For the Holy Land envisaged by sixteenth-
     and seventeenth-century cartographers see
     Tishby (2001), 80–105 and for the maritime
     maps see Whitfield (1996).
14   Timberlake (unpubl.), 63.
15   Timberlake (1603), 25; Timberlake (1609),
     31 – misprinted as p.23.
16   Timberlake (unpubl.), 65r.
17   Timberlake (unpubl.), 63r.
18   Blount (1636), 44; Chew (1931), 86.
19   Mitchell (1964), 149.
20   Hoade (1952), 30; Amico (1953), 68.
21   Mitchell (1964), 150.
22   Lithgow (1614) S2r.
23   Blount (1636), 44–5.
24   Amico (1953), 66–7.
25   Timberlake (unpubl.), 63r.
26   Timberlake (1603), 2–4.
27   E.g. Sandys (1673), 125–6, cf. Dimmock
     (2005), 2, n.8.

7: The 'Wild Arabians'

1   Timberlake (unpubl.), 63r.
2   [Rawdon] (unpubl.), 8v.
3   There was, for example, no idea of an
     'Arab Christian', only 'Greeks', 'Syrians',
     'Armenians', 'Latins', 'Copts' and so on;
     they are defined purely by religious
     denomination and language, not by
     ethnicity or culture.
4   Ray (1693/1738), 221–2.
5   [Rawdon] (unpubl.), 8r –10v.
6   Anon. (1603), 1–2 and 4.
7   Timberlake (unpubl.), 64r.
8   Timberlake (unpubl.), 63r.
9   Timberlake (unpubl.), 63r.
10   Timberlake (unpubl.), 63r.
11   Aldersley (1589/1903–5), 204.
12   Lithgow (1640), V3v.
13   Lithgow (1614), N5–6.
14   Sandys (1673), 139.
15   Sandys (1673), 140.
16   Bakhit (1982), 221–6.
17   Sharon (1975), 14–16.
18   Timberlake (unpubl.), 63r.
19   Sandys (1673), 137–40.
20   [Rawdon] (unpubl.), 7r.
21   See Auld and Hillenbrand (2000), 832.
22   Sandys (1673), 149–50.
23   [Rawdon] (unpubl.), 10r.
24   Timberlake (unpubl.), 64v.
25   Timberlake (unpubl.), 64v.
26   Timberlake (unpubl.), 64v.

8: The Dwelling of Abraham

1   Timberlake (unpubl.), 64v.
2   Sandys (1673), 150–1.
3   Moryson (1617), i, 217.
4   Singer (1995), 99–100.
5   Sandys (1673), 150.
6   Timberlake (unpubl.), 64v.
7   See Freeman-Grenville, Chapman and
     Taylor (2003), 151.
8   Taylor (1993), 90–91.
9   Hepper and Gibson (1994), 94–105.
10   Canaan (1927), 293.
11   Timberlake (unpubl.), 64r.
12   Timberlake (unpubl.), 64r, and what
     follows.

9: Heaps of Stones

1   Not all date conversions give the same date.
     This is due to the fact the new Muslim
     months require the spotting of the waxing
     crescent moon after sunset on the 29th
     or 30th day of the month to identify the
     beginning of the new month, and such
     sightings were not always consistent. There
     is also the question of how you correlate
     the days, given that the Muslim day begins
     at sunset and the western Christian day at
     sunrise.
2   [Biddulph] (1609), 113.
3   Chew (1974), 74.
4   [Bodington] (1693), 90. The name of the
     writer is given in Crouch's volume as 'T. B.'
     only, and the account is from a letter. I was
     able to discover his identity by comparing
     his initials with the list of English pilgrims
     recorded in the visitors' book of San
     Salvatore, Jerusalem, see Zimolong (1938),
     86–7.
5   Timberlake (unpubl.), 69v.
6   Maundrell (1963), 86–89.
7   For more detail see Bahat (1989), 80–119.
8   Ray (1693/1738), 224.
9   Said (1978/1995).
10   Ray (1693/1738), 224–5.
11   Ray (1693/1738), 224, cf. 214–5.
12   Sandys (1673), 154–5.
13   Rawdon (1607), 19r–20v.

10: Jerusalem

1   Timberlake (unpubl.), 64v.
2   Timberlake (1603), 6.

3   Timberlake (1625/1903–5), 489.
4   Lithgow (1614), O.
5   Peri (2001), 161–200.
6   Lithgow (1614), O4.
7   Chew (1974), 79.
8   The exact place where he was burnt was marked by the Franciscan artist Bernadino Amico in his plan of the Church of the Holy Sepulchre, see Amico (1953), 8, 89.
9   Forster (1931), 87–90
10   Cohen (1984), 117.
11   Forster (1931) 53.
12   Timberlake (unpubl.), 64v–r.
13   Timberlake (unpubl.), 64r, and for what follows.
14   Bent (1893); Dimmock (2005), 3–4, notes 18–19.
15   *NDNB* 54, 809.
16   Sandys (1673), 159.
17   Wood (1964), 34.
18   Moryson (1617), 241.
19   Moryson (1617), 241.
20   Raiswell writes: 'When he was visited by the Roman Catholic defender of pilgrims a short while later, he refused his help stating that he would rather place his trust in the Turk than the pope', *NDNB* 54, 809. However, the account does not imply that the Custos visited Timberlake in prison.
21   Timberlake (unpubl.), 65v.
22   See Auld and Hillenbrand (2000), 832.
23   Timberlake (unpubl.), 65v.
24   Le Strange (1890/1965), 202.
25   This room, though partly ruined, still exists in Jerusalem, even though most of the structure used as the Ottoman seat of government until 1870 is now destroyed, and the new buildings are part of a boys' school. The cloister is no longer standing. The *qibla iwan*, with its bipartite tunnel ceiling, where judgements took place, extends off a podium in the direction of the Haram esh-Sharif, where the large windows still afford a view of the Dome of the Rock, see Burgoyne (1987), 201–9, who lists also the literary evidence for the government building. I have used the descriptions by Elzear Horn and Van Berchem, and assume Amico's drawings and description refer to the courtyards exterior to the 'Praetorium' (cloister with *iwan*) itself.
26   Amico (1953), pl. 18, 78–9.
27   See Murphy-O'Connor (2003), 71–89 and Röhricht (1892).
28   Clark (2005), 96, has written that Timberlake 'once released' from prison

'with the assistance of a kindly Muslim' only agreed to lodge at San Salvatore on condition he was not forced to attend Mass. In fact, he was not released unless he agreed to conditions set by the Sanjakbey.
29   The manuscript mistakenly reads 'they'.

11: San Salvatore

1   See for a general overview Briggs, Linder and Wright (1977), 346–422.
2   Cohen (1984), 7–8.
3   Amico (1953), 8–9.
4   Cohen (1984), 6–7.
5   Cohen (1984), 26–8,
6   Cohen (1984), 34.
7   In the edition of 1603, the words 'but use that sort of prayer which is used in our law' is changed to 'but keepe my conscience to my selfe' (p.8).
8   Clark (2005), 96, writes that Timberlake 'had to field questions from the *custos* about why Queen Elizabeth I had not donated as generously to the upkeep of the Holy Sepulchre as her father had before he fell out with the Franciscans over his confiscation of their estates'. Actually, Henry VIII is not mentioned in Timberlake's reporting of the conversation, and Elizabeth contributed not simply 'as generously' as her father, but not at all.
9   Timberlake (unpubl.), 65v.
10   Moryson (1617), i, 240, and see in general 237–241 (there is no page 239 or 240).
11   Ray (1693/1738), 218–19.
12   Two copper basins probably used for this ceremony were found in 1863, and are now on display in the Museum of the Studium Biblicum Franciscanum in Jerusalem.
13   The traditions that link this site on Mount Sion to the actual place where the Last Supper (and foot-washing) were celebrated were ancient. There had been a small church on Mount Sion even before the Church of Hagia Sion was built in the late fourth century. This latter church was a huge structure that had survived burning by the Persians in 614, only to be destroyed in 1009 by Caliph Hakim, the Fatimid Caliph of Egypt, who also destroyed the great Byzantine buildings around Christ's tomb, at Golgotha. The Crusaders rebuilt the church, utilising walls that still stood, as the Church of St Mary of Mount Sion, and constructed also an Augustine monastery. When they were expelled from the city

in 1187 the site was entrusted to Syrian Christians until it was destroyed in 1219 by the Ayyubids. The Franciscans, with money from Naples (1335–7), repaired the surviving Cenacle, adding Gothic rib vaulting to the roof, and built their new monastery to the south. Part of the Crusader structure was subsequently requisitioned as the (Muslim) Tomb of David. In 1551 the Ottoman authorities banished the Christians from Mount Sion on account of the supposed tomb and allocated them a new residence in the north-western part of the city.

14 E.g. [Rawdon] (unpubl.), 11r; Sandys (1673), 170.
15 [Bodington] (1683), 98.
16 Timberlake (unpubl.), 65r. Clark (2005), 96, here writes that it was the Custos who knelt on the carpet and washed Timberlake's feet, but Timberlake says it was another friar.
17 Horn (1962), 161–3.
18 See Bilek (1986), 5–9.
19 [Biddulph] (1609), 117.
20 [Rawdon] (unpubl.), 11r–12 v.
21 Timberlake (unpubl.), 65r.
22 Timberlake (1603), 9.
23 Timberlake (1625/1903–5), 491.

12: The Pilgrim Trail

1 Thursday, 5 April in the Gregorian calendar.
2 Timberlake (unpubl.), 65r–66v.
3 Amico (1953), 80–81.
4 E.g. [Bodington] (1683), 85–6.
5 [Biddulph] (1609), 133.
6 [Biddulph] (1609), 120–1.

13: The Hammam

1 See Ze'evi (1996), 68–72.
2 An earlier tradition located the Ascension elsewhere, now commemorated by the Dome of Ascension (Qubbat el-Miraj).
3 For this and other details here see Rafeq (2000).
4 For descriptions of contemporary baths, see Dow (1996) and Dow (2000).
5 Timberlake (1603), 21. This section is part of the lacuna in the manuscript.
6 Ze'evi (1996), 62–8.
7 Timberlake (unpubl.), 69v.
8 Timberlake (1603), 24.
9 Timberlake (1609), 28.
10 Timberlake (unpubl.) 69r.

11 Its limits were more or less equivalent to that of the Holy Land. See for evidence the discussion by Gerber (1998).

14: Echoes

1 Timberlake 66v as also for what follows.
2 Sandys (1673), 197.
3 [Perrara] (1927), 26
4 [Biddulph] (1609), 134.
5 Lithgow (1640), 218, and see Peri (2001), 86–7.
6 Lithgow (1614), 03.
7 Lithgow (1614), 03–4.
8 [Biddulph] (1609), 142.
9 Sandys (1673), 199.
10 Amico (1609), xliv, plate 44.
11 Actually, the length of the Dead Sea is not 100 miles, but closer to fifty.
12 Timberlake (umpubl), 66r and for what follows.
13 Timberlake (1603), 19.
14 Timberlake (1603), 20–21.
15 Ze'evi (1996), 18, must also have recognised that Timberlake's note-taking on the Mount of Olives was perilously close to intelligence reporting, for he remembered incorrectly that Timberlake was put in jail *after* this activity, not before.
16 Timberlake (1603), 12.
17 Sandys (1673), 189. The tomb of Zechariah is sometimes also identified nowadays, on the basis of a Hebrew inscription, as the tomb of the Bene Hezir.
18 The manuscript mistakenly has 'fryers' (!) and then a correction.
19 Sandys (1673), 187.
20 Timberlake (unpubl.), 67v and what follows.
21 Lithgow (1614), R2r, and see [Biddulph] (1609), 127; Maundrell (1810/1963), 136. Maundrell notes that he saw bodies in various states of decay, which indicated that 'this grave does not make that quick dispatch with the corpses committed to it, which is commonly reported.'
22 In Timberlake (1603), 14 there is added: 'whether by the Friars poisoning them, or howsoever else it happened, but we thought it straunge, that all five should die together in one weeke.'
23 Moryson (1617), i, 238.
24 Moryson (1617), i, 236.
25 Sandys (1673), 186.
26 Amico (1609), xvi, Plate 46.
27 Ray (1693/1738), 262.

28   Maundrell (1810/1963) 131.

29   Timberlake (unpubl.) 67r.

27   Amico (1953), 47.

28   Amico (1953), 47.

15: Bethlehem

1   Timberlake (1603), 16. The manuscript here has a lacuna.

2   Sandys (1673), 176.

3   [Biddulph] (1609), 132.

4   Moryson (1617), i, 227.

5   Timberlake (unpubl.), 67r.

6   Bodington calls it 'Botechelle', Rauwolff 'Bethisella'.

7   E.g. [Bodington] (1683), 89.

8   [Rawdon] (publ.), 12v-r. 'Cratch' is an antiquated word for manger.

9   So Kootwyck (1619).

10 See Rafeq (2000), 68. 250 pipes from a water organ dating to the medieval period were found in archaeological excavations at the church in 1906, which are now placed in a reconstruction of a water organ in the Flagellation Museum, Jerusalem. See Freeman-Grenville (1993), 26–8.

11 Amico (1953), 59.

12 See Peri (2001), 70.

13 Peri (2001), 82–3.

14 Peri (2001), 70–6.

15 See Verniero di Montepeloso (1929), i, 238.

16 See Amico (1953) 10–12, 43–61 and the Ottoman firmans in Castellani (1922), nos. 213 and 215; Aquilante (1630), 273.

17 Peri (2001), 144.

18 Peri (2001), 91.

19 Amico (1953), 43.

20 Sandys (1673), 178.

21 Sandys (1673), 177; Ellis (1851), 36.

22 Alcarotti (1599).

23 Timberlake (unpubl.), 67r.

24 Amico (1953), 46.

25 From this point I have used the 1603 edition of Timberlake's letter (p.16), because the British Library manuscript breaks off in the middle of a sentence on folio 67r: 'then we went downe into a vault where was a chapell sett in the place of the Natyvitie of our Saviour which did inclose both that and the Manger where Christ was layd and where he was presented with giftes by the wise men. Now over this –' The copyist himself did not have the missing pages because the line break is not at the end of the sheet of paper but three-quarters down the page, a quarter of the way through a line.

26 [Biddulph] (1609), 133.

16: The Temple of the Sepulchre

1   Forster (1931), 294–5.

2   Dodd (1961), 92.

3   Amico (1953), 92.

4   Timberlake (1603), 17. Sandys (1673), 161 says that there were seven strings, one for each of the communities resident in the Church. Perhaps there had been some attempt to minimise the number of cords by Sandys' visit, or else Timberlake was exaggerating.

5   Clark (2005) mistakenly reads his passage as referring to '300 clergy and their families' (p.97) when he states in fact that there were 'above 300 persons, men and women' here in total. Later he gives the total as between 250 and 300, Timberlake (1603), 17.

6   Sandys (1673), 173.

7   Ray (1693/1738), 291.

8   Moryson (1617), i, 219.

9   [Bodington] (1683), 87.

10 See Peri (2001).

11 Rock (1989), 12–13. Punctuation altered.

12 [Bodington] (1683), 86.

13 Ray (1693/1738), 262.

14 [Rawdon] (unpubl) 14v.

15 Timberlake (1603), 18.

16 Timberlake (1603), 18.

17 Drijvers (1992), 11–16.

18 Moryson (1617), i, 232.

17: The Englishmen of Aleppo

1. [Biddulph] (1609), Preface, to Cv.

2   [Biddulph] (1609), Av.

3   Forster (1931), 147.

4   Moryson (1617), ii, 62.

5   Timberlake (1603), 18, and for what follows.

6   [Biddulph] (1609), Bv.

7   See Bakhit (1982), chapter 6, esp. 204–26; Sharon (1975).

8   For all of this, see MacLean (2004), 49–114, though the identification Maclean proposes between Biddulph and 'Lavender' is unlikely for reasons given below in Chapter 23.

9   The register was published by Zimolong (1938), 11. In the first version of this publication Timberlake's name is incorrectly

given as 'Kimberlare', but this is emended in the second version.

18: A Missing Journey

1   Timberlake (unpubl.) 68r.
2   Timberlake (unpubl.) 69r.
3   Timberlake (unpubl.), 68r.
4   Moryson (1617), i, 225.
5   Timberlake (unpubl.), 68r.
6   Lithgow (1614), Pr.
7   [Perrara] (1927), 56.
8   Dannenfeldt (1968), 189.
9   [Bodington] (1683), 101.
10   Maundrell (1963), 105-16.
11   Sandys (1673), 197.
12   Macintosh-Smith (2003), 25.
13   Mitchell (1964), 139-40.
14   Moryson (1617), i, 216.
15   Moryson (1617), i, 225.

19: Dromedaries from Gaza

1   See Chew (1974), 92-5 for the articles received when a pilgrim left Jerusalem.
2   Timberlake (unpubl.) 69r, and for what follows in this chapter.
3   Locke (1589/1903-5), 103-4.
4   Sandys (1673), 200.
5   Timberlake (1609), 29 30.
6   Ze'evi (1996), 10.
7   Timberlake (1603), 25.
8   Hancock (1984), 397.

20: The Hajj

1   Timberlake (unpubl.), 69r, and for what follows.
2   Timberlake (unpubl.), 70v.
3   Timberlake (1609), 32.
4   Timberlake (unpubl.), 70v.
5   Timberlake (unpubl.), 70v.

21: The Trojan

1   Timberlake (unpubl.), 70v.
2   Timberlake (1609), 33.
3   Forster (1931), 122-3.
4   From a note in *Purchas, His Pilgrimes*, in Forster (1931), 107, and see 121-3.
5   [Biddulph] (1609), 35.
6   Cartwright (1611), 6.
7   Moryson (1617), i, 242-3

8   Moryson (1617), i, 242
9   Forster (1931), 90
10   Forster (1931), 90
11   Forster (1931), xl.
12   Forster (1931), 123.
13   Forster (1931), 19
14   Forster (1931), 106.
15   Purchas (1625/1903-5), 9: 485-6.
16   Forster (1931), 19.
17   Forster (1931), 128.
18   Maundrell (1963), 41.
19   Lithgow (1614), L2v.

22: Disaster

1   Willan (1956), 15-16.

23: Publication

1   [Biddulph] (1609), A4v-r.
2   Timberlake (1609), 26.
3   [Biddulph] (1609), A4r.
4   [Biddulph] (1609), A4r.
5   [Perrara] (1927), 19.
6   [Biddulph] (1609), A4r.
7   [Biddulph] (1609), Bv.
8   [Biddulph] (1609), Bv, contra Dimmock (2005), 1, who writes that Timberlake's account was published two years after his return.
9   [Biddulph] (1609), A4v.
10   [Biddulph] (1609), Bv-r.
11   [Biddulph] (1609), Br.
12   Chew (1974), 48-9.
13   For this correspondence see Forster (1931), 259-64, and Chew (1974), 48-9. Maclean (2004), 51-5 suggests that 'Theophilus Lavender' may be a pseudonym for Biddulph, but given Lavender's ignorance of Palestinian topography it seems doubtful to me that he can be equated with Biddulph. Biddulph's own evidence – as reported by Timberlake – is reliable.
14   Dimmock (2005), 1.
15   *DNB* 56:401, see Calendar of State Papers, ed. Sainsbury (1862), 238 40.
16   *DNB* 56:401; *ODNB* 54:809.
17   'Hundred' was the name of a subdivision of a county of shire generally having its own court.
18   The information is found on the Timberlake family website, www.geocities.com/Heartland/Plains/7906/tidbits.htm.
19   *ODNB* 54: 809.
20   Hayward (1998), 112.

Epilogue

1   Vol. 29, folio 211: Henry Timberlake. Box
    9171/28–9.
2   A copy also exists in the National Archives,
    PROB 11/149, fols. 52–3.
3   The date of the wedding is shown in the
    Titchfield Parish register as 16 April 1624.
4   Wade and Watts (1989), 46.
5   Watts (1982), 68.
6   Smith (1997).
7   Smith (1997), 5.
8   Rowse (1965), 234–41 and see Akrigg
    (1968), 154–65.
9   Rowse (1965), 244; Akrigg (1968), 165.
10 Rowse (1965), 254–7.
11 Hayward (1998), 112.
12 *DNB* 56: 401.
13 Prerogative Court of Canterbury 3
    Barrington. I am grateful to Rachel Timlick
    for this reference.
14 Banks (1937), #63–4154.

Select Bibliography

Adrichomius, Christianus (1595), *A Brief Description of Hierusalem,* Eng. transl. by Thomas Thymme of *Ierusalem, sicut Christi tempore floruit, et suburbanorum, insigniarum, historiarm eius brevis descriptio...* (1584), (London).

Agostini, Ludovico degli (1886). *Il Viaggio di Terra Santa* (Pesaro).

Akrigg, G. P.V. (1968). *Shakespeare and the Earl of Southampton* (London).

Alcarotti, Gianfrancesco (1596). *Del Viaggio di Terra Santa* (Novara).

Aldersley, Laurence (1589/1903 5). 'The first voyage or journey made by Master Laurence Aldersley, Marchant of London, to the Cities of Jerusalem and Tripolis &c', in Hakluyt 5, 202–14.

Amico, Bernadino (1609). *Trattato delle piante et imagini de i sacri edifici di Terra Santa...* (Rome).

Amico, Bernadino (1620). *Trattato delle piante...* edition with hand-written amendations of the seventeenth century by an author familiar with Quaresmio, in the holdings of Essex University Library.

Amico, Bernadino (1953). *Plans of the Sacred Edifices of the Holy Land,* transl. by Theophilus Bellorini and Eugene Hoade, with preface and notes by Bellarmino Bagatti (Jerusalem).

[Anon.] (1603). *Letter written to the Right Worshipfull the Governors and Assistants of the East Indian Marchants in London* (London).

[Anon.] (1615). *Le pèlerin véritable de la Terre Saincte, auquel soubs le Discourse figuré de la Iérusalem Antique et Moderne de la Palestine est enseigné le chemin de la Celeste* (Paris).

Aquilante, Rochetta (1630/1996). *Peregrinatione di Terra Santa* (Palermo) repr. in *Corpus peregrinationum italicarum* 4 (4.1) (Pisa).

Auld, Silvia and Hillenbrand, Robert (eds.) (2000). *Ottoman Jerusalem: The Living City 1517–1917* (London).

d'Aveyro, Pantaleao (1593). *Itinerario da Terra Sancta, e suas particularidades ...* (Lisbon).

Bahat, Dan with Rubenstein, Chaim T. (1989). *The Illustrated Atlas of Jerusalem* (Jerusalem).

Bakhit, Muhammad Adnan (1982). *The Ottoman Province of Damascus in the Sixteenth Century* (Beirut).

Banks, Charles (1937). *The Topographical Dictionary of 2885 English Immigrants to New England (1620-1650)* (repr. 2002).

Barbour, Nevill (1965). *Morocco* (London).

de Beauvau, Henri (1608). *Relation journalière du voyage du Levant faict et descrit par Messire Henry de Beauvau* (Toul).

Belon, Pierre (1553). *Les observations de plusieurs singularitez & choses memorables, trouveé en Grèce, Asie, Iudée, Egypte, Arabie, & autres pays estranges* (Paris).

Benard, Nicolas (1621). *Le Voyage de Hierusalem et autres lieux de la Terre S., faict par le Sr Benard...* (Paris).

Bent, J. Theodore (ed.) (1893). *Early Voyages and Travels in the Levant I. The Diary of Master Thomas Dallam, 1599-1600, ii. Extracts from the Diaries of Dr. John Covel, 1670-1679. With Some Account of the Levant Company of Turkey Merchants* (London).

[Biddulph, William] (1609). *Travels into Africa, Asia and to the Blacke Sea,* prefaced and edited by Theophilus Lavender (London, repr. Amsterdam/New York, 1973).

Biddulph, William (1625/1903–5). 'Sundry the personall Voyages performed by J. Sanderson... (etc.) begun in October 1584, ended in October 1602', in Purchas 8: 248–304; 9:485.

Billings, Malcolm (1994). *London: A Companion to its History and Archaeology* (London).

Blount, Henry (1636). *A Voyage into the Levant. A Brief Relation of a Iourney, Lately performed by Master H. B. Gentleman from England...* etc. (London).

[Bodington, Thomas] (1683). 'A Journey to Jerusalem or, the Travels of Fourteen English Men to Jerusalem in the Year 1669', in Crouch, 79–104.

de Brèves, François Savary (1628). *Relation des Voyages de M. de Brèves, tant en Grèce, Terre Saincte, et Aegypte, qu'aux Royaumes de Tunis & Arger...* (Paris).

Briggs, John H.Y., Linder, Robert D. and Wright, David F. (eds.) (1977). *The History of Christianity* (Tring).

Brlek, Metodio (1986). *La Chiesa di S. Salvatore* (Jerusalem).

Burgoyne, Michael H. (1987). *Mamluk Jerusalem: An Architectural Study* (London).

Canaan, Tawfiq (1927). *Mohammedan Saints and Sanctuaries in Palestine* (Journal of the Palestine Oriental Society; facs. repr. Jerusalem, n.d.).

le Carlier, Jean (1579/1920). *Voyage en Orient. Publié avec des notes historiques et géographiques* (Paris).

Cartwright, John (1611). *The Preachers Travels. Wherein is set downe a true Iournall, to the confines of the East Indies, through the great Countreys of Syria, Mesopotamia, Armenia, Media, Hircania and Parthia...* (London, repr. Amsterdam/Norwood, N.J.).

Cartwright, John (1625/1903–5). 'Observations of Master John Cartwright in his voyage from Aleppo to Hispaan and backe againe', in Purchas 8:482–523.

Castellani, E. (1922). *Catalogo dei firmani ed altri documenti legali concernenti la Custodia di Terra Santa* (Jerusalem).

Chew, Samuel C. (1974). *The Crescent and the Rose: Islam and England during the Rennaissance* (New York).

Clark, Victoria (2005). *Holy Fire: The Battle for Christ's Tomb* (London).

Cohen, Amnon (1984). *Jewish Life under Islam: Jerusalem in the Sixteenth Century* (Cambridge, Mass.).

Conder, C. R. and Kitchener, H. H. (1881–83). *Survey of Western Palestine*, 3 vols. (London).

Coryate, Thomas (1625/1903–5). 'Master Thomas Coryates travels to, and Observations in Constantinople, and other places in the way thither, and his Iourney thence to Aleppo, Damasco and Ierusalem' in Purchas 10: 389–447.

Crouch, Nathaniel (Burton, Richard) (ed.) (1683). *Two journeys to Jerusalem, containing first, A strange and true account of the travels of two English pilgrims...* etc. (London).

Dannenfeldt, Karl H. (1968). *Leonhard Rauwolf: Sixteenth-Century Physician, Botanist and Traveler* (Cambridge, Mass.).

Davis, Richard Beale (1955). *George Sandys: Poet-Adventurer. A Study in Anglo-American Culture in the 17th Century* (London).

Dimmock, Matthew (2005). *New Turkes: Dramatizing Islam and the Ottomans in Early Modern England* (Aldershot).

Dodd, A. H. (1961). *Elizabethan England* (London/New York).

Doumani, Beshara B. (1999). 'Rediscovering Ottoman Palestine: Writing Palestinians into History', in Ilan Pappe, *The Israel/Palestine Question* (London).

Dow, Martin (1996). *The Islamic Baths of Palestine* (Oxford).

Dow, Martin (2000). 'The Hammams of Ottoman Jerusalem', in Auld and Hillenbrand, 519–24.

Drijvers, Jan Willem (1992). *Helena Augusta: The Mother of Constantine the Great and the Legend of her Finding of the True Cross* (Leiden).

Ellis, Henry (ed.) (1511/1851). *The Begynnynge and contynuance of the Pylgrymage of Sir Richard Guylforde* (London, repr. Camden Society Publications, vol. LI).

Ellison, James (2002). *George Sandys: Travel, Colonialism and Tolerance in the Seventeenth Century*, rev. ed. (Cambridge).

Epstein, M. (1908). *The Early History of the Levant Company* (London).

Favi, Vincenzo (1616). *Viaggio di Gerusalemme* (Cali).

Feiler, Bruce (2002). *Abraham: In Search of the Father of Civilisation* (London).

Forster, William (ed.) (1931). *The Travels of John Sanderson in the Levant 1584-1602*, 2nd ed. (London).

Freeman-Grenville, G. S. P. (1993). *The Basilica of the Nativity in Bethlehem* (Jerusalem).

Freeman-Grenville, G. S. P. (1994). *The Basilica of the Holy Sepulchre in Jerusalem* (Jerusalem).

Freeman-Grenville, G. S. P., Chapman, Rupert L., and Taylor, Joan E. (2003). *Palestine in the Fourth Century: The Onomasticon by Eusebius of Caesarea* (Jerusalem).

Finkel, Caroline (2005). *Osman's Dream: The Story of the Ottoman Empire* (London).

Gerber, Haim (1998). '"Palestine" and Other Territorial Concepts in the 17th Century', *Journal of Middle East Studies* 30, 563–72.

Gibson, Shimon and Taylor, Joan E. (1994). *Beneath the Church of the Holy Sepulchre, Jerusalem* (London).

Gibson, Shimon (2003). *Jerusalem in Original Photographs 1850-1920: Photographs from the Archives of the Palestine Exploration Fund* (London).

Golubovich, Girolamo (1898). *Superiori di Terra Santa* (Jerusalem).

Gómez-Géraud, Marie-Christine (1999). *Le crépuscule du Grand Voyage: les récits des Pèlerins à Jérusalem (1458-1612)* (Paris).

Gonzales, Antonius (1977). *Hierusalemische Reyse* (Cairo).

Green, Mary Anne Everett (ed.) (1857–69), *Calendar of State Papers Edward VI - James 1* (London: Her Majesty's Stationery Office).

Guerrero, Francisco (1592). *El viage de Hierusalem* (Seville).

Hakluyt, Richard (1589/1903–5). *The Principal Navigations, Voyages, Traffics and Discoveries of the English Nation made by Sea or Over Land* (London, repr. Glasgow).

Hammel, Ruth Victor (2000). 'Reality, Imagination and Belief: Jerusalem in 19th and early twentieth-century Photographs (1839–1917)', in Auld and Hillenbrand, 235–8.

Hampden, John (ed.) (1970). *Richard Hakluyt: The Tudor Venturers* (London).

Hancock, Ian (1984), 'Shelta and Polari', in P. Trudgill (ed.), *Language in the British Isles* (Cambridge), 384–403.

Harant, Kristof (1608/1972). *Putowánj...* (Prazskem), repr. in A. and C. Brejnik (eds. and transl.), *Voyage en Egypte...* (Cairo).

Harris, Bernard (1956). 'A Portrait of a Moor', in *Shakespeare Survey* 11, 89–97.

des Hayes, Louis (1624). *Voyage de Levant fait par le commandement du Roy en l'année 1621,* ed. Sr. D. C. (Paris).

Hayward, Keith (ed.) (1998). *Titchfield Parish Register 1598-1634* (Titchfield).

Hepper, F. Nigel and Gibson, Shimon (1994). 'Abraham's Oak of Mamre: the Story of a Venerable Tree', *PEQ* 126, 94–105.

Hoade, Eugene (1952). *Western Pilgrims* (Jerusalem).

Holm, John (1989). *Pidgins and Creoles: Reference Survey* (Cambridge).

Horn, Elzear (1962). *Ichnographiae Monumentum Terrae Sanctae (1724–1744)* (Jerusalem).

Hüttersroth, W. and Abdulfattah, K. (1977), *Historical Geography of Palestine, Transjordan and South Syria* (Erlangen).

Imber, Colin (2003). *The Ottoman Empire 1300-1650: The Structure of Power* (London).

Irwin, Robert (2006). *For Lust of Knowing: The Orientalists and their Enemies* (London).

Jullen, M. (1892). *The Virgin's Tree at Matarieh and the Crypt of the Holy Family at Old Cairo* (Cairo).

Kamps, Ivo and Singh, Jyotsna G. (2001). *Travel Knowledge: European 'Discoveries' in the Early Modern Period* (London).

Kemp, Peter (1978). *The History of Ships* (London).

Kootwyk, Johannes (1619). *Itinerarium hierosolymitanum et syriacum, in quo variarum gentium mores et instituta ... recensentur* (Antwerp).

Le Strange, Guy (1890/1965). *Palestine under the Moslems: A Description of Syria and the Holy Land from 650 to 1500* (Beirut).

Lewis, Bernard (1995). *The Middle East: 2000 Years of History from the Rise of Christianity to the Present Day* (London).

Lithgow, William (1614). *A Most Delectable and True Discourse, of an admired and painefull peregrination...* (London, repr. Amsterdam/New York, 1971).

Lithgow, William (1625/1903–5). 'Relations of the Travels of W. Lithgow a Scot, in Candy, Greece, the Holy-land, Egypt, and other parts of the East' in Purchas 10:447–492.

Lithgow, William (1640). *The totall discourse of the rare adventures and painefull peregrinations...* (London).

Locke, John (1589/1903–5). 'The Voyage of M. John Locke to Jerusalem' in Hakluyt 5: 76-104.

Loftie W.J. (ed.) (1884). *Ye Oldest Diarie of Englysshe Travell: being the hitherto unpublished narrative of the Pilgrimage of Sir Richard Torkington to Jerusalem in 1517* (London).

Lussy, Melchior (1590). *Reissbuch gan Hierusalem....* (Freyburg in Uchtland).

Macintosh-Smith, Tim (2003). *The Travels of Ibn Battutah* (London).

MacLean, Gerald (2001), 'Performing East. English Captives in the Ottoman Maghreb', *Actes du 1er Congrès International sur: Le Grande Bretagne et le Maghreb: État de Recherche et contacts culturels* (Zaghouane, Tunisia), 123–39.

MacLean, Gerald (2004), *The Rise of Oriental Travel: Early English Visitors to the Ottoman Empire, 1580–1720* (London).

Mandeville, John (1582). *The Voiage and trauayle of syr Iohn Maundeville, Knight, which treateth of the Way toward Hierusalem* (London).

Mantegazza, Steffano (1601). *Relazione del Viaggio di Gerusalemme* (Milan).

Maoz, Moshe (ed.) (1975). *Studies on Palestine during the Ottoman Period* (Jerusalem).

Matar, Nabil (1998). *Islam in Britain 1558-1685* (Cambridge).

Matar, Nabil (1999). *Turks, Moors and Englishmen in the Age of Discovery* (New York).

Matar, Nabil (2005). *Britain and Barbary 1589-1689* (Gainesville, Florida).

Maundrell, Henry (1963). *A Journey from Aleppo to Jerusalem in 1697*, with a new introduction by David Howell (London; repr. Beirut).

Mayer, Robert (1993-4). 'Nathaniel Crouch, Bookseller and Historian: Popular Historiography and Cultural Power in Late Seventeenth-Century England', *Eighteenth Century Studies* 27, 391–419.

Milton, Giles (1996). *The Riddle and the Knight: In Search of Sir John Mandeville, the World's Greatest Traveller* (London).

Mitchell, R.J. (1964). *The Spring Voyage: The Jerusalem Pilgrimage in 1458* (London).

Morris, Colin (2005). *The Sepulchre of Christ and the Medieval West* (Oxford).

Morton, A.L. (1979). *A People's History of England* (London).

Moryson, Fynes (1617). *An Itinerary written by Fynes Moryson. First in the Latin Tongue, and then translated by him into English.* 3 vols. (London, repr. Amsterdam/New York, 1971).

Moryson, Fynes (1617/1907-8). *An Itinerary...* (London; repr. 4 vols. Glasgow).

Murphy-O'Connor, Jerome (2003). 'Tracing the Via Dolorosa', in Molly Dewsnap Meinhardt (ed.), *Jesus: The Last Day* (Washington, D.C.), 71–89.

Parker, Kenneth (1999). *Early Modern Tales of Orient* (London).

Penrose, Boies (1942). *Urbane Travellers, 1591–1635* (Liverpool).

Peri, Oded (2001). *Christianity under Islam in Jerusalem: The Question of the Holy Sites in Early Ottoman Times* (Leiden/Boston).

[Perrara, Juan] (1927). *A Spanish Franciscan Narrative to the Holy Land*, transl. and ed. by Henry Luke (London).

Purchas, Samuel (1965/1903-5). *Purchas his Pilgrimes* (London; repr. Glasgow).

Quaresmio, Francesco (1639/1989). *Historica, Theologica et Moralis Terrae Sanctae Elucidatio* (Antwerp; repr. in original Latin with Italian transl. by Sabino de Sandoli (Jerusalem).

Radzivill, Nicolaus (1614). *Ierosolymitana peregrinatio a Thoma Tretero ex polonico sermone in latinum translata* (Antwerp).

Rafeq, Abdul-Karim (2000). 'Ottoman Jerusalem in the Writings of Arab Travellers', in Auld and Hillenbrand, 63–72.

Ragusino, Stefani Bonifacio (1875). *Liber de perenni cultu Terrae Sanctae* (Venice).

[Rawdon, John] (unpubl.) 'A Particular of my Journey with thosse Meane Observations I have collected', British Library MS 18 A XXXIX [also found in Add. 17,374].

Rauwolf, Leonhard (1582-3). *Aigentliche beschreibung der Raisz...*, 4 vols. (Laugingen).

Ray, J. (ed.) (1693/1738). *A Collection of Curious Travels and Voyages...* (London).

Raymond, André (2000). *Cairo* (Cambridge, Mass.).

Rock, Albert (1989). *The Status Quo in the Holy Places* (Jerusalem).

Roger, Eugène (1646). *La Terre Saincte; ou description topographique très-particulière des sainct lieux...* (Paris).

Röhricht, Reinhold (1892). 'Karten und Pläne zur Palästinakunde aus dem 7. bis 16. Jahhundert, *Zeitschrift für des Deutschen Palästina Verein* 15, 185–8.

Rowse, A.L. (1965). *Shakespeare's Southampton: Patron of Virginia* (London).

Rutherford, John Haynes (1986). *The Humanist as Traveller. George Sandys's Relation of a Journey begun An. Dom. 1610* (London).

Said, Edward W. (1978/1995). *Orientalism: Western Conceptions of the Orient*, with a new afterword (London).

Sanderson, John (1625/1903-5). 'Sundrie the personall Voyages performed by J. Sanderson... begun in October 1584, ended in October 1602', in Purchas 8: 305; 9: 412-86.

Sandys, George (1615). *A Relation of a Journey begun An. Dom. 1610.* (London).

Sandys, George (1625/1903-5). 'A Relation of a Journey begun Anno Dom. 1610 written by Master George Sandys and here contracted', in Purchas 8: 88-247.

Sandys, George (1673). *Sandys Travels, containing an History of the Original and Present State of the Turkish Empire, Their Laws, Government, Policy, Military Force, Courts of Justice, and Commerce*, etc., 7th ed. (London).

Schweigger, Saloman (1608). *Ein newe Reyssbeschreibung auss Teutschland nach Constantinopel und Jerusalem* (Nuremburg).

da Secli, Francesco (1639). *Viaggio di Gerusalemme* (Lecce).

Segal, Ronald (2001). *Islam's Black Slaves* (London).

Sharon, Moshe (1975). 'The Political Role of the Bedouins in Palestine in the Sixteenth and Seventeenth Centuries', in Maoz, 11–30.

Singer, Amy (1995). *Palestinian Peasants and Ottoman Officials: Rural Administration around 16th Century Jerusalem* (New York).

Smith, David G. (1997). *Four Centuries of the Earl of Southampton Trust* (Titchfield).

Strachan, Michael (1962). *The Life and Adventures of Thomas Coryate* (London).

Taylor, Joan E. (1993). *Christians and the Holy Places: The Myth of Jewish-Christian Origins* (Oxford).

Timberlake, Henry (unpubl.) British Library MS Sloane 2496, 62r–70v.

Timberlake, Henry (1603). *A True and Strange Discourse on the Travailes of two English Pilgrimes: what admirable accidents befell them in their journey to Ierusalem, Gaza, Gran Cayro, Alexandria, and other places,...* etc. (London, repr. Amsterdam, 1974).

Timberlake, Henry (1609). *A True and Strange Discourse on the Travailes of two English Pilgrimes: what admirable accidents befell them in their journey to Ierusalem, Gaza, Gran Cayro, Alexandria, and other places,...* etc. rev. ed. (London).

Timberlake, Henry (1625/1903–5). 'Report of the Voyage of Master Henrie Timberley from Cairo in Egypt to Jerusalem in fiftie dayes 1601' in Purchas 9, 487–92.

Timberlake, Henry (1683). 'A Strange and True Account of the Late Travels of Two English Pilgrims and what Admirable Accidents befel them in the Journey to Jerusalem, Grand Cairo, Alexandria, &c', in Crouch, 79-104.

Tishby, Ariel (ed.) (2001). *Holy Land in Maps* (Jerusalem).

Verniero di Montepeloso, Pietro (1929). *Croniche ovvero annali di Terra Santa...* ed. P. Girolamo Golubovich, 2 vols. (Florence).

Villamont, Jacques de (1596). *Les voyages du Seigneur de Villamont... divisez en trois livres...* (Arras)

Wade, Richard and Watts, John (eds.) (1989). *Titchfield: A Place in History* (Southampton).

Watts, George (ed.) (1982). *Titchfield: A History* (Titchfield).

Webbe, Edward (1590). *The Rare and Most Wonderfull Things which Edw. Webbe an Englishman borne, hath seene and passed in his troublesome travailes...* (London, repr. Amsterdam/New York, 1973).

Wheeler, John A (1601) *A Treatise of Commerce* (London, repr. New York, 1975).

Whitfield, Peter (1996). *The Charting of the Oceans: Ten Centuries of Maritime Maps* (London).

Willan, T.S. (1956). *The Early History of the Russia Company, 1553–1603* (Manchester).

Wood, A.C. (1935). *A History of the Levant Company* (Oxford).

Yahya, Dahiru (1981). *Morocco in the Sixteenth Century: Problems and Patterns in African Foreign Policy* (Harlow).

Yerasimos, Stephane (1991). *Les voyageurs dans l'Empire Ottoman (XIVe XVIe siècles): bibliographie, itineraires et inventaire des lieux habites* (Ankara).

Ze'evi, Dror (1996). *An Ottoman Century: The District of Jerusalem in the 1600s,* (Albany, N.Y.).

Zimolong, Bertrand (1938). *Ein Pilgerverzeidnis au Jerusalem vom 1591 bis 1695* (Palaestina-Hefte: 12–14: Cologne) repr. with corrections as *Ein Pilgezeichnis aus Jerusalem von 1561 bis 1695* (Cologne).

Zuallart, Jean (Eduard) (Giovanni Zuallardo) (1586). *Il devotissimo viaggio di Gerusalemme* (Rome).

List of Illustrations

Black and White Figures

Colour Plates

Index

If you are interested in purchasing other books published by Tempus,
or in case you have difficulty finding any Tempus books in your local bookshop,
you can also place orders directly through our website

www.tempus-publishing.com